17.XII.87.

The Explorations in Feminism Collective

Explorations in Feminism

Close to Home
A materialist analysis of women's oppression
Christine Delphy
Edited and translated by Diana Leonard

French Connections
Voices from the women's movement in France
Edited and translated by Claire Duchen

Gender and Schooling
A study of sexual divisions in the classroom
Michelle Stanworth

Geography and Gender
An introduction to feminist geography
Women and Geography Study Group of the IBG

Going up into the Next Class
Women and elementary teacher training 1840–1914
Frances Widdowson

Helping Women at Work
The Women's Industrial Council, 1889–1914
Ellen Mappen

In Other Words
Writing as a feminist
Edited by Gail Chester and Sigrid Nielsen

Man-Made Women
How new reproductive technologies affect women
Gena Corea et al.

Schools for the Boys?
Co-education reassessed
Pat Mahony

Seeing Red
The politics of premenstrual tension
Andrea Eagan, Valerie Hey and Sophie Laws

The Sexuality Papers
Male sexuality and the social control of women
Lal Coveney et al.

Well-Founded Fear
A community study of violence to women
Jalna Hanmer and Sheila Saunders

In Other Words

Writing as a feminist

Edited by Gail Chester and Sigrid Nielsen

Hutchinson
London Melbourne Sydney Auckland Johannesburg

Hutchinson Education

An imprint of Century Hutchinson Ltd

62–65 Chandos Place, London WC2N 4NW

Century Hutchinson Australia Pty Ltd
PO Box 496, 16–22 Church Street, Hawthorn,
Victoria 3122, Australia

Century Hutchinson New Zealand Ltd
PO Box 40–086, Glenfield, Auckland 10,
New Zealand

Century Hutchinson South Africa (Pty) Ltd
PO Box 337, Berglvei, South Africa

First published 1987

Set in 10 on 12 Linotron Plantin by
Input Typesetting Ltd, London SW19 8DR

Printed and bound in Great Britain by
Anchor Brendon Ltd, Tiptree, Essex

British Library Cataloguing in Publication Data

In other words: writing as a feminist.—
(Explorations in feminism; v. 12).
1. Women authors—Biography 2. Feminists
—Biography
I. Chester, Gail II. Nielson, Sigrid
III. Series
809'.89287 PN471

ISBN 0-09-164681-2

Contents

Acknowledgements 8

Introduction: writing as a feminist 9
Gail Chester and Sigrid Nielsen

Part One What Women Write

Imaginary ape or The one-eyed monkey answers questions 21
Suniti Namjoshi

Poetry – who cares? 25
Chris Cherry

The controversial feminist 30
Dena Attar

A double knot on the peeny 36
Joy Hendry

I tell my 3 year old she's real . . . : writing lesbian-feminist children's books 46
Caroline Halliday

Women and fiction: how we present ourselves and others 56
Rosalind Brackenbury

Meandering towards an ordinary job 62
Kath Fraser

The art of non-fiction (or the social construction of aesthetic divisions) 67
Catherine Itzin

Lesbian sexuality: joining the dots 73
Anna Livia

Writing erotica 78
Eileen Cadman

Part Two Taking Control

Lessons of history: beyond the male-stream classroom 85
Hilary Bourdillon

Working in the word factory 89
Ellen Galford

Producing a feminist magazine 93
Shaila Shah

They tried to rip me off 100
Diana Shelley

Why there's a light-box where my typewriter should be – being a feminist publisher 104
Joy Pitman

I am a feminist and a journalist . . . 109
Susie Innes

Translating as a feminist 114
Ros Schwartz

What the hell is feminist editing? 119
Marsaili Cameron

Part Three Writing About Ourselves

T. S. Eliot never called himself a clerk 129
Berta Freistadt

Writing for my mother 134
Pearlie McNeill

On being a late starter 139
Rosemary Manning

Writing as a lesbian mother 142
Caeia March

Words are weapons 149
Pratibha Parmar

Leaving it 'til later 154
Maggie Iles

An apology 159
Penny Cloutte

Writing as an Irish woman in England 164
Moya Roddy

Class conflicts 167
Jo Stanley with *Billie Hunter, Margaret Quigley, and Jennifer Wallace*

Young, gifted and getting there 174
Rosemarie Ademulegun

Imprisoning vision: towards a non-visualist language 177
Kirsten Hearn

Part Four Support and Communication

Making connections: the collective working experience 187
The Common Thread working-class women's anthology group

Writer/worker/feminist 194
Sara Maitland

Not chance but a community: women and élitism in poetry 199
Sally Evans

Women like us 203
Elsa Beckett

Broadening visions 209
Evelyn Conlon

Voice 212
Sigrid Nielsen

The script 218
Michelle Russell

Resources section 225
Compiled by Gail Chester

Notes on contributors 245

Acknowledgements

As feminists, we have stressed the need to be aware of other women's roles in making our writing possible. Working together, and with our contributors, has kept us going and changed our ideas – and we have benefited from the efforts of a great many women over the past fifteen years and earlier. However, some people have been particularly helpful in getting this book together, both directly and indirectly. The initial source of inspiration for the book and the conference from which it sprang is Ellie Siegel, who was instrumental in organizing the conference and would have been our co-editor if she had not had to return home to the United States. She has supported us from afar throughout this enterprise. We would also like to thank our contributors, for being so easy to work with; all the women who wrote papers for the Edinburgh conference, and all who volunteered their labour; everyone at Lavender Menace Bookshop, which handled much of the administrative work for the conference; Gay Jones and Prudence de Villiers of In Other Words Bookshop, Plymouth, for providing the book's title; the Explorations in Feminism Collective for encouraging us to submit the manuscript, and Claire L'Enfant at Hutchinson for accepting it and making many helpful suggestions; the members of our respective writing groups, for their support; and Cathy Burke, Eileen Cadman, Mary Collins, Daphne Davies, Jane Hustwit, Bob Orr, Pratibha Parmar, Laure Paterson, Cathy Phillips, Ros Schwartz and Lesley Sillitto for reasons too numerous to mention.

Introduction: writing as a feminist

Gail Chester and Sigrid Nielsen

This book has been written by women of many different ages and backgrounds, living in Scotland, Ireland, and England. Some of the authors have never before published a piece; others are established writers. They use writing for many different purposes: to earn their livings, examine their experiences, communicate their feelings, further their politics; and all of us are writing as feminists.

Each of the contributors would probably provide her own definition of feminist writing – and her own account of what led her to write from her feminist beliefs. The editors' own routes to writing have been completely different from each other: one of us wrote fantasy fiction about amazon heroines, dreamed of being a writer from an early age, and then stumbled on Shulamith Firestone's *The Dialectic of Sex* in a supermarket. The other saw writing as an ordinary skill, like mental arithmetic, and only began 'writing' when she joined a feminist group and discovered it produced a magazine. Despite these different approaches, writing plays a vital part in forming our perceptions of our lives as women, in working out our feminist views and in communicating them to others.

In the same way, writing has been crucial to the lives of women all over the world, in the past and now. Writing is essential to women's struggle for liberation from second-class status, poverty and enforced silence. Feminism, literacy and education for women are closely linked worldwide; illiteracy is a central part of women's subordination. Most liberation movements make a priority of teaching reading and writing to their supporters – and women have taken the lead in organizing and running such programmes (see, for example, the introduction to *Sisterhood is Global*, Robin Morgan (ed.), Penguin, 1985). Most totalitarian governments, on the other hand, realize that writing is a danger to their rule. A significant proportion of Amnesty International's prisoners of conscience are writers and journalists; and the authors and publishers of the original feminist *samizdat, Woman and Russia* (Sheba, 1980), were forcibly exiled from their country. One of the most moving sessions of the 1986 Oslo International Feminist Bookfair was 'Writing as a dangerous profession', where women from Spain, Kenya, South Africa, Northern Ireland and Uruguay spoke poignantly of being imprisoned by the authorities, and of being rejected by their own communities, simply for communicating in writing with others. Even in supposedly liberal societies, minority groups often experience difficulty in writing or getting an audience for their work.

Perhaps this is because writing can be a powerful force for change, not only individually, but by enhancing group effectiveness. NUPE, the trade union which represents mainly manual workers in the public sector, has made support for literacy its official policy – and together with other unions has developed a programme called Workbase, which provides literacy and numeracy classes. With their tutor, a group of women cleaners in Sheffield learnt how to organize their writing, take notes at meetings, and write down what they remembered later on. As a result, they gained the necessary confidence to challenge the hierarchy of their own union and elected the first woman shop steward at their largely female workplace.

This power of writing to give women control over their own lives is not limited to our own time. Recent research by Dale Spender (discussed in *Mothers of the Novel*)* shows that English women have been earning money from writing since the early seventeenth century; while in France, Christine de Pisan was writing for a living 200 years earlier (see *Medieval Women Writers*, Wilson). Since then, increasing numbers of women have followed their example, possibly because writing is one of the few professions which does not necessarily require formal training, expensive equipment, or a respectable front. Like many of the most exploitative women's jobs, it is often piecework. And since the writing is being bought, rather than the writer's presence, women have been able to publish under a male pseudonym, as the Brontës and many others have done.

Many of the papers in this collection show how thoroughly an education or a job can transform women's lives. 'Words are weapons' by Pratibha Parmar describes her determination to get a university degree and use her education and writing to improve life for all black people. 'T.S. Eliot never called himself a clerk' by Berta Freistadt explores the way a woman gains confidence by deciding to call herself a writer. Yet, vital as women's relationship to writing has always been, the feminism of the 1960s added an insight

---

* Biographical details are not given for books and authors listed in the Resources section.

which ultimately transformed feminists' views of their writing, themselves, and their opportunities, leading to new ways of producing, publishing, distributing, promoting, and criticizing women's writing.

This insight was simple, but it had many repercussions. Tillie Olsen, the writer who is probably quoted most often by our contributors, summed it up in *Silences* (Virago, 1980) by saying, 'The product can't be separated from the conditions of its production.' This is part of the most basic feminist lesson – that the personal is political; we don't leave ourselves out of the picture when we start writing and what we produce reflects the constraints under which we live as women: constraints of illiteracy, domestic responsibility, censorship and poverty, as well as lack of professional recognition.

As befits her status as a subspecies of 'real' writer, the woman writer is rarely reviewed (6 per cent of all books reviewed are written by women, according to Lynne Spender's figures), and even more rarely is she allowed a reputation that survives her lifetime (around 8 per cent of anthologized poets are women, according to Joanna Russ, and this figure has not increased over several generations). Feminist theory and practice suggest that any attempt to become an honorary man is doomed to ultimate failure. Feminists, instead, should write *as* women *for* women.

But writing as a woman for women is not as simple as it sounds. Over the years feminists have had to question some very basic assumptions. Style, vocabulary, subject matter, the methods used to produce writing and the credit a writer gives to those who support her, the role of publishers and the way they promote a writer's work, have all come under feminist scrutiny. The questions and the answers have led to a continuing dialogue between feminist writers.

For instance: should women's writing discuss parts of female experience which have traditionally been taboo, such as abortion and menstruation? Forbidding all mention of the female body has made women feel ashamed and constrained. In 'Lesbian sexuality: joining the dots', Anna Livia asks how women's writing has dealt with desires considered unfit to mention – and which some would still prefer to censor. Eileen Cadman's 'Writing erotica' talks about writing fiction which meets taboos head on – and breaks them.

What about the methods we use to write? Is it possible for a group to produce writing together? Collective working is an important feminist tradition, and writing collectively can help to develop a fluid intermingling of many voices, giving confidence to its participants and creating opportunities for a wider range of people to appear in print. Good collective writing is like good individual writing – it does not flatten out the individual voice and the new thought. The Common Thread, a group of working-class women who are producing an anthology, talk about their collective project in 'Making connections'.

Our thinking about writing is full of unspoken hierarchies. Published writing ranks above unpublished writing, and some forms, such as notes, jokes, songs and letters are hardly thought to be writing at all, yet they may play an important part in a woman's understanding of herself and her place in society. Elsa Beckett, who organizes Gemma, a network for lesbians with and without disabilities, examines the importance of letter-writing in 'Women like us'. Ros Schwartz asks why translation is not considered to be original writing, even though it demands creative effort and writing skill.

What does it mean to be 'a writer'? Who should feel able to consider herself 'professional'? (Chapter 1 of *Rolling Our Own*, Cadman et al. 'Women writers and the influence of feminism' is a useful discussion of this topic.) In the course of producing this book, we have encountered many feminists who have questioned their own credentials as 'real' writers. Some confessed to 'feeling a bit of a fraud' – either because of the type of writing they do, the amount of time they spend on it, or the fact that they haven't been published or earned money from it. Some of our contributors describe additional restraints which working-class and black women, for example, feel when starting to write. In 'Writing for my mother', Pearlie McNeill describes her lack of role models as a working-class writer who grew up reading novels about middle-class people; she began writing without the slightest assurance that anyone wanted to read about the fabric of her life. Women from oppressed groups also have to deal with a profound fear of stepping out of line, of betraying their group by exposing it to public scrutiny. For white middle-class women, as well as those who are 'other' twice over, validation of our work too often depends on a job or a publisher's contract, for which there is heavy competition.

Once her work is accepted for publication, a writer's problems are far from over. As the commercial market for feminist books has grown, so has a writer's need to be vigilant. Commercial publishers have most of the power and control – and all of the money – in the relationship. Feminists have tried to combat the more general forms of exploitation, such as inadequate advances, low royalties or delays in publication, while retaining a consciousness of feminist issues. Self-publishing, feminist publishing houses, and solidarity among writers are the most usual methods of doing so.

Self-publishing demands much time and energy as well as initial capital, but gives the writer a great sense of control, achievement and self-esteem. Many successful self-publishing projects have been undertaken collectively, as the work load can be shared. Some feminist publishing houses have begun like this, as described by Joy Pitman in her paper 'Why there's a light box where my typewriter should be'.

As feminists have become more aware of the massive suppression of women's viewpoint – past and present – more women's writing has come into print. Feminist magazines and publishers have been set up, and in just over ten years, have become highly visible, attracting internationally respected writers and uncovering a whole new readership for women. But feminist writers who are able to publish with commercial concerns must exercise caution and cynicism, and have a thorough knowledge of the control they may be relinquishing. Will the writer have a say in the internal design, the cover illustration, or the selling price? Might a black or a Scottish publishing house be more appropriate for her work, as well as more efficient at promoting the book so that it reaches the proper audience? Would a Jewish or disabled woman, for example, prefer to entrust her work to an editor who might identify with its message from her own experience?

Every writer needs support. One of the cliches of writing is the genius in the garret – but far from struggling in splendid isolation, he generally has his clothes washed and his meals cooked by his devoted mother, wife, 'mistress' or sister. What can we do as women to find support systems and to acknowledge those that already exist? Sally Evans, in 'Not chance but a community', looks at the cult of 'great authors' and how it limits *all* writers' access to support. Michelle Russell's article, 'The script', asks whether women playwrights can find support in mixed writing groups, while Maggie Iles explores the crucial issue that women are often unable to start writing at all because of the burden of their domestic responsibilities. This theme is echoed by other contributors, such as Penny Cloutte.

Even for those who do manage to start, there are still many problems connected with writing as a feminist. Is it possible for a feminist writer to further her beliefs if she is employed in a partriarchal institution such as a school, a newspaper or a multinational publishing company? Can she subvert her job to incorporate her politics, and what can she do if they conflict openly? 'Working in the word factory' by Ellen Galford and 'I am a feminist and a journalist' by Susie Innes examine some of the dilemmas of feminists in the media, while Hilary Bourdillon in 'Lessons of History' shows what can be achieved by a determined feminist history teacher.

For many women, the conflict of being a writer and a feminist is not intimately connected with earning a living. But conflicts still arise. Feminist activism is demanding in terms of time. Personal problems, insecure living situations, lack of confidence, absence of role models and poor education all diminish women's potential for writing. Can feminism help us be more productive, given the difficulties women face? In 'Meandering towards an ordinary job', Kath Fraser tells how learning to write collectively gave her a skill which she was able to use later when her personal life was in confusion. Sigrid Nielsen's paper examines what happens in our thoughts when we write, and how learning about other women's experiences and working methods can help us with our own writing.

Helpful as feminist analysis is, feminist activism may not be conducive to doing much writing. We have often wondered if some of our activism isn't a way of avoiding the hardest task of all – picking up a pen. For, well-established as feminist writing may seem, the world of which it is a part can only be maintained by actively defending the gains we have made. State censorship, violence against bookshops which emphasize their commitment to feminist publications, and especially the formal and informal censorship of the mass media, all demand our attention. Nevertheless, we believe that writing can flourish best in a supportive environment of activism, which it can also help to create.

As long ago as 1920, Virginia Woolf wrote that group support was the element women writers had always been denied. By the early 1980s, feminist writing groups existed in many parts of the country, growing out of feminist traditions of collective working practice and the ideas of writers such as Virginia Woolf. Yet most feminist writers, and many who might have been interested had they known how to find each other, were still working in isolation. In 1983, both of us belonged to writing groups where we read each other's work and provided practical and personal support. We both benefited greatly from them and we wondered if other women would benefit from an extension of the conversation we enjoyed. With Ellie Siegel, a friend who was in a writing group in the United States, and with help from many other women, we organized the Edinburgh Feminist Writers' Conference, which attracted 150 women from all over the country and abroad. We wanted to learn why women wrote, what they wrote about, how they saw themselves involved as feminist writers, what support their involvement gave them, and what difficulties it caused. In collecting the papers for *In Other Words*, some of which are versions of papers written for the conference, we have tried to extend the range of women participating and offer the benefits of a writing group to an even wider circle of women. We have tried to capture some of the ways very different feminists are using writing, and we hope our readers will be able to use these experiences to clarify their own.

But one of the things we learned from the conference – and which has been brought out frequently since – is that 'experience' is not a completely straightforward concept. In the first consciousness-raising groups, women attempted to analyse their common experience of oppression, but often found different assumptions, based on different backgrounds, which were by no means easy to integrate. Initially, published writing by feminists reflected the myth that most were middle-class, white, gentile, able-bodied and heterosexual. Thanks to the determination of women with very different experiences struggling to make themselves heard, the situation is beginning to move closer to reality.

Feminist writing and publishing, though still overwhelmingly weighted in favour of more privileged groups, is coming to reflect a wider view; many women who were previously stifled by narrowly western-centred outlooks are now struggling into print. In some cases the response to their work has outstripped all expectations. *The Color Purple* (The Women's Press, 1983), an outspokenly feminist novel by black writer Alice Walker, won the Pulitzer Prize, sold 3 million copies in the USA alone, and has been successfully filmed. *The Bone People* by Keri Hulme (Picador, 1986) is an even more striking example – a novel by a Maori woman, written from her experience of two conflicting cultures, which was initially turned down by mainstream publishers as 'too difficult'. Published in New Zealand by Spiral, a small feminist collective with both Maori and white members, it went on to win the Booker Prize in 1985 and became a bestseller in Britain as well as New Zealand. Spiral and other independent publishers are playing a crucial role in making books from many cultures available, regardless of fashion and in defiance of racism and censorship. To make sure that such work is not submerged again, feminists need to find a balance between taking the opportunities commercial publishers can offer and maintaining the small feminist presses. For those of us who come from so-called 'minority' groups, it is a matter of our very survival.

The hard-won successes of a few feminists do not amount to any final victory over racism. Black writers have appeared only recently in feminist booklists; and black British writers were published years later than black writers who had already become known in the USA. Many black and third world writers feel that they are now being used because they have become the latest fashion, just as feminism in general has been used. Meanwhile, feminists in the third world are starting their own publishing ventures, for example, *Manushi*, an Indian magazine, *Mujer/Ilet*, a Latin American monthly newsletter, and Kali for Women, an Indian book publisher. At a workshop in Oslo on feminist publishing in the third world, women from some of these groups explained that their enterprises are often tied to western fashions in publishing, even when the needs of their own countries are entirely different. Nevertheless, they continue to work with western publishers, not least because of the money they and their authors can earn from foreign publication. Feminist publishers in the third world are confronting western-centred attitudes – and their struggle must be supported by *all* feminists if it is to succeed.

This new priority is reflected in many of the papers in the book. 'Producing a feminist magazine' by Shaila Shah shows how one group responded to black women's invisibility even in the feminist media, and established a newspaper for women, *Outwrite*. 'I tell my 3 year old she's real' by Caroline Halliday asks how feminists can create children's books which welcome different abilities in women from many cultures, while also depicting lesbian relationships honestly. 'Imprisoning vision' by Kirsten Hearn explains how her writing is affected by language which assumes that everyone is able-bodied, and also relates her experience of being blind. 'Class conflicts' by Jo Stanley *et al.* examines the way women's class background affects their writing, and the conflicts that can arise from assuming that all writers are middle class. Joy Hendry looks at a group of Scottish women writers whose work has been suppressed. Many other papers mention similar topics; it is difficult to be a feminist these days and remain unaware of such issues, even though we have some way to go before becoming a movement 'for all women'.

Feminist writing has gained perceptibly as women continue to describe their experience, painfully re-examine established positions and expand old insights. Alice Walker expressed the gains very well when she described her idea of 'womanist' prose based on black women's vision: ' "Womanist" is to "feminist" as purple is to lavender' (*In Search of Our Mothers' Gardens*). But at the same time, there is a new note of caution, or even pessimism, in some assessments of the state of feminist writing today. Some feminists suggest that working on the visibility of the new woman-centred writing is a soft option, a dangerous distraction from the serious business of feminist politics. We heard this view at the Edinburgh conference both from a socialist feminist and a revolutionary feminist. It goes along with another view which deplores 'cultural feminism' – believing that art can only be used as a substitute for political action, rather than as part of it. Because women's experience is not so straightforwardly similar as feminists once thought, some writers want to deny that common experience can exist or that it can inspire political action. According to this view, women unite because they intellectually perceive that they have the same interests, not because they can identify with each other's lives. And writing is held to be political, or feminist, only if it concerns itself explicitly with those interests and the need to act on them.

We do not feel that everything published by feminist publishers or every account which reflects women's lives should be beyond criticism. Criticism and questioning of our writing have been going on since the women's movement began, and are healthy and important parts of our effort to speak out. But some of these criticisms go beyond the idea that certain writings explore experience more consciously and usefully than others, and deny the political value of encouraging women to write at all.

We believe this book shows that the act of writing itself can be political for women. Learning to organize thoughts on paper, to express feelings, to respond to others, is an enormous extension of women's power. It allows communication over time as well as distance. Writing that is not primarily feminist, by women such as Emma Goldman and Rosa Luxemburg, has been instrumental in bringing women into politics, giving insights and background which led to the creation of the women's liberation movement. Others like Margaret Sanger and Marie Stopes spread knowledge of birth control to give women power over their own bodies, which enabled them to make other choices about their lives. Writing has also been one of the major means of spreading feminist ideas. Though feminist action takes place in groups, it starts with each woman's personal conviction, formed when she first encounters feminist ideas – and that often happens through the written word, particularly in areas where feminists are hard to find. And since radio and television barely acknowledge the women's movement, books and magazines are the only means of communication with the vast majority of women who still have no first-hand experience of feminism.

This book shows the personal importance writing has for women, and our overwhelming need to communicate. We may not have a shared language, but that does not mean we will never have one. We may not have identical experience, but that does not mean we cannot share our different experiences. In writing for other women, we reinterpret our own experience in a way which brings us closer together. And women's experience is not only the sum total of each woman's memories, but a collective possession, a tradition which shapes the way we view our individual lives. We are all engaged in creating this tradition. Much of this book is a record of the process, based on conversations between the two of us, between us and the contributors, and between the contributors themselves. We hope we have shown how one woman's impasse can become another's insight: and how the energy released by creation can be important in sustaining feminism in the years to come.

Gail Chester
London

Sigrid Nielsen
Roslin, Midlothian

December 1986

PART ONE WHAT WOMEN WRITE

Imaginary ape or The one-eyed monkey answers questions

Suniti Namjoshi

The one-eyed monkey was perched on a pedestal. Two or three people were gathered about. She wondered briefly if they would settle after all for something short of total enlightenment. A simple and partial explanation perhaps? She assumed her most unassuming expression. A very young woman was glaring at her. Sooner or later the questions would start. The monkey waited.

At last the young woman blurted, 'Why do you write?' Well, it could have been worse. They could have required a considered solution to the unemployment problem, a precise gradation of the six best writers, a judicious comment on the latest atrocity in the latest headlines. She had once considered confessing publicly that she never read the papers and that she knew almost nothing about pretty well everything; but had been advised against it. Such a remark might be misconstrued. She had decided to keep quiet. But the intense young woman was still glaring. The one-eyed monkey essayed a smile. What was the duration of a smile she mused. How long could it delay answering a question?

The one-eyed monkey smiled again. 'Why do *you* write?' she asked. A question in return was sometimes useful.

'Oh, I'm not a writer!' The young woman sounded quite startled. But then she hesitated. 'Well, I mean, I do write a little. Poems and such. And I haven't shown them to anyone. I – I write in order to know what I think. I guess it's just self-expression.' She was now glaring at the stony ground in a perplexed fashion.

The one-eyed monkey was about to inquire why the young woman hadn't shown her poems, but it occurred to her that the young woman might thrust them at her. 'You're an egoist', she scolded herself silently, but she didn't ask.

'But isn't art supposed to be relevant?' This was a young man, who might or might not be connected with the young woman. Did they get on? A question had been asked. Relevant, relevant. . . . Did the 'r' roll, did the

'I' lilt? Was something relevant to something else? Oh yes, art – was it relevant? 'Poetry makes nothing happen.' Was that the wrong answer? Was it incorrect these days to quote Auden? If it was the wrong answer, her image would suffer; if her image suffered, her books wouldn't sell and that was relevant. She decided she had to say that art was relevant. But the young man hadn't waited for an answer. 'What I mean is', he was saying, 'that I think people matter. And I am a feminist, so I think women are people. And what I think is that poetry that's just an exercise in aestheticism is pure self-indulgence. It ought to be banned. What I mean is that you ought to be saying something specific to someone, to the people, so that there can be progress and change and revolution. You ought to be writing for and to and from the people. In short, what do you have to say to the ordinary man? To someone like me for instance?' He paused for a moment. 'I don't understand why you insist on writing about monkeys and cows and all sorts of animals. They are not people.' He concluded with a final and ferocious frown.

The one-eyed monkey wanted to frown back. But being rude to people wasn't good policy. And if she said to the young man that she had absolutely nothing to say to him, except that she wished he'd go away, he wouldn't buy her books. But perhaps that needn't matter so much if someone else would?

'The fable', she began soothingly, 'is an ancient and respected form.' Should she throw in a word about its being Indian? It would work like a trigger. They'd draw themselves up and immediately assume a liberal stance. Revolting idea. 'Well, yes, as I was saying', she began again, 'I use the form of the fable because. . . .' But she didn't know why she wrote fables. If only she could find a plausible explanation.

Her third questioner came to the rescue. 'That is precisely the area I wished to discuss.' She appeared to be a middle-aged academic, probably on sabbatical. The one-eyed monkey alerted herself. Academic attention was almost certainly a good thing. 'Now, don't be facetious. Be civil at all costs, even solemn', she told herself urgently. But the middle-aged academic had rounded on the young man. 'Art', she informed him, 'is anthropocentric. Literature is written by human beings and read by human beings. So that even a tale about ape-men has human meaning.' The young man didn't say anything. He was thinking about a tribe of heroic ape-men; he liked the idea.

The academic now turned on the young woman. 'The difference between mere self-expression and literary expression has to do with distancing. The latter is distanced, the former is not. The one-eyed monkey is not merely a protagonist, but – as in this instance, for example – almost a narrator, indeed even a persona – if we stretch the term slightly. The question you should have been considering is the exact relationship between the one-eyed monkey' – she nodded at the monkey perched on her pediment – 'and the one-eyed monkey in quotation marks, so to speak.'

The one-eyed monkey felt dazed. She had begun to invent a story about a one-eyed monkey who once had a sister who was also one-eyed, or perhaps a friend. . . . She pulled herself together. The academic was addressing her directly.

'The device of the one-eyed monkey is in the tradition of the alien observer, the man from another planet, the traveller from Persia or, in reverse, the visitor to Utopia. All that is perfectly obvious. What is, perhaps, more distinctive, is your choice of a monkey. It follows that there must be a play, albeit implicit, on the verb, "to ape". In other words, you are aping the tradition as a means perhaps of attempting to mock it. The essential stance is hardly humanist. It lacks authority. And this connects in turn with another feature I have examined carefully. Your monkey is one-eyed. I was misled at first by my research into mythology. Was there a connection with the god, Shiva, or possibly with Hanuman? But though Shiva has a third eye, having three eyes is hardly the same thing as having only one. And as for the monkey god, there is absolutely no evidence that in the matter of eyes he was in any way abnormal. Moreover, your monkey is female. As I pondered the point the symbolism of the "one eye" suddenly became clear. It is an admission surely that the vision is limited. It explains satisfactorily the narrowness of perspective.' The academic paused. She beamed at the others, 'Now, if you like, you may ask your questions.'

But the one-eyed monkey had been feeling more and more unhappy. By now she was acutely uncomfortable and cross. She decided to get in a few statements first. She addressed the young woman, 'As you said, I write because I want to know exactly what I think.' Then she turned to the young man, 'The exercise of pure aestheticism gives me pleasure.' And then she growled at the academic, 'As for you, why don't you write your own stories? The one-eyed monkey is a one-eyed monkey. And I don't know why I write about her.'

'But you haven't explained anything', her questioners protested.

'Why should I?' cried the monkey.

'Because you've set yourself up as a writer', they said. 'You ought to be able to explain yourself.'

'But I can't explain', replied the monkey, 'all I can do is excuse myself.' And with that, she scrambled down the pillar and quickly made off.

Meanwhile the itinerant academic pulled out a notebook. 'Pillar and pilloried', she jotted down rapidly, 'probably some sort of hidden significance.'

Poetry – who cares?

Chris Cherry

On a beautiful summer's day when I could be lying in the park soaking up the sun, or at the beach; walking in the woods or talking with friends; on a beautiful summer's day when I don't have anything special to do or anywhere special to be, I choose to write about poetry.

The old conflicts start up again. 'What do you want to do that for? Pretentious, self-indulgent, anti-social, useless . . . why don't you go out and *do* something instead . . . ?'

Caught between desire and censorship, unable to relax and unable to work, I droop, shuffle down to the park, half-heartedly scrawl a few inarticulate sentences, return for coffee and sandwiches, flick through the pages of a book, gather myself again for this act of commitment called writing.

I write because I have to; because I want to; because I love to.

I knew I wanted to be a writer at the age of 7. Amidst constant family rows – my father's wrath, my mother's tears – I was expected to be quiet, uninitiating and dutiful. I escaped from these unpalatable messages into fantasy adventures full of people, action, and excitement. These I both acted out in play and wrote down when I had to be inside and amuse myself.

Once I got to secondary school my teachers discouraged my long stories. My 'education' sacrificed imagination and creativity to facts, rules, and accuracy. In this dualistic world of good or bad, right or wrong, success or failure, there was no room for risk, discovery, or self expression. No one sought or wanted my opinions, feelings, experiences, or my dreams. A straight road led through this desert of boredom and passivity to university and back to school as a teacher.

Having barricaded myself behind my school-books to avoid the worst violations to my person that my home environment represented, at 22 I made the sanest choice then available to me and got married, taking a copy of the just published *The Female Eunuch* with me on my honeymoon. Three years later I joined my first women's group, demanded a room of my own and started writing a novel. Three years after that I left my husband, moved into the country, and lived a year of solitude, getting to know myself for the first time.

During this year, poetry started to flow – suddenly and delightfully. And it seemed then that the poems wrote themselves, that there was an unending store of thoughts, feelings, images, ideas, just waiting to be released and expressed – in a lunch hour, at the launderette, driving my car and especially during the long, lonely winter nights, words and images poured through me onto paper, speaking more than I consciously knew. High on poetry, I fell under her spell.

That year I met up with other women writers and we started a group which kept me going for the next five years. Squeezed into odd hours between paid work, friends, emotional traumas, poetry keeps coming back to demand my attention.

I've discovered that there's a difference for me between writing prose and poetry. I can sit down on demand and struggle with prose, arriving at some adequate approximation of what I'd hoped to say. I don't find it easy, it can be lonely, I'm never completely satisfied with what I've written, and it's hard work. But I know I can do it.

But poetry can't be so forced and disciplined. She comes and goes of her own volition. When she's with me I move into another dimension, feel connected both to my inner world and the world around me. I fill out, I flow, I spark; see significance, patterns, and meaning where before there was none. Words resonate on several different levels of consciousness, bringing past and future into the present. Everything becomes symbol and metaphor. But poetry will only stay around if the conditions are right, and she can disappear as suddenly as she came, returning me to a two-dimensional world, flat and incomplete.

For me poetry is more than words on a page and need not be written down to be experienced. Poetry is connectedness. It is uncovering, knowing and accepting my feelings and inner voices so often drowned by the rush of everyday survival. It is going back to uncover again and again what has been found and lost. It is being with others and allowing the flow of sympathy and antipathy in a mutual present in which I do not seek to pretend to be other than who I am. It is sensing acutely the moods, rhythms, and cycles of nature and being responsive to my own moods, rhythms, and cycles. It is feeling connected to my own loving, living, creative, sexual energy without apology or shame. It is taking the time to look and hear and smell and taste and touch; to bring everyday things into focus and see them as if for the first time, knowing that each flower, tree, cloud, wall, shadow, cup is unique and perfectly itself and at the same time part of a great, universal network of finely balanced correspondences. It is knowing that I am not alone and separate and arbitrary but part of a common humanity whose feelings and experiences are more alike than different beneath surface appearances, the habitual distortions of race, culture, and gender.

Poetry is a form of meditation with its own inward and outward movement, inspiration, and exhalation. If my mind were an iceberg the top ninth would be above water and visible; the rest below water, unseen and unheard. It is from the unseen and unheard that poetry comes bubbling up as words and images. Images can come at any time. I need not always remember them first time. Like dreams, if they're important they'll come back. But if I want to write poetry, I have to learn to value and respect them, welcome them, pay them attention, and be prepared to work on them.

The first stage of the work involves exploring and expanding the original image. This requires an uncensoring mind and a state of total concentration. I have to become the image – the desert, the sea, the mountain, whatever it was that came into my mind – get right inside it, feel my way around it, see it, hear it, smell, and taste it until I know it. I write down any connection that comes to me until I've exhausted the present possibilities. Then I bring the more rational, analytical part of my mind into play to order, shape, and form the material. I weed out what is superfluous, pay attention to the rhythm and music of the words, the pauses and silences, the shape of the poem on the page, juggle the lines until the whole thing dances together complete in itself.

This poem 'Iceberg' begins to describe this process:

1

I could draw poetry out of silence
with the patience of a fisherwoman
I have cut my circle in the ice
and wait.

2

I want to find the courage to dive deep
beyond conception,
to hammer diamonds from the glassy wall
such hard at meaning

to make transparent the opaque.
I want to trace with burning fingers
the unique and perfect pattern
of each frost flower
to wear a skin so thin
my blood's heat
will melt the edge of ice
and make the inert flow.

3

I want to write poetry with muscle
– words that can't be pummelled into submission
but swagger seeking across a page.
I want a new vocabulary for living,
a grammar for contradictions
where mind and body rhyme
and my heart's beat
sounds in the sea.

Poetry is a way of knowledge. By giving myself over totally to my inner life in these moments, I make a commitment to myself and, consequently, to all those to whom I am connected. In doing so I risk discovering both my power and my limitations. I take responsibility for who I am and dare to speak who I am. Self-centred, it is not a selfish act; only through knowing and accepting my own pain, joy, desire, despair, fragility, my own human condition, can I know and accept yours. By daring to speak it, I break the conspiracy of silence which keeps us separate. And if you can understand me, through my words, which are never quite right, or adequate, but all I have with which to reach you, we are both a little less alone, a little more connected.

Adrienne Rich describes this commitment in these extracts from 'Diving into the Wreck':

First having read the book of myths
and loaded the camera,
and checked the edge of the knife-blade,
I put on
the body-armor of black rubber
the absurd flippers
the grave and awkward mask.
I am having to do this
not like Cousteau with his

assiduous team
aboard the sun-flooded schooner
but here alone . . .
. . . I came to explore the wreck.
The words are purposes.
The words are maps.
I came to see the damage that was done
and the treasures that prevail.
I stroke the beam of my lamp
slowly along the flank
of something more permanent
than fish or weed.

I can only write as I am – a woman of this time and culture – and I have made apologies for poetry for years, calling it self-indulgence. But my biggest block has been fear. My rational mind fears the unconscious – her desires, her power, her knowledge, her chaos, and unpredictibility. I fear what I most desire. I fear that if I let myself down into the under-water world, I will never come back. I fear speaking my words to another, risking both their criticism and rejection and their acceptance and expectation. I fear discovering the void inside me, finding nothing to say and nothing to offer. I fear the loneliness that precedes solitude.

But I come more and more to know that words are powerful and liberating. Speaking out and writing and publishing are ways of breaking the silence that binds us, of connecting with a common humanity which is all we have.

The controversial feminist

Dena Attar

We need a feminist polemic. The dictionary defines 'polemic' as controversial discussion. I would define feminist polemic as writing which is for and about feminism, unashamedly persuasive and political. We have such writing already, of course: in newsletters, magazines, and journals both internal to the Women's Liberation Movement and more generally available (*Wires, Spare Rib, Outwrite, Trouble and Strife, Feminist Review*, a few other nationally available titles and many more local ones), in anthologies of feminist writing usually taken from these journals, and occasionally in other full-length books brought out mainly by feminist publishers. Countless women have experienced the impact of such direct writing and found it useful in our personal lives, while the Women's Liberation Movement (WLM) could hardly have existed without it. A lot of us can remember the effect of reading for the first time books and pamphlets which were full of anger but also gave us a sense of our own power – it could have been *The Dialectic of Sex, Sexual Politics, Against Our Will, The Female Eunuch, Redstockings' Feminist Revolution* (to name only those I have heard women of my generation single out as early influences for them) amongst many others. It does not matter what we think of those books now – ideas move on, we learn and change and we are hardly likely to read them again uncritically. The point is, they set something in motion. Yet such writing is still hard to find in spite of the success of feminist publishing ventures generally. Why?

Typing this at the last possible minute, ten months behind schedule, I certainly do not underestimate the problems women have to overcome before they can sit down to write anything at all. Still, it does strike me that women find it easier to start on a full-length novel (even if finishing one is another matter) than to attempt a short non-fiction article. I formed this impression at the conference which sparked off this article, where most discussion groups concentrated on the writing of fiction, poetry and autobiography, and I find it confirmed every time I go into a bookshop and see the range of books now appearing with a feminist imprint. Feminist writing has virtually come to *mean* feminist fiction, poetry, and autobiography, rather than referring to the written versions of the political discussions going on in the WLM. Feminist ideas continually evolve through the activities and discussion of our groups, meetings, and conferences – but most of this is never written down. In other words, we lose a lot of our work, and ironically this is happening just at a time when there is a growing audience for feminist literature (though *Catcall* – a unique political journal of feminist controversy – folds, while *Women's Review* – inspired by the tremendous current interest in women's writing – opens). I want to consider here the particular hazards of political writing which deter us from putting our arguments and ideas down on paper – what happens in-between those moments of sudden insight in discussion, or after some revealing experience, when we feel we have something to say which we ought to communicate to a wider audience (promising to do it, even, as editors know) and the point when we give up the idea as impossible or not worthwhile.

Before we can even begin to write we face the problem of form – how to set about saying what we want to say. Writing directly about your ideas and experiences takes a different kind of confidence from that required by women writers-as-artists: you may not have to worry about the artistic merits of your work, but on the other hand you are obliged to write as yourself. You have to own what you say. You are free to disown your ideas at a later date, of course, but you cannot deny that *was* once what you thought. This is a worse problem for us precisely because we are feminists, and we do not play the game of pretending to be neutral, objective, and uninvolved in what we write. Liz Stanley and Sue Wise in *Breaking Out: Feminist Consciousness and Feminist Research* (Routledge and Kegan Paul, 1983) do an excellent demolition job on the myth of objectivity which male academics in particular build up around their work. It can still be hard for us to break away from the impersonal essay/textbook model of writing, whether because we have been exposed to so much of it that we think it is the only 'correct' way to write serious non-fiction, or because it does provide a refuge for the writer, allowing her to keep a safe distance between her writing and herself. There are now plenty of books which are *about* women as seen by social scientists, historians, anthropologists, and others writing as 'observers', which are not necessarily feminist books at all. They may indeed reveal that women are oppressed, although they are less likely to say that it is men who oppress us, but if they are written as academically respectable 'objective' texts, they are probably unable to make the reader feel that oppression matters. For that, we need writing with no pretension to objectivity, which is fully involved, as fierce, angry, and passionate as we want to make it.

The essay/textbook style is not the only one to be wary of, for the publications of other, non-feminist political organizations on the left offer us a different model. I have heard feminists saying they wished we had an equivalent paper to *Socialist Worker* and its counterparts to sell to women; I have also heard it said that we need a feminist *Capital*, a single authoritative text to wave (presumably) at our opponents. I disagree. I find the versions of its political writing which the mixed left produces for popular consumption – sometimes quite cynically – deeply disrespectful. In its worst form it treats the audience merely as a target for propaganda. As feminists, we have not only to include our own experience, but somehow leave room for the reader to include hers. We learn about our oppression through our own lives, not through simple slogans, and while we may want to challenge other women into debate and into re-examining their opinions or behaviour, for example questioning heterosexuality, we cannot ask that women accept feminist ideas passively. If the WLM goes on dealing in slogans it will go on excluding and alienating groups of women. Think for example of 'Free abortion on demand – a woman's right to choose' which formed one of the basic demands of the WLM in the 70s, and how long it took the Movement to reconsider it in the light of the different experiences of Black women, women from minority groups, and infertile women. As for needing the one right book which says it all, analyses every woman's oppression, and tells us what to do, I can hardly tell if I think it's a dream or a nightmare, but I cannot see how a movement founded on the experience and involvement, potentially, of all women could give birth to such a one-dimensional creature.

Throughout its history, in its efforts to create a non-hierarchical movement, the WLM has properly been wary of authoritarian creeds, demands, and manifestos, but as it gets harder to produce definitive political statements, the danger is that we will find it hard to make definite statements of a political nature at all. Whatever our doubts about the purpose of the seven demands, gradually adopted by the WLM in Britain at various national conferences in the 70s, these demands at least provided a statement, admittedly limited, of what we wanted to change and of what we wanted for ourselves. If we make no such statements, it is much easier for our opponents to claim that feminism is merely a matter of dress and style, or that it only applies to a few women, or that we have already achieved everything we wanted.

Faced with the difficulties I have described, many women have found that an obvious solution is to adopt a personal and expressive form of writing, which fits in well with feminist theory and process generally – 'the personal is the political'. It is easier both to write and to read, but if the writer never generalizes from her own experience, this can have the disadvantage of undermining the value of her statements. Personal writing can be extremely powerful in its own way, but it can also be dismissed more easily than the words of a woman who insists 'this means you too', particularly when separate individual accounts can appear to cancel each other out. The anthology *Why Children?* (The Women's Press, 1980) is an example of a collection of separate personal accounts of having or deciding not to have children which somehow never adds up to anything, so that I find it impossible to say what, if anything, the book contributes to the feminist debate about motherhood. Letters pages in journals can also give me a sense of clashing personal histories which never quite turn into a debate. A further problem of purely personal accounts is that they can be used in a token way, meaning that a one-off story implies a one-off experience and an exceptional woman. Sometimes the point we want to make may indeed be that our experiences differ, and that no one woman can represent another. But this should not be taken to mean that we have wholly different concerns – as if racism, violence, sexuality, could be issues for some women but not others. When a woman writes about experiences she has had which have not been shared by most of her readers – describing a specific religious upbringing, perhaps, or writing as an incest survivor – there will still be connections between the readers' experience and the writer's. It may be particularly important to spell them out, to stop readers assuming that because the writer's personal history seems completely different from theirs, she is not able or entitled to make comments relevant to other women's lives, even to those who don't share her experiences.

The political is after all more than the personal. We can learn a lot from telling our stories to each other, but as we can never hear every woman's story, that on its own is not enough. In any case, we do sometimes want to set out what we know to be true without limiting it to our direct personal experiences or qualifying it in any way. We have to take the next step towards creating a politics based on our experience of oppression and make brave, quite bald statements.

Feminism has produced a form of its own for expressing such direct political statements, a poetic-polemic where the writing itself claims our attention as much as the ideas swept along with it. I find it a mixture of ancient and new, with echoes of the Old Testament prophets. Reading the work of feminists experimenting with this form in their political writing – Adrienne Rich, Robin Morgan, Andrea Dworkin, Susan Griffin – I am sometimes irritated at having to clear a path through to what they are actually saying. As a reader you are given more time to feel but less time to think. Perhaps it is no coincidence that many women I know who thought Mary Daly's *Gyn/Ecology* beyond criticism when it was first published are now having second thoughts.

I am not saying, and I do not believe, that there is an ideal feminist form for political writing waiting to be invented, but I would argue that since anyone who writes has to make a decision about the form in which she writes, the least we can do as feminists is make sure we think about it consciously. The WLM has already produced guidelines we can use: steering us away from false objectivity, expecting us to acknowledge the contributions of other women, and above all *not* expecting us to be utterly sure of ourselves or to wrap everything up neatly.

If we get past the difficulty of finding the right way to write, there is another obstacle – can we phrase what we want to say 'correctly'? The idea of 'correctness' implies that there is some higher authority waiting to judge what we write. As we have become more aware of oppressive forms of language, so feminists – mainly middle-class White feminists – have acquired a fear of inadvertently betraying themselves in speech or through the written word. I encounter these fears mainly in discussion with other women about proposed pieces of writing, but I also believe that some women stay silent altogether rather than risk criticism for saying or writing something that others may interpret as racist, heterosexist, imperialist, class-biased, oppressive towards disabled women or mothers, and so on. I do not wish to trivialize the serious study of language, or to dispute how important it is for us to take care when we write not to use offensive words and phrases. But we need a more open way of confronting one another and of keeping debate going. At the moment, we avoid a lot of possible confrontations, because some of us who are confident that we know the right words to use go unchallenged, while others of us, afraid of using the wrong ones, stay silent. Words do not have fixed meanings, and when we pay obsessive attention to correct and incorrect vocabularies we are not necessarily changing what we think; we could just be learning a new set of rules. Meanwhile women who fear that they do not know the rules become discouraged, rather than thinking through or working out on paper their insecurities, while other women who feel that they do know, who may for example have been able to attend racism awareness courses, can become complacent.

Rules which stop women being articulate about their ideas and experience, which mark out exclusive groups from those not in the know, can hardly help us in developing and communicating feminist politics. From any number of examples I can recall two which seemed to me entirely unhelpful. One was the rule that you should never say 'girls', always 'women', because it is oppressive and trivializing to call a woman a girl – but a child of 8? The other was a whole set of rules invented by a group of women (wimmin, womyn) in defiance of patriarchal spellings and in particular aiming to avoid English word-forms which included the letters 'he' or 'men'. Women using the feminist variants communicated to each other, and to other women, that they belonged to an exclusive group of pioneers, but I could not and still cannot see that the variant spellings communicated much else about language and oppression. We need discussion rather than prescription, and we also need to deal more with what women say, not just with how they say it.

Poised to write, what do you do now about the worst fear of the lot – how will other women react when they find out what you really think? The writer is vulnerable – the difficulties I have just listed remind me just how vulnerable she is. Our most important source of help here is the support of other women to give us the courage and confidence to go ahead, which may sometimes mean seeking out women who are likely to agree with what we want to write. Women who set out to write explicitly feminist articles do not have the protection of a party line, or of a sense of academic detachment, or of a literary persona. There is also usually no money in it (though there may eventually be for someone else). But we need the written word because ideas get lost, are forgotten or distorted, because there are always new aspects of our oppression for us to understand and analyse, our strategies need changing, we get tired and pessimistic and want new sources of inspiration. So many good discussions go unrecorded, so many groups and campaigns leave hardly any traces of their existence, of what they achieved and of what they learned. We need to know about our successes and our mistakes. We need to know about our fears and doubts, we need to talk about being wrong as well as about knowing we're right. We need to criticize each other's writing without condemning, and to read and write without fearing to criticize. We can change the world, and a feminist polemic can help us to do it. We have a lot more to learn from each other than we can ever learn face to face in meetings.

A double knot on the peeny

Joy Hendry

Being a woman is difficult enough. But being a Scottish woman is more difficult still because of Scotland's position as an oppressed colony of England, and a nation with severe psychological hang-ups. There is the popular myth that the Scottish male is more domineering, his attitudes about women more 'primitive' than other men. Certainly, we have the same problems as women everywhere, but perhaps in more extreme form.

If the myth is true, then Scottish manhood is not entirely to blame. A look at Scottish history provides some reasons for men's behaviour: the loss of Scottish nationhood (an experience something like castration), a continuous and deliberate erosion of Scottish culture, the trauma of the Clearances, the greater levels of poverty, all these have brutalized the Scottish male, alienating him from his more natural self, from his native roots. Remove from people the sense of belonging in a particular place, deprive them of their language, their natural expression, the fabric of their traditional ways and customs, their art, their habits of thought, and you also remove a sense of responsibility to the environment, to other people. I believe the Scottish male has suffered even more from this process than the Scottish woman has.

Apart from this, Scots Presbyterianism has taken an exaggeratedly masculine form, and been historically anti-female, blaming on the female all the sins of the flesh (witness the monstrous witch-burnings in Scotland – thousands more than in the more populous England). It has also lacked the traditionally female virtues of compassion, sympathy, sensitivity, and so on, which it has begun to aspire to in this last century.

Is the Scottish dimension something every Scottish feminist must reject, turning instead to her sisters internationally and to the feminist movement? Indeed, some Scottish feminists do identify with London-based culture and fail to recognize the importance of Scottish autonomy and nationhood. As both feminist and Scottish separatist, I believe both are vital. Women have to learn to be women everywhere, but they also must relate to the environment they belong to. For Scottish women, that is a problem.

Becoming a feminist is a political and psychological revolution for a woman. She achieves a new perspective on the world, as do people from Wales, Ireland, Cornwall, Brittany, or Scotland, who come to recognize the thorough-going oppression of their nations by English imperialism, which affects even the minute fabric of life and culture. Both realizations involve a radical change of consciousness, a true revolution.

I do not want to see feminism imposing a khaki uniformity on women world-wide, but to see it encouraging self-liberation within a particular political and geographical context. The kind of nationalism I advocate is internationalism in a very real sense – a celebration of the differences of people everywhere, and their right to their own distinctive identity. As a Scottish woman writer, my concern is to engage in the feminist struggle within the Scottish context. My culture is under threat of extinction: both the Scots language and Gaelic hang on by the merest thread; Scottish culture has been and still is being eroded, diluted, Anglicized. Scottish women have been silenced. All that is very much my business.

Male dominated though it seems, the Scottish tradition is in many ways superior to the English ways which are gradually superseding it in many fields – in law, in education, in general philosophical outlook, as well as in more everyday aspects of life. It is tragic to see so much of worth disappearing. Being fundamentally egalitarian, the Scottish tradition is more compatible with feminism; belief in the importance of the people has been there in Scottish society for centuries. In education, for instance, the Protestant reformers decreed four centuries ago that education should be available for all, female and male, and a hundred years later had achieved much towards this end. Scottish education has always favoured a philosophical approach to studies, encouraging the individual to question presuppositions and advocating a widely-based general education, in direct opposition to the specialization favoured by English educational thinking. But little of this distinctive character remains: the Scottish system has been forced over the years to incorporate largely English 'reforms'.

Women's contribution to the development of the Scottish tradition has been considerable, but not easily visible. Particularly in pre-Reformation days, women often held whole estates together. Within clan society, they had their own respected place. During the Clearances, when the Highland population was forcibly removed from the glens and replaced with sheep, it was not the men, but the women who offered physical resistance to the officers sent to evict them. The triumph of women during the Glasgow rent strike is well known.

Writing is a claim to power. Scottish women are at one further remove from the seats of power by being first female and secondly Scottish. You can't deal with one without the other. Scottish culture as a whole is a neglected area, lacking in status and prestige. A Scottish woman writer shares that neglect with her male colleagues, as well as being overlooked and underestimated because she is a woman. Thus, the woman writer, rare enough anywhere, is even rarer in Scotland. The Scottish woman writer must overcome the inferiority feelings stemming from her femininity, and also those stemming from her Scottishness. It's the double knot on the peeny.

It's not easy for the Scottish woman to explore her Scottishness because knowledge of it is largely denied her in the educational system. And when she looks around for Scottish women writers of previous generations, she will seem to find very few.

Looking at anthologies and literary histories, you would be forgiven for thinking that the Scottish women writer didn't exist. Women tend to be mentioned in these volumes not for their writing, but for being the mother, mistress, wife, sister, or daughter of a male poet. The coverage of the few women (chiefly novelists) who do peek like a sunbeam through the male nimbus, is scanty and patronizing.

The woman novelist seems to be more readily accepted by the male literary establishment: the novelist deals with social and emotional matters – territory to which women have established their right. And the nineteenth-century novelists Mrs Oliphant and Susan Ferrier *have* had their writings recorded (but not much more) in the literary histories. In the twentieth century, reasonable coverage is given to novelists like Muriel Spark, Naomi Mitchison, and Jessie Kesson, but comparing that afforded to, say, Lewis Grassic Gibbon, it is hardly adequate, and many fine novelists are ignored altogether.

Scotland is not alone in this, but many women who wrote – diaries, novels, poetry – destroyed their writings prior to their death, because writing was not a seemly occupation for a lady. Many women passed their writings off as being by other people. It's not that they didn't write; of course they did. As early as 1700, a majority of Scottish people, men *and* women, could both read and write, so this is not the reason for the almost total lack of Scottish women poets prior to this century. The answer lies in the strength of the Scottish oral tradition and the tendency for it to be dismissed as an inferior branch of literature.

Scotland has one of the finest oral traditions in the world: look, for instance, at the richness of the Scottish ballads. This is a world of song and story, rhyme and riddle, legend and epic, a world which perpetuates itself not in print, but by word of mouth, passed from one generation to another by tradition bearers. A major role in oral literature has been played by women, as both creators and communicators of oral lore, of which little printed evidence remains.

There is a wealth of anonymous literature in the oral tradition, but you have to guess what originated from whom. Here is one example, taken from Burns's collection, *The Merry Muses of Caledonia*, traditional pieces, bawdy and appealingly uninhibited, which I suspect could only have been written by a woman. It is 'John Anderson, My Jo' from which I quote the second verse:

> John Anderson my jo, John,
> When first that ye began,
> Ye had as guid a tail-tree,
> as ony ither man;
> But noo it's waxen wan, John,
> And it wrinkles to and fro;
> And I've twa gae-ups for ae gae-doun,
> John Anderson, my jo.

Burns collected this piece, and later bowdlerized it, producing the better known version which is pale and sentimental by comparison.

The distinction between poetry and song is meaningless in the oral tradition, and has been vamped up by literary and music critics for their own reasons. For the art for art's sake school, song is too much of-the-earth-earthy to be admitted into the rarified world of poetry, which must be preserved in splendid isolation. In the Scottish poetic tradition, this is arrant nonsense; poetry always has been earthy and vigorous, unsympathetic to the polite, the mannered and the refined, but rooted instead in ordinary life, both glamorous and tedious. To see that the distinction between poetry and song has always been blurred, we need look no further than Burns himself. It is worth remembering that Scotland only nine hundred years ago was almost entirely Gaelic speaking, and at the back even of the very different Lowland tradition, there is much Gaelic influence.

In the Gaelic world, there is no relegation of poetry to cloudly Elysium or ivory towers; we have instead the bardic tradition, in which the bard enjoys real status and is an integral part of society, with a real duty and responsibility towards it, in all its aspects, however humble or elevated. It is hard for those brought up in the Anglo-American tradition to imagine a society in which poetry actually mattered to almost everyone and was an important part of life. This was certainly true of the Gàidhealtachd and is still, to an extent. Furthermore, to distinguish poetry from song is almost impossible. One of the strongest motivations for the Gaelic poet, Sorley MacLean, is to reproduce in poetry some of the greatness and subtlety of the old Gaelic songs.

With the exception of some present-day feminist writers, almost all Scottish women poets have been strongly influenced by this fertile oral tradition, and by the ballads in particular. Many have seen themselves as tradition bearers, and when they wrote, did so to add to that tradition. This is true even of women from the upper echelons of society. Not surprisingly, it is the aristocratic women who survive in print, to be roundly dismissed by literary critics as writers of song, rather than 'Poetry'. To name a few, these women are Lady Nairn, Lady John Scott, Lady Grisell Baillie, Elizabeth Hamilton, Alison Rutherford, Lady Anne Lindsay. Perhaps best known is Jean Elliot, 1727–1805, responsible for 'The Flowers of the Forest', the lament for the dead at the Battle of Flodden, 1513, when the Scots were heavily defeated by the English. Her words, set to an old lament, capture the sense of loss and tragedy for the community. I quote the first and third verses:

> I've heard the lilting of our yowe-milking,
> Lasses a-lilting before the dawn o' day;
> But now they are moaning on ilka green loaning;
> 'The Flowers of the Forest are a' wede away.'
>
> In hairst, at the shearing, nae youths now are jeering,
> The bandsters are lyart, and runkled and grey;
> At fair or at preaching, nae wooing, nae fleeching:
> The Flowers of the Forest are a' wede away.

Jean Elliot and another, Alison Rutherford, are dismissed by Maurice Lindsay in his *History of Scottish Literature* as 'one-song poetesses who, after the custom of the time, pretended that their productions were by other hands'. These women all chose to write in the 'Scottish vernacular' or Scots, despite social and political pressures to write in English which drove many, including the great philosopher David Hume, to employ Englishmen (and even Irishmen) to purge their writings of all Scotticisms. The women song-writers helped to preserve a pure tradition of writing in Scots, past the death of Burns and into the nineteenth-century Kailyard period; at this time writing in Scots became increasingly debased and parochial, as Burns's imitators fastened on the 'coothy', the sentimental, the home-orientated aspects of his writing. Their work gave all too rosy a picture of a Scotland which, far from being rural, happy, and peaceful, was being wracked by the Industrial Revolution.

The songs written by these women are rich in texture, both in melody and lyrics, and extremely various in content and mood. 'Caller Herrin', by Lady Nairne, is a market-place cry from a fisherwife such as could be seen in her striped apron (peeny) selling her wares on the streets of Edinburgh. But it also describes the dangers faced by the fishermen when catching the herring, a fish despised by the well-to-do, who 'cast their heads and screw their faces' at the fisherwife as they pass her in the street. But this fish, for the poor, for the 'wives and mithers, maist despairin', is called 'lives o' men'.

Lady Nairne's spirited 'Laird o' Cockpen' is a piece of humorous satire:

> The Laird o' Cockpen he's proud an' he's great,
> His mind is ta'en up wi' the things o' the State;
> He wanted a wife his braw house tae keep,
> But favour wi' wooin' was fashious to seek.

His male pomposity is roundly debunked when the lady refuses him with a brusque 'Na!', but in a nice touch in the last verse, he is found riding through the glen thinking, 'She's daft to refuse the Laird o' Cockpen.'

These are two of many. What matters is that the inspiration for the songs comes directly from the oral tradition; the language in which they are written is a muscular, lively and authentic Scots, a language much more vivid and down-to-earth than the more sophisticated effeteness of English. The contribution made by these women to Scottish literature has not been properly appreciated. They speak with a distinctively female voice, and it is to them that Scottish women must look for our historical antecedents.

In 1980, Alexander Scott, a well-known Scottish poet, denied to me that there were *any* Scottish women poets. He spoke not out of ignorance, but contentiously, denying that any Scottish women had written poetry worthy of attention. But around the beginning of this century, we find two women in particular, Violet Jacob and Marion Angus, who, like their song-writing predecessors, maintain an authentic Scottish voice despite the nineteenth-century Kailyard sentimentality. They are direct descendants of the song-writers and the oral and ballad tradition, employing many of its conventions in their writing. At times their poetry is marred by Kailyard nostalgia, but on the whole, their direct, simple, and honest writing marks them out. Both write largely in Scots.

Violet Jacob (1863–1946) was an aristocrat, the daughter of the eighteenth Laird of Dun. A poet and storyteller, she produced novels (*Flemington, The Interloper, The Sheepstealers*) and short stories. The novels are long out of print, but her short stories were recently republished. Her prose work is due for re-evaluation.

Her poems are best remembered. They are deceptively easy to read and come in a variety of moods: nostalgic poems of exile, poems about places; lively, witty pieces. Often she assumes various characters: a ploughman, a shepherd, a young girl, and produces a poem which is essentially dramatic in nature. In one of her best known poems, 'Tam i' the Kirk', she captures the first exhilaration of love, highlighted by the austere setting of the Scottish kirk. This is the first verse:

> O Jean, my Jean, when the bell ca's the congregation
> Owre valley an' hill wi' the ding frae its iron mou',
> When a'body's thochts is set on his ain salvation,
> Mine's set on you.

Rarely does she write without assuming a dramatic mask, except in the poems written about her only son, killed in the First World War.

Marion Angus (1866–1946), born in Arbroath, daughter of the United Free Presbyterian manse, lived with her family most of her life. Her use of Scots is possibly stronger than Violet Jacob's (who learned it not from her family, but by being 'aye in and oot amo' the ploomen's feet' – see *Octobiography* by Helen B. Cruickshank). She has been disparaged for writing about the supernatural world, but one must remember that the world of the fairies was real enough to the common folk not so very long ago. The most striking quality of her verse is its ability to evoke deep sympathy in the reader, as in this poem, 'Ann Gilchrist':

> As I gae by the Bleedie Burn
> Whaur's nayther leaf nor tree,
> Lat me nae hear Ann Gilchrist's feet
> Nor sicht her evil e'e.
>
> As I gaed by the Bleedie Burn
> Tae the witches' howff I cam' –

Ann Gilchrist's in among the whin
  Seekin' a wandert flamb.

She's ta'en it frae the thorny buss,
  Syne thro' the moss and fern
She's croonin' it and cuddlin' it
  As gin it were a bairn.

An' I wuss the whins wis nae sae shairp
  Nor the muckle moss sae weet,
For wha wull gie Ann Gilchrist fire
  Tae warm her clay-cauld feet?

I quote the poem in full because it illustrates her ability (shared with Violet Jacob) to tell a story in a few verses. She can also produce startling, but sensitive portraits, like the much anthologized 'Alas Poor Queen' about Mary Queen of Scots.

It is, in fact, the political dimension which is absent from their writing, inevitably, given their sex and circumstances. Helen B. Cruickshank (1886–1975) was born an important twenty years later than Jacob and Angus, and became involved in suffragism while in London, and later, in active Scottish Nationalism. Unfortunately, she fell prey to circumstances all too common for women then and not unknown now: she had to look after her widowed mother, giving up her freedom until too old to pick up the threads again. However, she had a public life too; she was a life-long civil servant (her sex and lack of money debarred her from university education); she was secretary and founder member of Scottish PEN; she had a very active social life, keeping open house for her many literary friends, including Hugh MacDiarmid, holding as many parties as her limited means allowed.

What I find extraordinary about her poetry is its quality of compassion and generosity. She had two love affairs, neither of which led to marriage, one of them because her commitment to her mother forced her to say 'goodbye to my hopes of being able to wed my penniless artist'. This was a major blow, which she faced with characteristic bravery and unselfishness, evident in this poem, 'A Prayer':

Oh, Thou who dost forbear
  To grant me motherhood,
Grant that my brow may wear
  Beneath its maiden snood
Love to distressed Mankind,
  And helpful sympathy

For all whom Fate doth bind
 In Sorrow's company.

She also wrote extensively and well in Scots. There is considerable range of subject, mood, and voice, often combining humour and seriousness in a way which is typically Scots. She can be spirited as well as sad: in the sonnet 'At the End', she claims 'Fire will I have for my swift and perfect lover.' She can be both profound and controversial, as in 'Comfort and Puirtith' in which she compares the children of poverty, who will 'warstle tae the fore/Wi' hunger-sharpit brains!' with the 'pudden thrang' bred by 'creeshy W'alth'.

The critics are patronizing about Jacob and Angus, seeing them essentially as 'poor dears'. Alan Bold, in his book *Modern Scottish Literature*, typifies the male critics' attitude when he compares them to a male contemporary, Lewis Spence: 'Spence was no shrinking Violet or a home-made Marion, but a man who put his patriotic ideal to a public test.' The Scottish poet Hugh MacDiarmid, however, knew better. On more than one occasion, he acknowledges his debt to Jacob and Angus for advancing the cause of literature in Scots, for paving the way for the revolution in Scottish literature which he brought about in the 1920s and 30s. If the work of Jacob (and Angus) is limited in scope, MacDiarmid sees this as inevitable given the political circumstances of Scotland. He refers to

> her apparent obliviousness to the vital problems confronting Scottish nationality today [which] a better orientated spirit with her raciality of character could not have refrained from addressing. In other words, the present position of Scotland as a nation has deprived us of all but a shadow of the Mrs Jacob whom in less over-Anglicized circumstances we might have had.

By a 'better orientated spirit', MacDiarmid means, I think, her political and social position as a woman, preventing her coming to grips with the vital issues of her day, the lack of self-confidence and endemic reticence which has led many women to content themselves with more trivial and peripheral subjects. Of Jacob's understanding of, and love for, Scottish life and culture, and of her unfulfilled potential, he clearly has no doubt. So MacDiarmid agrees that there is a double knot on the peeny. These Scottish women, and many others, writing in the non-Gaelic tradition, have been much derided and ignored. They deserve a better fate.

More fortunate, however, are the Gaelic women poets, operating in a society where poetry matters fundamentally and in which women have always been accepted as poets and bards (although there *has* still been discrimination in favour of the male poets). I am not competent to deal with the Gaelic tradition, but it must be mentioned. There have been several major Gaelic women writers whose importance is recognized. To name a few – Sìleas na Ceapaich (Julia Macdonald of Keppoih), Mairi Nighean Alasdair Ruadh (Mary MacLeod) and Màiri Mhòr nan Oran (Great Mary of the Songs), the bard of the Land League Movement of 1882 in Skye.

At least two Gaelic women poets were buried face downwards to prevent their restless spirits and powerful words continuing to exert influence over the living. That is testament to the standing that they, and others like them, had in their community. It is also a powerful symbol for women struggling to write now in Scotland. And for those who are dead, may it make them turn in their graves.

I tell my 3 year old she's real . . . : writing lesbian-feminist children's books

Caroline Halliday

Reading a bedtime story is not as calm as it used to be. Not if you are a lesbian mother with a daughter who has a disability. A child needs to find her/his self, her likeness in the books she uses, not some patriarchal notion of the 'normal' child. With some exceptions, children's books promote stereotypes of physically perfect, white, middle-class children who live with mum and dad. In 1983 there was not a single English book which depicted lesbian or gay life styles for young children. So when my daughter was very young there were no books which matched our reality, which said to me and to her, 'You're *real*. . . .

Of course, you can swallow the anger and frustration at night after night of other people's reality telling us that lesbians and our children don't exist, and that racism and violence are acceptable. I don't want that. Or you can turn every book into a lesson in politics, changing the 'he's' into 'she's', pointing out that the lack of Black children doesn't depict her friendship group. You can remind her and yourself that she has three mums and no dad at all and so do many of her friends. And you can search in vain for books that have children with disabilities as characters, rather than subject matter. The only other possibility is to demand new books from publishers. And write them yourself.

When my daughter was 2½ I began to sketch out stories which put us and our lives into the centre of the story and the images – our reality, amongst the lesbians we know, Black and white, disabled and able-bodied – books which said, 'You can be yourself, a girl with a short arm and a full length arm and hand. This book is about *you*.'

Writing for children in this context demands thinking out and expressing the most exciting politics I can manage, to present positive and accurate images of children and adults with disabilities – a community where child care is child-centred, and where adult women are friends to each other and the children, and not necessarily biologically linked – and at the same time reduce the racism and class stereotypes.

To describe this child-centred world means unlearning our adult concepts and beginning to understand liberation for children. This might include being more relaxed about time and about 'efficiency' and 'rationality', and envisaging a world where children could make their own decisions about their clothing, food, eating, sleeping and playing times. It would not be a situation where they were at risk or were oppressing adults, but an altered world of work, home, and community which respected children. So activities would happen which were geared to a child's level, where cupboards, sinks and safe cookers could be reached. Comfortable play areas would be integrated with houses and shops, and 'grown-up' activities such as car maintenance and building work would include children as participants or observers. This would be a community where adults and children could move in and out of each other's living spaces whilst respecting privacy and the wish for solitude.

Feminist children's books must show the multiracial society in this country, in which children and women live in different classes and are affected by race and class divisions. The books must explain how people live in different ways here and all over the world, often in the face of extreme difficulty and oppression. White, middle-class writers cannot write books which 'accurately reflect the Black perspective', nor which are 'relevant to Black children'.[1*] And that includes Black children who are in different classes and who may well be disabled. These books must be written by Black and white working-class feminists and those from all different identity backgrounds, all of which include disabled women.

The problem for women in these groups in the past has been access to the necessary resources, both of time and of encouragement to write and illustrate, and the resources of publishing, money and influence. Women who have had greater access must recognize this and respond by widening the spectrum of women involved at all stages of the production. And at the same time they must make sure they do accurately represent people different from themselves. (See a good article in *Racism and Sexism in Children's Books*.)[2]

I also want men to write and present alternative images of themselves, and of boys' lives, to the macho, role-playing stereotypes of Tarzan, or daddy out washing the car. There is a new generation of images now, Superman and his friends, but the details haven't changed. Men, as writers

---

* Superior figures refer to the References at the end of chapters.

and illustrators, must look at all aspects of their images, and publishers must check this out minutely. It is not enough to show girls in active roles if the specific details of what they are doing don't support that possibility, and if the overall context puts boys in the lead. Boys must have their counterpart choices presented seriously. Our boy children require models to identify with, of men and boys capable of sharing their emotions, feeling fear, and expressing physical affection to each other. Girls need to get support from these presentations of their small male friends.

I wanted to write books showing lesbians in the foreground and others with us in the background, taken for granted. (Just as mummy and daddy are never explained.) Books are like bricks: some lay the foundations then another layer takes off into the clouds. A girl and her mothers in a spaceship need no explanation to my daughter. But maybe we won't be able to write these fantasy stories until our ordinary lives and our hopes for the future have been described for children, displayed in bookshops, and discussed by reviewers, and most important, taken on board by publishers, schools, and librarians.

The books I worked on in 1982–3 were simple experiments in these directions for ages two and a half and upwards. *Everybody's Different*,[3] which has now been published by Dalston Children's Centre, was a workshop production in conjunction with Ingrid Pollard, who did the illustrations, and with mothers at the Centre. In it, Jessy, a child with a short arm, goes to a party of lesbian mothers and children where there are face-paints and a summer witch to give out presents, and she meets up with a friend who has a minor disability. In the second half of the book, she is at her multiracial nursery which includes children with physical and learning disabilities. Jessy and the staff deal with the interest of a new child in her short arm and the replies the children can make on the theme 'everybody is different':

> 'Everybody's different', Lisa says. 'Think about it. Some of you have got brown hair and others have got fair hair. It's just the way you were born.'
> 'And I've got brown skin and Kevin's got pink skin', Pauline adds.
> 'And Shaun wears glasses and I don't', Kay says.
> 'Kay is small and I'm big', Jessy points out.
> 'And Chantelle can't talk but she likes being tickled.'

Another story was called 'Jessy has three mothers' and used the idea of a map to explore the area where Jessy lives in two different households, with her three mothers and other adults who care for her. Another text, 'Sometimes we all shout', showed children and women shouting out of hurt and anger, and in celebration, pride and joy, 'Girls and women can be strong. . . .'

In 1985 a group of us* worked on a children's book for under–5s commissioned by the Greater London Council (GLC). It had to express their four policy guidelines of being anti-racism, anti-sexism, anti-heterosexism, and pro-disability. The book plan we presented concentrated on images of ourselves and our children living in the lesbian-feminist community. The aim was to have full colour photographs, text in two languages and braille. The book showed fun times and work, celebrations and rows.

Here are our friends and our mothers. Lots of them are lesbians and that means they are women who love themselves and each other.

It had photos of a girl on roller skates pushing her adult friend in a wheelchair, a son helping his disabled mother wash herself, girls and women learning woodwork and British Sign Language and going to meetings, as well as watching television and so on . . .

We meet people who don't like our mothers being lesbians. Some of them shout at our friends or tease us as school. BUT WE DON'T AGREE WITH THEM, and we talk to our friends about it and decide what we should say to THEM.

The project was not completed for the GLC because of lack of funding (and even the GLC wanted men in the book). We will take the manuscript[4] to an independent publisher eventually; its value has been in working out ways of expressing our lesbian-feminist politics in suitable ways for under-fives, and in the formal and informal passing on of ideas about children's books which resulted from it. A project like this is also significant as it slowly builds up the collaboration between women who are disabled, and Black and white women. The use of photographs, of course, puts our safety in question, especially as Black lesbians, lesbian mothers and disabled lesbians, in a way most heterosexuals have no notion of, and tests the extent we as lesbians can know and trust each other across boundaries which potentially divide us.

---

* Ingrid Pollard is a Black photographer, illustrator and filmmaker, committed to exploring the wide range of ways 'people' can be, to counter the dominant view of 'normal'. Pat Rock is a white working-class woman with a disability who was co-founder of Sisters against Disablement, and is active in disability politics. My thanks go to both of them, and to the many friends who have contributed to the ideas in this article and to the radical changes in my thoughts about disability over the last five years.

Personally, it has helped me to re-evaluate feminist but able-bodyist concepts which I unconsciously incorporated into the first drafts. Most noticeable was the emphasis placed on active 'doing', something which comes from a desire to counter the sexist notion of 'passive' girls. Parallel to this was the idea of girls' and women's 'strength', which went unchallenged in the initial stages. The necessity, of course, is to recognize the other side of these concepts and incorporate a changed awareness. We are not actively 'doing' all the time, whether we are able-bodied or, most obviously, if we are disabled. And although 'strength' is an inspiring ideal sometimes, it is and must be tempered by accepting our vulnerabilities, welcoming the sharing and relief they can bring – by recognizing we have real fears (of attack, of lifts, etc) and acknowledging our uncertainties about ourselves and our abilities ('I can't do that . . .', 'I'm afraid of . . .').

For children and women with considerable invisible or visible disabilities or illnesses, life is full of awareness and feelings, many painful, unpleasant, slow, depressing and unwanted. Some of these feelings are exacerbated by an environment and society which prevents people with disabilities from participating, and increases rather than alleviates their difficulties. Others are inherent in the nature of the illness or disability. This aspect of reality must be brought into the themes of children's books.

As an able-bodied woman writing this article I am indebted to the challenges to my thinking by friends with disabilities. Working in collaboration is an important stage, but to transcribe a previous quote (p. 47), 'Can able-bodied writers accurately reflect the "disabled" perspective?' Clearly not.

In the community I feel part of, we are beginning to develop or rediscover patterns to mark out life events and crises. In a joking conversation a few years ago I invented . . . the winter witch. She comes to give out presents and has taken hold of our children's imaginations, arriving at any suitable event during the winter. As female symbolic images become used more automatically by women, it is important that we place them inside our books, strengthening our children's minds against the violent destructive imagery they experience elsewhere on television and video.

I would like them to have a story based on the celebration for the life of Sue Cartledge, which we attended with my daughter and where we participated in the laughing, the songs, the stories about Sue's life, music and crying. I was very moved that we could both be part of this significant celebration, an alternative to just mourning, an alternative made actual. In the Christian tradition there is a tendency to hide death away, especially from children, (which is not present, for example, in the Jewish tradition). This tendency produces illusions of living for ever, it reinforces a belief that it is possible to be perfect and rejects anything 'not perfect' – illness, disability, change. It is hard to incorporate pain, illness, and death when we are only beginning to deal with these things differently as a community, but often something 'difficult' for an adult changes its impact through explaining it to a child, and enables us to note the conditioning which has produced our responses.

What about books including children with disabilities? The information books are coming through, though they are sadly lacking in any political dimension, and there are a few poetic books, but they don't combat 'normalism' – the central concept of our society – that anyone who is not normal is *inferior*. For 'normal' read 'white, male, heterosexual, middle class, gentile, able-bodied, good-looking, and fast at learning male concepts . . .' or any cluster of these attributes with a pecking order depending on how many of them you've got!

Most of us are totally indoctrinated by normalism. One of my major difficulties in writing books for my daughter lay in working out my own attitudes to disability so that I could get beyond 'don't show disability in a negative way', and take on an approach which expressly *welcomes* physically and mentally different people and celebrates them. Take a minute or two to think what that means to you. An approach which also shows their creative solutions and ideas in relation to their disability. As an able-bodied mother of a child with a disability I can be an 'ally' in political terms of people with disabilities. I don't claim to have reached the level of awareness described above, but I know where I want to go. Neither have I yet managed to use my imagination or observed my child enough to describe how she feels within and about her body. The current active work by women with disabilities will produce books which are closer and more real.

There is a new child in the nursery today. He keeps pulling at Jessy's arm because he's never seen someone different from himself.
'You haven't got a hand', he says.
'I have got a hand *and* an arm', Jessy replies firmly.

Helga shows Jessy a photo of her riding a bike on the farm.
'My short arm is very strong', Helga tells her, 'because when I was at college I used to work in the bar and lift a lot of heavy crates.'
'I like being different', Jessy says. 'Everybody's different.'[5]

I would like to have books which deal further with normalism – books which explain to my child why an older boy at the paddling pool came up, saw her arm and said 'Ugh'. I was very angry and he later apologised. Or why a mother in another playground could say to my friend about her son who has a hand with no fingers, 'You should put a glove on that!'

The Blue Rose by Gerda Klein[6] expresses a little of this. It describes a girl called Jenny who has a learning disability and it tries to deal with her pain and sadness about 'children who taunt [and] who say I'm retarded; Mommy, what does retarded mean?' The book approaches Jenny lovingly and imaginatively, but at the same time it complacently accepts the normalism in the lives round her, featuring a white, heterosexual family, weddings, and brave male astronauts!

Another book, *Sally Can't See* by Palle Petersen,[7] contains some mixed messages:

> Sometimes [Sally] meets strangers who are sorry for her and curious about her blindness. This makes Sally upset and cross, because people seem to think there is something strange about her. And all she wants is to be treated as much like other children as possible. So if you *ever* meet a blind person, remember Sally who is learning so much *although* she cannot see.
> (The italics are mine.)

I am sympathetic to the author's aims and the first two lines are great. Sally has every right to feel cross and upset. My daughter and I have role-playing and shouting sessions where we recreate the scenes that have hurt and made us angry. If the people round us were all better informed, and if people with disabilities hadn't been forced into 'special' places, or to stay at home, then the able-bodied would not be curious about the physically different people they interact with.

But 'if you ever meet . . .' makes it sound pretty unlikely, as if blind people were extremely rare, rather than part of our society, and divided off and made to segregate themselves from the 'normals'. And does Sally want to be treated 'as much like' other children as possible? In some ways, yes. She doesn't want to be singled out *because* of her blindness, but to have her particular needs recognized appropriately. ' . . . although she cannot see' contains another hidden negative; Sally's blindness doesn't affect her ability to learn unless society is unwilling to choose teaching methods she can use.

We have to search out and reject the books which casually depict people with disabilities as cruel, odd, and ugly. Books that have value in other respects could be used as learning material to demonstrate anti-disability stereotypes. Libraries and schools could make use of stickers at the beginning of the book which state the book contains negative images around disability/

race/class/gender identity and advise teachers, pupils, and parents to discuss and think about the issues.

An example for outright rejection of a book came recently at my daughter's school. She came home with a picture book of *Three Blind Mice*,[8] for practice reading. Not only were the mice wearing dark glasses, which only some blind people choose to wear, but they were carrying the brown walking sticks with curved handles mostly used to help people with walking, not the white sticks which blind people have a purpose for. The editors would no doubt claim that these old-fashioned images were appropriate to the historical period of the nursery rhyme. Considering how distasteful they were, I would demand wholesale rejection of the rhyme as a vehicle for learning to read.

The severed tails were unnecessarily obvious. We are dealing here with the delicate area of images, impressions which can evoke and reinforce traditional stereotypes. Disability is seen in many negative ways – as evil, fearful, a stigma, a punishment, ugly, gruesome, ridiculous, even contagious. Many of these connotations have been reinforced by religion, traditional tales, and in literature in general – from three blind mice to Captain Hook. They damage our children's minds and it is time editors took a position against it. We must demand books which celebrate difference, give accurate information and which welcome the idea that really to *include* all of us would improve life *for* all of us. Our children deserve this.

Children under 5 are well aware of oppression, and the prejudice and stereotypes that go with it. Once they have grasped the idea and been given words for the *concept* they can apply it themselves.

'Why aren't there small toilets in houses?'
'You grown ups turn the taps off too HARD.'

Learning the words for oppression, racism, antisemitism, heterosexism, gives children *power* over their environment, enables them to discriminate between one set of ideas or behaviours and another, and ultimately to choose where their allegiances will go. Learning these concepts begins well before five. To show children what different kinds of oppression are is therefore education in its truest sense, enabling better life choices. But for the adults around them it can be frightening, because it threatens our power over oppression of them.

Think how challenging it is for patriarchal society when, in a conversation about the film *Supergirl*, with R, aged 5, she said, 'There are too many heterosexual bits in it . . . *but* you don't have to look'; and when our daughters say at 4 years old, 'I'm a lesbian too, Mummy.'

At home we have two different versions of the story of Snow White: one in which the pale princess is kissed and is passive, and a feminist version from *Once and Future Tales*,[9] in which Snow White rebels against the queen and leads the people against the soldiers. To me this is a laudable piece of alteration and the story is dramatic and moving. But it manages this at the expense of *not* examining the continuing racism in the title of Snow White, the equation of white with good and black with evil. The negative role of stepmothers in many fairy tales also needs to be re-examined.

K and I had a thorough discussion and role-playing session about what 'princesses' are shown as doing and what *real girls* can enjoy. This is teaching the concept of sexism. Today I heard her say to her friend that the crossing light was a green person, not a green *man*.

As K grows older these new stories encourage her to write her own. But we need hundreds of them to show her and other readers, even those who live in a nuclear family dominated by a male, that there are many more possibilities for a different kind of life that 'normalist' society offers us: the supportive lesbian community K and I have helped to create versus the pink princess; massage as a way of relaxing and healing versus guns and bombs; these are the choices as I find them. I want stories to read which make these choices real to children.

Everybody's Different has now been published and K helped to sell some. 'This book is about me', she said proudly.

References

1 Albert V. Schwartz, 'Sounder: a black or white tale?', in *Racism and Sexism in Children's Books* (Writers' and Readers' Publishing Cooperative, 1979).
2 Carla Stevens, 'The image of gypsies in children's literature', in *Racism and Sexism in Children's Books*.
3 Ingrid Pollard and Caroline Halliday, *Everybody's Different* (Dalston Children's Centre, 1984).
4 Ingrid Pollard, Caroline Halliday and Pat Rock, 'Hooray', unpublished manuscript.
5 *Everybody's Different*.
6 Gerda Klein, *The Blue Rose* (Lawrence Hill & Co., 1974).
7 Palle Petersen, *Sally Can't See* (A & C Black, 1975).
8 Aidan Warlow (ed.), *Three Blind Mice, Start with Rhymes* (Ginn and Co. Ltd).
9 'Snow White: Once and Future Tales', 53 Sandown Lane, Liverpool L15, reprinted in *Hard Feelings, Stories from Spare Rib* (1979).

Contributor's note

I have attempted to change the language in this chapter which expresses things in able-bodied terms, which are as oppressive as negative language about blackness. The chapter has also caused me to think in depth about 'looksism', the rejection of people on the basis of how they look which works alongside normalism. Both work through fear of difference.

Women and fiction: how we present ourselves and others

Rosalind Brackenbury

In the course of both reading and writing fiction over the last fifteen years, I have found it interesting to see how our idea of ourselves as women has affected the way we have presented ourselves in print, and the way we create both our female and male characters. The Women's Movement has had a profound effect upon literature throughout the world; and just as our actions and decisions create our literature, so in turn we are represented by that literature, given back a new reflection of ourselves in portraits of other women, united by what we perceive we have in common. Over the last decades especially, there has been a growth in women's publishing, women's criticism, women's journalism, women's political theory, as well as, and dependent upon, a mass of new women's writing of fiction. I think it is better to be a woman writing now than it has ever been; as the Women's Movement has encouraged us to find our true voice and tell what we know, so the new institutions of publishing houses and women's studies have pushed new standards of criticism and theory into the world, to be made accessible to men as well. I see the theory as inseparable from the practice. Nobody writes in a vacuum, away from the political and social structures in which we live. We breathe the air of today's thought, we digest it in everything we read and consider; also, we create it. This is largely the role of women today: to create, present, and consider a new world. We are doing it in very many ways. I think the point can never be to exclude men, but rather to initiate, to insist upon change, to share our thinking with them as we do it.

So I want to consider the way that we as women writers experience and interpret ourselves and the world. First, ourselves. Women's fiction has a range, a power and a public presence that it has never had before. I think perhaps I would rather say, women's writing. For we have seen the connections of 'fact' with fiction and dared to make bridges between the two. In order to make plain truths that were veiled or only guessed at, women writers have had to risk themselves, talk about themselves openly, put themselves on view. We can no longer hide behind our characters, manipulating them as puppets on stage, presenting shadow plays for public amusement. The 'writer as God' could never have been a woman. From Charlotte Brontë's impulsive 'Reader, I married him', on through confessional fiction, into the literature of the personal–political stance, the masks are down, the movement is towards truth-telling, towards demystification. Barthes' description of the writer 'pointing to the mask he is holding in front of his face' can hardly apply to women writers of the last two decades; in very many cases the masks have been down, faces have been shown, the veils have been removed. Women have said more about themselves and each other than possibly ever before; there is a vast literature of telling, of showing, of sharing, of analysing how it has been. As in consciousness-raising groups, so in fiction; telling each other how it has been is immensely reassuring. It has given us courage to write, to tell it, too. Other women's daring has been a stepping stone, has created a bridge.

I am thinking here of so many women who have been for me, in various ways, part of that bridge: the women in the 1960s who talked about child-rearing and housework and the drudgery of the kitchen sink; the women who have talked openly about their sexuality – Erica Jong's ebullient heroines, Mary McCarthy in *The Group*, Doris Lessing in *The Golden Notebook*, to name a few; the women who have been political, openly angry. Then there are the women who have taken apart the whole structure of what 'the novel' is supposed to be: many Frech women writers here, for me, who have seen the connection between language and oppression, and who have been radical in 'telling it differently' – Hélène Cixous, Marguerite Duras, Benoîte Groult, Catherine Clément – women who have told of themselves, from their own unique point of view, and changed the grammar of storytelling in doing so. Then again there are Angela Carter and Judy Chicago; Germaine Greer; Anais Nin, with her insistent insight that the way was inward, through the personal, to reach what was universal, whose diaries changed millions of women's lives. It is good to name a few of them, my literary god-mothers, the ones who built the bridges I have been able to cross.

But a question occurs: why, with such examples of confidence and daring, with such a tradition now of excellence, is it still so difficult for so many women to trust themselves to write? I think the answer lies with the outer and the inner image, with the gap that still exists between the two. We write, we create, we act, we take power, we describe the new worlds we envisage, and still we feel uneasy. There is still the voice in our ear that suggests that we ought to be doing something else, cleaning the house, doing '*real*' work, doing something for somebody else. It is still the voice of Virginia Woolf's 'angel in the house', killed off fifty years ago, yet coming back to be finished off over and over again. If the angel in the house were really dead, thousands more women would be writing, making their voices heard. For those of us who are writing, there is often still the insidious murmur, suggesting that this is not what we should be doing, that it should be more important. The conditioning has been so heavy for most women that it cannot perhaps disappear overnight. Yet, as we do transform our world and as men perceive their own role changing, the outer situation is capable of change. The voice of the angel in the house may linger on for some years yet, an ever-fading whisper, increasingly out of date, but while it is still there, I think we have to keep on arguing back. I think of Tillie Olsen, author of *As I Stand Here Ironing* and *Silences*, so aware of what has silenced women over centuries and what silences us still: others' needs, poverty, overwork, ridicule, the whole weight of an oppressive society. This society, though changed and changing, is still with us; and this is why I see writing and social change as inseparable, interlinked. Unless we can change the structures, the assumptions from the past, we cannot change our own way of thinking, being, writing. I think this is widely understood by women now, but particularly for older women, for women with husbands and children, for women involved in the family structure in any way, the problems do not automatically get solved.

How we see ourselves, then, is still linked with and determined by the ways in which society has seen us. To what extent this is true may be seen by how many writers write in reaction. We have not been listened to, and so we will be heard. There is a strand in women's writing which is reactionary in this way; I mean, in reacting to the status quo. We have not been listened to, and now we will be heard. It is good to talk of childbirth, periods, masturbation, rape, men and how they have oppressed us, all the subjects that have been taboo. It is the step on to the first stepping stone, or even on to the one after, or the one after that. We will tell each other, share with each other, and inform men; and here we are, mid-stream, looking about for the next foothold. And where shall it be?

Recently, in a women's bookshop, I was browsing, reading, enjoying the evidence of what women have done. Yet in among the shelves of fiction I was all at once struck by a certain sameness, a certain sense of repetition. I thought all at once – what shall we do next? We have told, explained, described, analysed, what it is like to be a woman. A woman in relation to other women, to children, to men, to our parents. But, centrally, to be a woman. To have breasts and periods and a certain view of the world, a view that has for a long time been mostly unexpressed. To have our own way of seeing things, saying things, understanding things, and our own way of working. We have now in writing fiction at least, put ourselves back firmly at the centre of our own worlds. The effect, the great effect of women's fiction upon women's lives over the last few years, has been to create this change in emphasis, so that now we can believe in the worth of our own experience. No woman now will have to believe that what a man says about her sexuality must be the 'real' truth. No woman has to bow down uncritically to the axioms of Freud. No woman has to think that to be a poet, a playwright, a novelist, you either have to be, or pretend to be, a man. The evidence is there, in the bookshops, available, at last.

But as I read and browsed, and sat on the floor surrounded by books, all books by women, I thought how slow I had been to dare to put my own experience at the centre. I appreciated the work of the women all around me, who had been more daring, perhaps more perceptive than I, or who were younger, born in a different time; and I thought – what shall we do next? What direction shall we go in now? If we were yet more confident in ourselves, we should dare to speak not only of ourselves, but of the world. We would dare to include men, to see them as human beings like ourselves. We would break open, finally, the old structures that allow us to go on seeing ourselves as less than completely powerful, and men either as incomprehensible or the enemy. We would write of a world in which men exist as our brother, friends, and equals. For this is what I think has been missing from women's fiction. Yes, we have turned the tables; used men sexually perhaps in their turn, berated them for sexism, excluded them when we needed to exclude them, when it was sensible to exclude them; but what now? For as long as we write in reaction to sexism, our writings will be reactionary. Sure of ourselves as women and as artists, surely we can look now at the whole picture. Men share the world with us, yet in much of women's fiction have been presented as cardboard figures, ogres, or dwarfs. A balance that needed to be redressed has been redressed. But, as I see it, no man ever consciously chose to behave in a sexist way, and nobody would ever play the role of 'baddie' unless mistreated first. Men are not the enemy in society, for they are human beings too; but more importantly here, where the discussion is of art and writing, I do not think that writing can flourish which excludes or distorts out of fear.

This does not mean that I want male 'characters' flooding back into fiction wearing their old disguises, flourishing swords and moustaches, taking over the show once again. I doubt if the traditional idea of 'character' as something separate from the subjectivity of the author can survive in the novel or be resurrected; we know too much now of the workings of our own minds and of how society moulds us. As women writing, we will not be able to pretend to be men, either in the sense of writing as if we were men, or by being male 'characters'. We know too much of the distortion and pain of pretence. As we will never again take ourselves to be Lady Chatterley or Anna Karenina or Madame Bovary, so we will never again, I think, assume the painful necessity to 'be' men. This does not mean that we will not pay attention to what men writers are trying to say about themselves when they write about women, or that we will give up trying to understand the men we may write about. When I talk of welcoming men back into our world, in writing, I mean in a spirit of truth-telling, inviting truth-telling in reply, in the spirit we have begun to develop over the last two decades while talking about ourselves. As I write this, I think of Doris Lessing's treatment of the man, and the male principle, in her novel *The Marriage Between Zones Three, Four and Five* and of the momentum that book has as a result.

In our lives, as we welcome men back as friends and potential equals, so we can welcome them back into what we write. But it will be on new terms, in a tone that is initiatory rather than reactionary – truly revolutionary, truly creative. A structure that has to change in order to allow this has already changed in many women's lives. We do know men who are not automata ruled by a push-button sexuality, and it is time we said this. The conspiracy to pretend that we are all of us, men and women, governed only by our sexual urges, has been propaganda to keep us in our place – men aggressive, women passive. So-called sexual liberation was often personal enslavement. Portrayals of men and women together in fiction have concentrated on the sexual connection, men with constant literary erections, women either welcoming or reacting to them on every page: sex war or sexual binge, two sides of the same phenomenon. This has been true of 'quality' fiction, though disguised tastefully enough; in pulp fiction it reaches absurdity. In the grip of propaganda by pornography, we have been made to forget what we are really like, made to consider ourselves powerless, manipulable, unable to change our relationships and thus unable to change the world; separated off from each other, doomed to misunderstand each other, closed in our own separate worlds. The political aspect of this vision of helplessness is not far to seek.

As the Women's Movement, women in general, have agreed to reject the image of ourselves put out by the propagandists – the glamour image, the perfect mother image, the image first invented by men and internalized by ourselves through no fault of our own, the image of the 'angel in the house' – so, now, we could reject this image of ourselves in our connection with men. We could reassert our ability to communicate with each other, our basic humanness, the way we share this planet, the things we have in common. We could carry on telling how it really is, and invent how we want it to be. We could say that the era of the voracious prick and the insatiable cunt has had its fling, that we want to begin listening to each other again, that this is how the real world must go. In doing so, we would be making art, in our writing, because art is concerned with the complexity, the two-sidedness, the interaction of things.

This just a beginning. I think it is important to realize how much has changed in the last decade or so, in order to appreciate how much we are capable of change. In 1971, it was possible for a whole debate to take place around Norman Mailer's book, *The Prisoner of Sex*, in which the whole problem was seen as who was fucking and who being fucked. Germaine Greer asked at that time for a re-invention of the whole grammar of sexual connection, perceiving that until this could happen, men's and women's writing would be characterized by this assumption of exploitation, and she was right. Essentially, the insights of the Women's Movement and what it has offered to men of liberation from their own fixed roles, have changed male-female relationships for ever. Now, I think it is time that we caught up with the fact of this change, both in our statements about our lives and our writing of fiction. Even though it may sometimes feel as though nothing much has changed, and as if the 'brave new world' which Shakespeare saw is still out of reach, the fact is that we have lived through a revolution. If we realize and rejoice in this, our writing will move effortlessly away from the defensiveness of propaganda. I cannot yet fully imagine what it will become, but I delight in its possibilities, for they are boundless. Now, I would like to hear from other women how you envisage the future of the novel, and what it will imply to you, as writers, to accept no limits on your creative power.

[This article was first presented to the Feminist Writers' Conference in Edinburgh in 1982, and was subsequently published by *Cencrastus*. A few changes have been made. R.B.]

Meandering towards an ordinary job

Kath Fraser

'You've written a novel? You've actually written a whole book? *I* couldn't imagine. . . .'

When I wrote the novel, I couldn't imagine finishing it either. My reasons for writing and my feelings about it changed as the novel progressed – and I hope this account will demystify a task many women see as impossible.

I had never written a novel before – and most of my previous writing was poetry, social science essays, and exam papers (or, how to convince the reader the padded information you include is relevant). For two years I had worked on a collective, making *Women's Report*, a feminist news magazine. We produced an issue every two months. I co-wrote the pages on women's health and helped write news items and book reviews. It was all a strong exercise in giving information clearly and briefly and I had to be aware of the language I used – an awareness I'm still developing. There was an awful lot of material to squeeze into the number of pages we could afford to print – and the weekend of 'subbing', where we all read and severely edited each others' efforts, made for even further economy. I enjoyed writing collectively with other women, learning to write in shorter sentences, and grappling with the task of accessibility. In the process I had to think hard about the purpose of my writing, both for other women and myself.

For much of this time I was 'unemployed' and desperate for structure and meaning to my days. I wrote in a journal nearly every day, something I had begun years earlier because a woman to whom I was attracted had kept a diary. Now, much time and many diaries later, during a period of intense conflict, pain, and frustration – not knowing whether to accept a situation I did not want, or to try to change it – I wrote in my journal. Round and round it would go, arguing, railing, wailing. I realize now that my conflict wasn't only about a particular relationship – it was the familiar choice between acceptance and revolution, the problem for all of us about how to have less than everything. At the time, however, I was sickened by the writing in my journal. All it did was confront me with my own impotence. When I needed to be strong, it felt weakening.

Sometimes I could escape this emotional turmoil by deliberate distancing – a temporary fire-door rather than a rigid barrier between me and the conflict I couldn't solve. I began to wonder if I could use writing in a different way – to carry on with the routine of journal-writing I'd established, but to get some distance through 'making things up'. A few times in the past I had started stories – once or twice at school, half a chapter of a novel two or three years before, and more recently, fantasy images. But I had always wanted to be scrupulously honest, even literal – which stood in the way of fabrication. The idea of inventing a whole reality – a relief from habitual ways of seeing myself – was new. If I let it come out without censorship or conscious moulding it would be me on a different level. I still needed that reassurance – that it would help me *understand*. Now I see it as a way towards control, a natural struggle out of oppression – somewhere women can have influence, feel our power. I made a few faltering starts, and then a year later, some friends and I organized a writing group – I don't know how far I would have gone without it. In October 1978 I wrote in my journal, 'Re-encouraged to write the novel.'

So I sat at my typewriter and typed. What came out was often directly autobiographical, but from all over the place in my life rather than following a time-trail. I did not know what the story would be when I started. I knew I wanted to write a novel, a substantial body of work that hung together in one piece. I wrote partly to find out whether I could persist at it and partly to give a continuity, a long-term project – even a reason for living – when other dreams might fail. It is interesting, if unsurprising, that the first page of my first draft is about a personal search:

> I look through the job ads in the local paper, the national daily, the evening paper, the weeklies. Every day the ritual. Throw the I Ching, look at the work market, throw the I Ching and make a few phone calls or write a couple of letters. Telling strangers I might be all right as an employee. You got to sell yourself, my father used to say – he never did himself – but what do I write when I am not clear who wants the job? Today I am a van driver, yesterday I was a cleaner, the day before that a gardener, and so on except for secretarial work. Draw the line at that. Today I could get a job if I owned a four-door saloon, but I don't, so I have finished that task enough to satisfy my conscience.
>
> Out in the street I stand still and don't know where to go. Or which order to do things, or whether I am still in the mood for complicated socializing. I walk north in the direction of the river. I think of people I know first, of what I would say to

them if I could be sure they'd understand. I temper accusations with flattery. Gradually I take my hands out of my pockets – I have to gesticulate to my audience – and realize I can't bite my nails smoothly and comfortably while walking along. So must I walk all the time to have healthy hands and to know what I really want to bite? I am walking over Waterloo Bridge looking at the concrete playground of the arts complex not yet bought by the Army, still talking to my internal audience, waving and pointing and jumping up and down, happy to be alone with my imagination. Always I shall keep my distance and shout, I think. On one upsweep of my right arm I am stopped by collision. A brown bundle stares at me or through me and I say, 'Sorry I hit you, I was conducting my thoughts. . . .'

I have said I did not know what the story would be – yet there were questions I was conscious of wanting to answer: about morality, determinism, will, and other grand and vague ideas. It seemed important to have *some* guidelines, however loose and bendy. The more I wrote, the more themes emerged for me and characters became people. I imposed constraints, selecting more and more of what followed from what was already written. The bigger the volume of paper the more careful I had to be about consistency. There came a point at which I was researching into my own novel – the referring back, the searching for earlier information to build upon.

By the time I was choosing deliberately what came next in my developing adventure story, I think I had already established a 'style'. I needed the free-flowing non-censoring stage to do that: my experience in writing poetry laid the base, and concise journalism had given me the skill to refine what my imagination produced. As I told my story I moved freely between first and third person ('I' and 'she') and between present and past tense. This was meant to give a sense of different ways of seeing reality – different levels of involvement in it. I used the third person past tense to convey relative detachment, the present for closer involvement of the character in her experience. Later, on the basis of other women's reactions, I changed all the tenses to third person past in order to avoid confusion. Whilst writing, I hadn't pursued the idea of switching deliberately enough. (I would still like to try it in another piece of writing.)

For me, writing the novel was a process of making conscious what was unconscious or dimly formed. Early on I needed the freedom and richness of the unknown. Later I had to see the patterns and carve them into a shape that I, as well as others, could more easily recognize and assimilate. The material of expression comes first, construction afterwards. The importance of the latter surprised and excited me: the feeling of *making* something, and with so few tools. A writer is a weaver and a builder.

As I said, I didn't know if I could finish a whole book when I started. Writing became increasingly routine and increasingly essential to me. When I began I wrote erratically – from the need to know I could be or create something beyond undirected pain and rage. 'Everyone' said I would need discipline and hard work. With the constant stimulus of the women in my writers' group I held on to the confidence and determination to continue and enjoy. So, in 1979, I set myself a not too outrageously demanding routine. I decided to write for a minimum of half an hour a day, Monday to Friday, and that's what I did for two years, through changes in surroundings and activities: full-time gardening work in London, six months travelling abroad, a year-long horticulture course in the country, several women's projects, periods of celibacy, and then a close relationship which led me to Lancashire where I still live. Half an hour a day doesn't sound much time, but it was my continuity, the external life-line I needed. It reminded me that I was the common factor in all my experiences: something we as women often have to relearn.

Eventually I 'finished'. Then I read the novel through finely, making notes, sifting for inconsistencies, contradictions, and errors in chronology. I enjoyed this. I also tried to clarify meanings in the book in the light of what I now thought it was about.

After minor editing, I gave the manuscript to a feminist publishing collective to read. When they sent it back I was angry and hurt: 'They don't understand!' Even if you are expecting rejection, it is difficult to take. This was another time when women's support was important, probably essential, for me to go on. In time I could accept the publishers' comments as well as the criticisms of other women. I realized that if women did not understand what I was trying to do, I was not doing it successfully. By now I wanted the novel to be read and so I had to make it readable.

Listening to the criticisms of other women was the only way I could learn to do this. The more women read my book, the more I could see what was general shortcoming and what was the result of incompatibility between me and a particular reader. The parts others found awkward more or less coincided with the ones I didn't like. I preferred to cut those out altogether rather than struggle with changing them. One friend read the manuscript thoroughly and made notes, and through discussions with her, I began to learn to trust my own judgement.

In 1982 I set to work editing the novel again; I am now, in June 1983, typing what I hope will be the final version. Like many others I discovered that the least satisfactory parts were the beginning and the end. At the beginning, I was still searching for direction. Endings are difficult as well: sometimes I never wanted the novel to finish, other times I wanted to get it over with as quickly as possible. How many loose ends to tie up? A neat denouement or something more open-ended? How do you leave the reality you have invented, say 'no more'? I preferred to leave questions behind, unanswered: I felt there must be something left for readers to think about.

Now, after two and a half years' part-time work as a handyperson, I have become officially unemployed again. Writing is my 'job'. It still feels arrogant to say this – how long does it take a woman to stop feeling guilty? How many times during the writing have I had to shut up internal judgements: 'Stop taking yourself so seriously'? Many more times, certainly, than if I had had access to a women's writing group. I also suspect that, although I began this first novel as a 'coping mechanism', it is not necessary to suffer misery to write. Pain may provide need and material, just as joy may, but oppression in itself is no help in getting it down on paper.

As my life becomes calmer, the discipline of writing comes more easily. Writing is a job as much as anything else I do, like gardening. I write regularly because it is easier, smoother, with practice. The effort of will is less as routine takes over. I take it for granted I shall write. I write because I need to have an ordinary job. I do know that the freer I feel as a woman, the more the words come. If we were all free, then thirty-six years of living would surely be preparation enough for a hundred books.

The art of non-fiction (or the social construction of aesthetic divisions)

Catherine Itzin

There is a hierarchy in art and literature, just as there is a hierarchy in the class system: aesthetic divisions which determine that some kinds of writing are deemed better than or superior to others. At the top comes fiction – poetry, plays, novels (perhaps even in that order): 'creative' writing. Lower down the aesthetic ladder you will find the 'working class of writing': non-fiction. These are the books about this or that – history, biography, autobiography, cookery, philosophy, politics, psychology, gardening, sociology and so forth: the prose, prosaic.

There is, of course, a caste system within the category of non-fiction, too. Authors of cookery or gardening books are definitely not in the same class as the academics (whatever their discipline), and the writers of 'how to' books hardly regarded as writers at all.[1] Writers for children are the lower middle class of the fiction system.[2]

For sheer *quantity*, non-fiction publications far outstrip fiction (see library or bookshop shelves for evidence), though you would not realize this from the paltry amount of publicity and prestige they receive compared with fiction. But for *quality* – or what is regarded as 'quality' – fiction is apparently untouchable in the aesthetic hierarchy.

As a former journalist and now a non-fiction author, I find this system – these aesthetic divisions – as oppressive as I do the class and gender divisions that deem me 'inferior' as a working-class woman. I am, of course, aware of some of the ways that the class and gender divisions interact with the cultural hierarchy. It is obviously no mere accident that within the non-fiction class we find topics such as cookery and child-care ('women's work') at the bottom, and that the forms of writing most available to women (letters, journals, diaries) should come in the lesser category of non-fiction. Romantic fiction – by, for, and about women – is predictably regarded as artistic rubbish.[3] Nor is it by chance that the forms of writing with the most 'formal' structures (poetry and plays) should be so highly regarded, given that these 'formal' forms have to be learned and acquired, mimicked, imitated and internalized through years of educational experience. They require success in the educational system, itself a key middle-class social institution and transmitter of middle-class culture with 'examination gates' to control the flow of working-class traffic to its higher echelons. It comes as no surprise that the higher art forms are the most intellectual and the lowest the most practical.

Just as socialism questions the apparently inherent values of the social class system, and feminism questions the biological determinism of gender divisions, and Black liberation challenges the myth of racial inferiority and exposes racism and imperialism, so too should the aesthetic class system be challenged. And not just from the point of view of the exclusion of women, Blacks and working-class people from participation in it. Their – our – absence (or invisibility) amongst those who write poetry or plays (classics of any kind) has been much discussed and (correctly) interpreted as the effect of sexism, classism, and racism restricting the opportunities of people from these groups to 'become' poets or playwrights. But we haven't sufficiently questioned the *appropriateness* of these *forms* for the expression of 'our' experience and visions, or really questioned why certain forms and kinds of writing should necessarily be regarded more *highly* than other forms. Why should a poem be regarded as more aesthetically valuable than a letter? A play more important than an essay? A philosophical analysis more 'authoritative' than an autobiography? Says who? Who benefits from saying so? Who loses? What is lost?

High art – or the culture of élitism – was attacked in the 1960s and 1970s by the left who propagandized for popular art forms and arts for the people. This was, for example, the ideology at the heart of the socialist and feminist and community theatre ('political theatre') movement whose achievements I worked at editing, reviewing, compiling and writing about for over a decade.[4] There was a similar pattern in the education system over this period – a radical reaction against the élitism of the academic curriculum and its inaccessibility to the majority of Black and working-class people who make up the (school) population. Popular art (a night out and a knees-up) and permissive education (learning foremost as fun) were advocated with great energy and enthusiasm (not least by myself) on many anti-establishment and egalitarian fronts. The motivation was a genuine sense of the injustice of oppression and a sincere belief in equality of opportunity for everyone.

But we (on the left) made some serious mistakes. Quite rightly and courageously we campaigned to put popular art and its innovations (new forms, new language, new audience) on the cultural agenda, and successfully persuaded the cultural establishment (the Arts Council) to subsidize the new alternatives.[5] But wrongly we wanted to get rid of the old (high) art. Our anger and frustration with the hierarchy – its exclusivity and the exclusion of the majority of people from it – confused us into believing there was something inherently wrong with certain art forms, when the real problem has always been the hierarchy itself. Nor is it just a matter of the majority of people being deprived of access to and appreciation of 'high art', but also the exclusion of the élite from popular culture (the attitudes that 'despise' pop music are just as socially conditioned as the ones that 'hate' opera). The divisions are also, I suspect, reflected in the lowly position of popular culture in the aesthetic league tables, the denial to non-fiction of the status of creativity, and its exclusion from the category of art at all.

The consequences of this aspect of confused left ideology in the education system have been extremely damaging. Several generations of young people – largely Black and working class – have not only been disinherited from the received cultural tradition, but denied the opportunity to create or re-create their own or to 'compete' in the social system, having been deprived of knowledge of the old and the skills to make the new. (Half of all young people are failed by the examination system and leave school without qualifications.) They lack not just literature, but literacy.

Of *course* learning should be fun and the old authoritarian rote learning modes are not the way, but success in the economic system still depends on success in the educational system (including exams) and it is a betrayal of the already oppressed to maintain the pretence that this is not the case. Now there is a left-wing 'backlash' in the literary world which wants to re-establish a hierarchy of high art and classic literature within socialist ideology and to cultivate the belief that this is created by a gifted élite.[6]

These feelings are understandable, perhaps, given the enormity of the confusion about cultural value there has been on the left in the last fifteen years, and the great loss this has created for precisely the people the left wanted to help – the already disadvantaged. This recent revisionist challenge is correct in claiming 'articulacy and literacy as the best weapons of the powerless' but profoundly mistaken in still wishing to change the order of classification rather than the aesthetic class system itself. The reality must be that there are different kinds of aesthetic experience, different kinds of art and literature (culture), all of value and importance: a continuum or network (rather than a hierarchy) which *includes* (rather than excludes) Shakespeare and stand-up comedy, grand opera and the Ceilidh, Royal

Shakespeare and Spare Tyre, Milton and Michele Roberts, Rudyard Kipling and Alice Walker.

What's wrong at the moment is:

1 the exclusion of *any* people from *any* of this experience (the majority from the impact and thrill of Shakespeare or opera, and the 'educated élite' from the inspiration and joy of Spare Tyre or Irish dancing);
2 the aesthetic class system which claims inherent values for different kinds of art and literature, and which dictates that non-fiction is not art at all.[7]

Excellence is not the issue, but who defines it. Now we can turn to feminist writing, both fiction and non-fiction, for a model of literature without aesthetic divisions. For feminism has demonstrated that the division of writing into creative and polemic is artificial and meaningless. Feminists are both, and consider both to be creative writing.

Gradually, and as a result of the persistence over many years of many people, there has been a shift in regard for women's writing and feminist fiction – from contempt to acclaim.[8] Previously invisible bodies of work from the past and new creations have begun to acquire their (rightful) status – as art. New forms are receiving cultural accreditation: including increasingly the writing of Black women.

Feminism also offers evidence of a need for the 'elevation' of non-fiction to the level of art and creativity. The Women's Movement has spread and taken root as the largest and most successful world-wide liberation movement this century, arguably surpassing even the great socialist revolutionary movements in insight and achievement. This Movement has taken hold largely as the result of ideas communicated primarily in the form of non-fiction – in the writings of such women as Simone de Beauvoir, Kate Millett, Germaine Greer, Suzie Orbach, Mary Daly, Adrienne Rich, Dale Spender, and the other legions of 'women of letters'. Women have also discovered that truth is not only stranger, but often stronger, than fiction – and have transformed the forms of life history, biography and autobiography, into revelations and sources of shared power: breaking the silence, revealing the realities of women's lives.[9]

This 'art' – of clear thinking communication of the meaning of women's oppression – has taken the *creative* non-fiction form of:

1 ideas that have transformed consciousness, awareness, and understanding, and motivated, i.e. moved, often in a process of catharsis, millions of women to transform their own lives and change the system which oppresses them;

2 ideas that have transcended centuries of received 'wisdom' and ways of thinking;
3 ideas that have stirred the imagination of millions of women and inspired personal and social change;
4 visions.

Is this not creative writing?

It is this non-fiction that has been the 'art' of the feminist movement and it has, arguably, been the very art of this non-fiction that has inspired the Women's Movement and fuelled its success. On what grounds, then, does this form of writing become relegated to a lesser category in the literature of the times and ages? Here is evidence at last of what we have come to discover about all other forms of oppression. Aesthetic divisions are just as socially constructed as the divisions of class, gender, and race. None are inherent or immutable, all are open to revaluation, redefinition: revolution.

It has been the feminist art of non-fiction that has stimulated a sea-change in consciousness (crossing race, religious, and class divisions) and laid the foundations of a world-wide liberation movement.

It's a fine art.

Notes

1 I am the author of *How To Choose A School: A Parent's Guide* (Methuen, 1985).
2 As a result of ageism and 'adultism', children's low status (i.e. oppression) in society means that those who care for them and write for them share their low status.
3 There are, of course, real objections to romantic fiction for reinforcing sexist stereotypes, but the same could also be said of highbrow fiction.
4 I founded and edited *Theatre Quarterly*, *Theatre Pacts*, and *New Plays* from 1970–7, was regular drama critic for *Tribune* from 1972–80 (and occasional contributor on theatre to *Time Out* and the *Guardian*), am editor of the annual *British Alternative Theatre Directory* and *Directory of Playwrights, Directors and Designers* (1983) and author of *Stages in the Revolution: Political Theatre in Britain 1968–1978* (Metheun, 1980–2).
5 See *The Republic of Letters: Working-Class Writing & Local Publishing*, edited by Dave Marley and Ken Worpole (Comedia, 1982).
6 'Only imagination can create the new discourses of politics and culture, and only artists of high talent can invent the liberatory images . . .' (Tony Dunn and Howard Barker, the *Guardian*, 10 February 1986). Like any 'right wing backlash', the left's is dimissive of the feminist, Black, and gay 'minority' (sic) constituencies, betraying the White heterosexual male bias.

7 A recent televised debate featured luminaries of the literary establishment (including Germaine Greer) who debated the proposition that 'Biography was the pestilence of English literature.'
8 Feminist publishers like Virago, The Women's Press, and Onlywomen as well as individual women writers.
9 Some of the many examples: Jean McCrindle and Shiela Rowbotham (eds.), *Dutiful Daughters* (Pelican, 1979); Susan Hemmings, *Girls are Powerful* (Sheba, 1982) and *A Wealth of Experience* (Pandora, 1985); Karen Payne, *Between Ourselves: Letters Between Mothers and Daughters* (Picador, 1984). I have often used life-history interviews in my work, e.g. in *Splitting Up* (Virago, 1980).

Lesbian sexuality: joining the dots

Anna Livia

Polly and Sadie are sitting in the back garden. It is hot. Polly is trying to get on with her thesis and keep an eye on Sadie. Sadie, it seems, is crazy. Sadie begins to speak, answers a question half-formulated in Polly's mind. The answer brings relief, as when a nameless fear is shared, solved by articulation. Polly looks at Sadie: her height, her wide face, her smooth skin. The sun shines persuasively. Sadie smiles and Polly no longer thinks her crazy, no longer thinks, only wants her, wants Sadie.

While striving not to close the kitchen curtains discreetly, draw a veil of lilac buddleia over the proceedings, but to go all the way and describe two women making love, I found I had written of 'passionate biting and scratching, kissing so hard it bruised'. Horrible stuff, also untrue, as I hate being bitten and cannot imagine it pleasant. Why was I writing about sex at all? How should I do it so it said something I could recognize? I do not believe in an essential, purely sexual experience which it sufficeth to describe accurately and in detail, but rather that the words we choose create the experience; bestow context, metaphor, image, connotation; forge parallels with other, seemingly disparate, experiences: cunt as lotus blossom, pomegranate, dried apricot half, black hole, split beaver.

Writing sex located it, the words its wedge into the world. Gone were the days of mute embarrassment when I couldn't say what I wanted because I wasn't sure which bit was my clitoris, let alone how to pronounce it. I began looking for predecessors, wondering in which contexts I had seen that word 'clitoris', why violent sexual imagery came so quickly to mind.

My search led me back along my bookshelves through lesbian literature to Radclyffe Hall and coy avoidance: 'for now she could find no words any more . . . and that night they were not divided',[1] which seemed to state my problem admirably: a) how to find the words, and b) how to join the dots.

Believing Jane Rule when she told me[2] that it was still unclear whether, according to Gertrude Stein's complicated code, 'cow' meant turd or orgasm, I passed on to Djuna Barnes, and her mystifying imprecation:

Look for the girls also in the toilets at night, and you will find them kneeling in that great secret confessional crying between tongues: 'May you be damned to hell! . . . May you die standing upright! May this be damned, terrible and damned spot! May it wither into the grin of the dead, may this draw back, low riding mouth in an empty snarl of the groin!'[3]

– which you read three times in perplexity only to conclude that women you know don't do that, or at least not kneeling in the toilet. And hell's teeth, the 'empty snarl of the groin'? I think I prefer Hall's 'terrible nerves of the invert'.

But what about the sexual celebration? What about my positive self-image? Jane Rule poses the problem as one, again, of vocabulary:

Now that our experience is increasingly available to us as a subject of contemplation, we have to extend our language to express our new consciousness until we have as many words for sexuality as the Eskimo has for snow.[4]

How is this 'new consciousness' achieved, if not through language? How do we recognize it? Is it not the words which make it available? For the words are not lacking; we are not doing anything unheard of, lesbianism has, after all, its own history. Rather the words for it are more common in anatomical, perhaps, or pornographic descriptions, carrying these overtones into lyrical or emotional contexts. Hence, perhaps, our reticence to turn our struggle to live out sexual contradictions into a possible turn on for men, the consequent flight into floral or violent imagery, the dot dot dots, the language of the damned: the 'always already', that time-honoured repository of guilt and desire. Given only the choice between the wicked and the victim, evil sounds more exciting. Djuna Barnes' creatures of the night are far more memorable than those who 'sew a quiet seam', whereas Stephen (*The Well of Loneliness*) Gordon's relationship with Mary is peculiarly undynamic, a petrifaction of desire versus guilt, as though struggles between the women must be silenced, subsumed to the greater struggle of taking on the world – like the Ladies of Llangollen, who must never admit to quarrels or coolness, lest the Irish relations think the ideal friendship hasn't worked. The girls in the toilets mouth 'between tongues' alternately their damnation and the activity they are damned for.

Was it not part of the 'new consciousness' to say that as our lives must be lived in open defiance of male opinion, as simply to live and breathe and be a lesbian is to express hostility, so our writing will honour only its own purpose, and if men have a little wank on the offshoots, so the world is full of little wankers? Monique Wittig, with the excruciating precision of the scalpel, enumerates the layers of *The Lesbian Body:*[5]

A/I pull starting at the labia, it slides the length of the belly, . . . A/I pull starting at the loins, the skin uncovers the round muscles and trapezii of the back, . . . A/I reveal the beauty of the shining bone traversed by bloodcells. . . .

If words like 'trapezii' make *The Lesbian Body* read like an anatomy textbook, doesn't an anatomy textbook now read more like *The Lesbian Body*? Oblivious of sentient reaction, it accepts only the resistance of the body.

Sexual descriptions which are without contradiction (either *vis-à-vis* a hostile world, or within the relationship itself) seemed pornographic in their unproblematic throbbing, possibly because only when a body is entirely objectified does it offer no resistance. Contrast Jane Rule's:

Then they were lying together on the couch in a long kissing, for Kate so sweet a relief that she wanted nothing but to go on and on kissing into opening desire, the longing of body for body there was finally an answer for, brief but absolute, against all ugly and grieving loneliness.[6]

with Mountainspirit's:

My finger finds her open. It is warm inside, inviting. I lick her and push my open mouth over her, my tongue circles the opening. She is moaning softly and pushing herself against me.[7]

We have moved on to the 1970s, the guilt and damnation have disappeared. The vocabulary of sexual desire with its repetitions, its image of two bodies open and vulnerable to each other, is similar in both descriptions. Yet Mountainspirit offers only unity, the immediacy and eternity of sex, whereas Jane Rule counterposes the insight 'brief' to her 'absolute'. Kate and partner lie together against a background of loneliness. The central contradiction shifts from guilt versus desire, to sex versus loneliness, violence versus vulnerability. The limits imposed are internal, the violence of desire translating sometimes into physical violence. Witness Ginny's desire (in *Brainchild*) to

pin [Irene] up against a wall. . . . tear her clothes off, push her down, fuck her hard and when she cried 'Stop' . . . then do it harder.[8]

Sometimes guilt has become embarrassment, a state of perplexity, of being caught between conflicting emotions: brazen and apologetic. Often the conflict is resolved by laughter. The sad tale of Dix and Eunice, those despicably unpoliticized gays of *Rubyfruit Jungle*, nearly caught by straight room-mates in the shameful act Djuna Barnes (almost) describes, was the first thing I read that indicated other women like licking. Dix's confession: 'So one night I'm over there and well, you know. I was – uh – I was going down on her', seeks only temporary refuge in dots and dashes and manages to say what she was doing, even though this is immediately followed by divine retribution. Dix gets her tooth brace caught on Eunice's pubic hair; her unenviable alternatives are 'to go blind, shit, or run for her life'.[9]

Finally she bolts for the closet. (Closet, eh, d'yer geddit? Eh, do yer?) The scene is funny, perfectly accepts they didn't oughter of been doing that. Joanna Russ, with similar, slightly exaggerated humour keeps the embarrassment strictly between friends. No sign of self-deprecation.

We were both rather wary of touching each other again. . . . I was blind, deaf, overwhelmed. I kept wanting to put my finger through the central hole of the last bagel because it struck me as such an extraordinarily good joke.[10]

After this rather hurried leafing through half a dozen lesbian classics to find the descriptions of sex – instantly recognizable as those places where the pages were brownest – I had before me a wide variety of precedents from the soft sunset and roseate dawn, the tortured and damned, the coded and dotted, the anatomic, the pornographic, the embarrassed, funny, or violent as the narrative tension revolved around outcasts and normality, male voyeurism and female experience, relations of dependence and vulnerability with a chronological increase in lesbian autonomy.

My page remained before me, calmly waiting, and I concluded that here, certainly, the how and the why, as for any other subject, were entirely up to me. My sex scene should take its context from the rest of my story, not leap off with a life of its own.

For barely the second time since entering the house Sadie smiled. Polly had a stream of hazy, soft, smooth, warm liquid thoughts starting with the calm of lying in the sun, stretching out, lazy. Then not so lazy, kissing wetly and the kiss spreading, the wetness spreading, the warmth growing, heat. 'Sex!' thought Polly blatantly.[11]

Notes

1 Radclyffe Hall, *The Well of Loneliness* (Jonathan Cape, 1928). Known as a 'lesbian classic' because it most nearly expresses the classic anti-lesbian position that women are better off dead than dykes.

2 J. Rule, 'Sexuality in Literature', essay in *Outlander* (Naiad, 1981). A collection

of short stories and articles by Jane Rule, author of the wonderfully passionate *Desert of the Heart* (Pandora, 1986).

3 Djuna Barnes, *Nightwood* (Faber and Faber, 1936). A novel to learn by heart for the beauty of its language, not its sentiment.

4 'Sexuality in Literature'.

5 Monique Wittig, *The Lesbian Body* (Peter Owen, 1973) – metaphor made flesh.

6 'Pictures', short story in *Outlander*.

7 Mountainspirit, 'The Bus Ride', story in *A Woman's Touch*, edited by Cedar and Nelly (Womanshare Press, 1979), a collection of lesbian who-puts-what-where.

8 Eve Croft, *Brainchild* (Onlywoman Press, 1980). Little known, brilliantly worded novel etched with a scalpel blade.

9 Rita Mae Brown, *Rubyfruit Jungle* (Corgi, 1973). Alternative classic (see note 1 above). Deadpan trivialization.

10 Joanna Russ, *On Strike Against God* (Out & Out, 1980). Woman academic comes out. Enjoys a beginning, a middle and an end. Unusual for this (temperamental) author.

11 Anna Livia, *Accommodation Offered* (The Women's Press, 1985). Three love affairs: Polly's with Margot; Sadie's with Africa; Kim's with feminism.

Writing erotica

Eileen Cadman

Eroticism is one of the basic means of
self-knowledge, as indispensable as poetry. (Anais Nin)

I started writing erotica as an experiment, to see if I could write something that would turn other women on, something different from the very partial and distorted fantasies of women's sexuality produced by men and purveyed as pornography.

The urge to write erotica did not just fall from the sky, neither did the fact of getting something down on paper. I did not simply think, 'Ah, no one's written any feminist erotica lately, I'll just sit down at my desk and fill this gap in the market. Tap tap tap, hey presto!' Like other forms of writing, it emerged as a need within the context of my individual development. The kind of erotica we write reflects us back to ourselves, and this is its challenge.

Writing erotica is an act of gratuitous pleasure which I think women would benefit from doing more of. It can be rather alarming at first because your erotic imagination moves in what are sometimes completely unfamiliar regions; it is not predictable. Writing erotica is also fun. I enjoy meeting friends and saying 'Hey, I've written some more erotica!' and seeing their faces light up as they say 'Ooh, can I have a read?' I enjoy the discussion some of my pieces have provoked, it broke down some barriers. And the writing turned other women on.

I first harnessed my ability to draw human figures to my desire to express sexual feelings at about the age of 8 or 9. The result was masochistic, or pornographic if you like, although I didn't know pornography existed. The pictures were of a prince ordering a male servant to maltreat a partially clothed peasant girl. In my teens I used to write pornographic stories for myself, then tear them up into tiny pieces and throw them away almost immediately. I call them pornographic because they were masochistic, centring on an anonymous woman who was humiliated by, and sexually submissive to, an anonymous man. But there were also fragments where I tried to be assertive and forthright about my sexuality. Some years later I wrote more pornography/erotica with a lover. Some of this was strongly masochistic in character, but other parts were also funny.

I wrote my first deliberately erotic public piece with the encouragement of a feminist writing group. It's hard now to realize how difficult it was to even think about writing that first piece. I wouldn't have done it without the support of other feminists at the time. It was rather abstract; typically, the characters were just talking about it! I showed it to the group rather nervously and they said, 'It's good as far as it goes, but you haven't got them *doing* anything.' 'What', I said, 'you mean get them *doing* something?' 'Yes', they said. So I did, and the result was called *Bananas*.

Bananas is about three women: Mary, a lesbian, Nicola, who is bisexual, and Sarah, a heterosexual who has never appreciated the range of pleasures of the banana – she only eats them. But Mary and Nicola have developed quite other uses for this innocent fruit, which Sarah rather nervously agrees to try. She is finally persuaded by the spirit of fun in which they conduct the whole ritual and calls out 'Up with bananas!' as she herself comes to climax.

In *Bananas* I wanted to think and write about sexuality in a way that wasn't serious, and I wanted to send up pornography. I wanted to convey the idea that sexual activity can be funny sometimes. Making it funny was also the only way of allowing myself to write about explicit sexuality at the time. I took a deep breath and sent the story to *Spare Rib*, who turned it down. At that time the collective felt it wasn't possible to explore women's sexuality using the old pornographic forms in any way. However, several heterosexual women said they found it very funny and a turn-on. One lesbian found it erotic, and another said it verged on anti-lesbianism. When writing erotica you absolutely cannot please all the people all of the time.

These days I tend to adopt Anais Nin's view that there are

> a million forms of eroticism, a million objects of it, situations, atmospheres, and variations. We have, first of all, to dispense with guilt concerning its expansion, then remain open to its surprises, varied expressions, and (to add my personal formula for the full enjoyment of it) fuse it with individual love and passion for a particular human being, mingle it with dreams, fantasies, and emotion. . . . (From 'In Favour of the Sensitive Man', essay in *Eroticism in Women* (Star Books, 1981) p. 11.)

One of the crucial points here is that of the 'personal formula'. No woman can speak for other women as to what they ought or ought not to find erotic.

But it is also true that, in so far as we are social beings, there are bound to be themes and patterns in what people find erotic. They reflect deep-seated emotions over which we have no direct control (this is not to imply that they are unchangeable).

This is why women can be turned on by pornography, a fact which seems to run counter to deeply held political convictions. Being oppressed and repressed sexually does not remove the fact that we are independent sexual beings and that we want certain things. Sexual oppression and repression make it sometimes impossible even to think what it is we want, let alone demand it directly. In order to get what we want therefore, we have to use the oppressed (i.e. indirect) mode to get it. Until women feel able to take responsibility for their sexual needs without feeling guilty, we will continue to use other ways of getting some level of sexual satisfaction.

As we gain more control and confidence in our lives, negative images will hopefully be replaced by something more positive. And with that in mind, after I wrote *Bananas*, I wondered how to write heterosexual erotica which could be satisfying to women. Coming from a pornographic culture, I felt completely ignorant as to how to go about it. To some extent I felt that I had copped out by writing a piece with all women in it. Nevertheless, you have to start from where you are and go at your own pace.

I have not by any means solved the problem of writing good heterosexual erotica for myself, and this reflects the ambivalences I have, at some level, in my sexual relationships with men. While reading Nin's writings I came across the phrase 'power of surrender'. Now the act of surrender is not new to me, what is new is the concept of it as a powerful and active thing to do. Surrender is not submission, which means giving up power and responsibility and simply being dominated. But it still seems easier to me to show surrender between women and not confuse it with submission. Can surrender of a woman to a man be seen in our culture as anything but submission? I think it is possible, we must make it possible.

However, the first piece I tried to write was unsatisfactory in that the man (in order that he should be incapable of dominating the scene) was only known as X! Give them a personality, I felt, and they'll just take over again. I now think this was silly, but at the time it seemed a way out of my dilemma. Another piece, written more recently, was better in that both the main characters exhibit their emotions as well as their bodies.

As I have continued to write erotica it seems to me to be important that women should write deliberately erotic pieces, not just include sensual scenes in other more 'meaningful' writing. Why?

Because sometimes women are lonely or alone, or maybe decide to be alone, and sometimes want material to draw them into the land of electric flowers, and all there is available is pornography. Because erotica is a great opportunity to let yourself go and let your imagination run wild. Because we need to use our talents as writers to create new visions of the erotic, we need to produce myriads of images which women can try out, reject or embrace as they wish – images which strengthen them and give them a greater insight into their power and vitality. And if, as we suspect, men get less out of pornography than they are reputed to do, we may show them – as a side effect – a glimpse of something better also.

I do not think it is possible to draw a clear distinction between erotic and pornographic writing. But we still want to draw boundaries, both political and moral, around what's acceptable and what's not. I think that this will always be the case, and that some people will also ignore those boundaries. Further, I think that the effort which goes into trying to draw this distinction would be better used in creatively broadening the horizons of our erotic imagination, thereby putting pornography – which has become the model of the erotic in our culture – in its place as the preference of a minority.

I believe that there can be an erotic writing which is not exploitative of either women or men and that women must explore its possibilities. We have to break new ground in creating images of women's sexuality; if we don't, we will remain imprisoned by the masculine view of it. Men are still the purveyors and producers of images of women's sexuality. Since these images are so distorted we must create true images showing who we are and what we want.

References

Erotic writings by women

Lonnie Barbach, *Pleasures: Women Write Erotica* (Futura, 1986).
Angela Carter, *Black Venus* (Chatto/Hogarth, 1984).
Cedar and Nelly (eds.), *A Woman's Touch: an anthology of eroticism and sensuality for women only* (Womanstore Books, 1979).
Nancy Friday, *My Secret Garden: women's sexual fantasies* (Virago, 1975).
Nancy Friday, *Forbidden Flowers: more women's sexual fantasies* (Pocket Books, 1975).
Kensington Ladies' Erotica Society, *Ladies' Own Erotica* (Arrow Books, 1986).

Anais Nin, *Delta of Venus* (Star Books, 1978).
Anais Nin, *Little Birds* (Bantam Books, 1979).
Anais Nin, *The Journals of Anais Nin*, vol. 3 (Quartet, 1979).
Anais Nin, *Spy in the House of Love* (Penguin, 1983).
Derek Parker (ed.), *An Anthology of Erotic Prose* (Sphere Books, 1983). Contains extracts written by women.
Sherley Anne Williams, 'Meditations on History', in *Any Woman's Blues: stories by contemporary black women writers*, M.H. Washington (ed.) (Virago, 1980).

Essays on erotica and the erotic

Angela Carter, *The Sadeian Woman* (Virago, 1979).
Maurice Charney, *Sexual Fiction* (Methuen, 1981). Contains lengthy bibliography.
Audre Lorde, 'Uses of the Erotic: the erotic as power', in L. Lederer, ed. *Take Back the Night: Women on Pornography* (Bantam Books, 1980).
Clark Orville, 'Anais Nin: studies in the New Erotology', in Robert Zaller (ed.), *A Casebook on Anais Nin* (New American Library, 1974).
Eileen Phillips (ed.), *The Left and the Erotic* (Lawrence and Wishart, 1983).
Sharon Spencer, 'The Erotica', in *Collage of Dreams: the writings of Anais Nin* (Harvest/HBJ, 1981).

For lists of some of the standard and classic erotic and pornographic works see:

J. A. Cuddon, *A Dictionary of Literary Terms* (André Deutsch, 1979) (entries under 'Erotic Poetry' and 'Pornography').
A. Preminger (ed.), *Princeton Encyclopedia of Poetry and Poetics* (Macmillan, 1979) (entry under 'Erotic poetry').

PART TWO TAKING CONTROL

Lessons of history: beyond the male-stream classroom

Hilary Bourdillon

There are many reasons why all teachers, but especially women, find they have to write their own materials for use in the classroom. First of all, there has been an increasing awareness of the sexism and racism in text books. To give pupils a critical understanding of the racism and sexism in most of these printed words and pictures, and to provide positive images of women and Black people, we have to write, lay-out and print our own material, to counterbalance the predominantly White male 'knowledge', as constructed and transmitted by writers of text books and setters of examination papers.

There are, though, other reasons why women teachers spend quite a lot of their free time writing their own materials. In part, it is a necessary response to working in a hierarchical organization based on male values of competition and the individual pursuit of knowledge, where keeping order in the classroom is based on the ways men traditionally relate to each other, relying on the use of physical punishment, loud voices, shouting and the threat of physical violence, particularly in mixed-sex and boys' schools. Women teachers are seen as being 'soft', because we can't and do not wish to keep order in this way. Instead, we become very concerned about using materials which have an intrinsic interest, to motivate pupils without threats of punishment. My own involvement in writing materials for classroom use began in my first year of teaching, when I realized that being a 'good' teacher was measured by, quite simply, the maintaining of a low noise level in the classroom.

I began teaching history in a split-site mixed comprehensive behind Waterloo station in the early 1970s. The school was streamed and so were the teachers. New, young teachers like myself were given the bottom band forms. Whilst my head of department taught the 'O' level classes in relative peace and quiet, I taught lower school and generally lower band pupils in an enormous multi-layered 1876 Board School building – 'the annexe'. My tutor group – 3J – was the bottom stream in the third year. For some of the older members of staff, they provided the justification for the continued use of the cane and the slipper. The pupils hated their position as the 'thickies' in the school and resisted this by living up to their reputation.

In order to survive with 3J, I had to wrack my brains for entertaining and fascinating ways of presenting my lessons. Daily I wrote work-sheets and turned the banda machine handle. I even resorted to hiding duplicating paper and white spirit (no photo-copier then!) to ensure an adequate supply of work-sheets.

To interest and thereby 'discipline' my form was not the only reason why I began to write my own materials. The language in the available text books was far too difficult, or in the few cases where the reading level was appropriate, the content was babyish and the tone patronizing. The questions accompanying the texts concentrated on testing factual recall and comprehension. They did not use historical documents, or present pupils with the problems of interpreting historical evidence, but assumed that history is a collection of non-negotiable, pre-existent facts, truthfully recorded. They contained a narrative, peopled by upper and middle-class men, where women might occasionally appear in the history of social reform, family, or fashion.

Fortunately I had a lot of support from other teachers in a similar position. Several of us (women and men) expanded the area of our writing to produce collectively a termly magazine (which we had commercially printed once we had done the writing and the lay-out), which was distributed through bookshops and to subscribers, in which we analysed the function of schooling, the curriculum, pupil resistance (mainly male), racism, and sexism. The collective (with a fluctuating membership), continued for many years, until it finally exploded and disintegrated over the issue of sexism.

Fourteen years later I still have to write my own classroom materials. Published materials have changed during that period, showing the influence of the official curriculum developers, i.e. male-dominated organizations like the Schools' Council, now the Schools' Curriculum Development Project, as well as radical pressure. They do now include extracts from historical documents, and pupils are asked to interpret and assess the bias and limitations of this evidence. Yet the fact that the areas of history which are considered significant enough to study concern the public world where men operate, and not the private sphere of women's activity, is never questioned. Patriarchy is never considered as one of the filters which distorts the construction of the past. The history of women and Black people must also be included to remove the inaccuracies of male-stream history.

To overcome the isolation of teachers working on women's history, a group of women teachers began to meet at the ILEA (Inner London) History and Social Sciences Teachers' Centre, in 1980. The aim was not to become 'writers', but to put together resources for teachers to use, and to counter the claim that it was impossible to teach women's history because there was no material. The group was approached by an educational publisher interested in producing a series of topic books on woman's history (C. Adams, P. Bartley, and C. Loxton (eds.), Women in History Series (Cambridge University Press, 1984). I became involved in this as a co-writer for the series. So far, three books in the series have been published, with others in the pipe-line, written by feminist history teachers and historians.

Work we submit for publication is obviously going to come under close scrutiny. The ideas and expectations of a long-established publisher about what is 'good history' are going to be different from the ideas and expectations of feminist history teachers, so getting the books through the publishers has been a somewhat tedious task. As feminists, we have come to expect criticism and objection to what we think is important.

Eighteen months ago, I finished a book on women healers for the series. This is having a slow and difficult passage through the publishers. The recommendation from the series editors that the book be included was questioned by the Press Syndicate (a group of academics, mainly retired, who advise the publishers). The synopsis and one chapter had been vetted by someone 'in the field' and as a result of his comments I was advised

> to be a little more circumspect in how you make certain points. It is vital that a school book on this subject could not be attacked as being overtly polemical or too strident. The view that the history of medicine equals a story of progress is being challenged now, but we must avoid aligning ourselves with some of the newer and most radical approaches to the subject. . . . We are not advocating a dilution of your material . . . but a more tactful and circumspect approach. (Letter from publisher, 14 February 1984)

Comments like this they do not surprise me, and I record this not as a tale of woe but as a description of the problems we encounter in writing feminist history for school. The series is seen by some people at the publishers as being 'controversial'. The humanities editor and the series editors stand by the book, yet despite this support and strong recommendations, the advisor is able to hold up the publication. This struggle continues and we expect to succeed in the end! By writing this history we do challenge the framework of academic history.

The success of getting the books through the publishers has largely depended on the series editors, who are strong and principled feminists and extremely supportive to the series writers. It's tempting at times to concentrate on producing materials to distribute to schools through the teachers' centres. Yet it is important that feminist teachers do persist in getting work commercially published. The printed word does, after all, carry status and respectability; it is much harder to dismiss text books than material turned out on the school duplicator. The pupils I teach who use the book in the series on the Middle Ages think I'm 'very clever' to have written it, without noticing that they have been using my work sheets for years!

It's no good waiting for publishers and other people to provide us with the materials we need. In an article in *The Times Educational Supplement* in April 1985 on the teaching of women's history, an editor for an educational publisher admitted

> For some reason, the writing of school history books has become the preserve of retired male teachers. I would be delighted if more practising female teachers would write in to us suggesting books they might write.

On the other hand a different publisher said

> It's ironic that just when so much women's history is being produced, we have to recognize as publishers that there is a limited market for such work in schools. . . . I think this is a subject that exercises a lot of London teachers, but I'm not sure how widespread it is in the rest of the country.

I'm not an expert at market research, but one important thing about the Women in History series is that it does sell, and not only in London.

Teachers are not passive consumers of the products publishers choose to print. We have some degree of autonomy in our classrooms, and as long as the publishers' materials are racist and sexist, and ignore the contributions teachers make to curriculum development they will not meet our needs. We will continue to write our own materials because, after all, we are concerned about writing for good educational practice, while publishers publish for profit.

Working in the word factory

Ellen Galford

'You're all whores', says the consultant, pocketing his fat fee and retreating back to his vine-covered hillside in the south of France. He comes and goes when we need him, but we're here all the time, churning out ideas, outlines, words and pictures for a vast multinational publisher. (Books are only a tiny part of the empire, along with glossy magazines, television networks, computer software, video, etc., etc. The books I work on are translated simultaneously into German, French, Dutch, and sometimes Italian, Spanish, Japanese and Icelandic. Somebody pushes a button and the copy I write in London shoots out of a machine in Washington, DC.)

I suggested once, after buying guru-consultant yet another dinner on expenses that maybe he was just a higher-priced whore himself, since we both live in the belly of the same beast.

'No, it's not the same thing at all', he sneers, swirling the last of his (subsidized) cognac in his glass.

He's right, of course. He's an artist. The rest of us are hacks.

That's only during the day, of course. At night I step into a telephone box, slip on my lavender cape, and become something different.

My own writing (feminist fiction, a little poetry, lesbian story-telling) is the most important thing I do. I have always written, but it took me until my 20s to start – and finish – my first novel. Until I'd done that, I couldn't admit, even to myself, that my own writing was a priority, and I think it will be some time yet before the external circumstances of life and career catch up with that fact.

In the meantime, I'm doing what writers have always done – struggling to improve and develop my own writing, but simultaneously using the same skills to earn a living. For most of the past fifteen years, I've been selling words – writing, editing, tuning other people's copy, figuring out new ways to say the same old thing twenty times over. I know how to make complicated subjects look simple, and how to make silly subjects look serious. I've written television scripts, dust-jacket blurbs, film programme notes, recipes, catalogue copy, instructions, introductions, even – goddess forgive us – television commercials for toy cars and slogans for deodorant soap (but that was a long time ago, and in another country. . .).

I don't consider myself particularly ambitious in career terms. I'm anything but a hustler, in an industry that is full of them. And although my present job is a very good one, I sometimes wonder if I should be there at all. The contradictions between my 'creative' job and my 'real' writing are sometimes intolerable.

Anyone who has any kind of paid employment in these evil times is privileged, and I'm aware that in my present job I'm luckier than most. But I think it is important for us to look hard at the effects that our working (or non-working) lives have on the ways we write, and on the ways we struggle to make the time and find the energy to do it.

I'm not sure if the word-games I play for a living affect my own writing for good or ill. My paid work entails writing and editing glossy, heavily illustrated non-fiction on subjects that range from current affairs to cookery; my own, 'real' work is writing lesbian feminist fiction. Light years apart.

In the office, every text is written, rewritten, edited, sent back for more alterations, and ultimately is dependent on the initialled approval of other people in the hierarchy. Theoretically, the purpose of this agonizing is to make the text as clear, concise, and lively as possible, but – in practice – it doesn't always work out that way. This monolithic organization takes pride in its high standards, and heavy editing is an integral part of the culture. (I should add that I've played several roles: as a writer asked to re-write by an editor, as an editor asking for re-writes, and as a senior editor asking an editor to go back and fix the damned thing yet again.)

Meanwhile, at home, I'm working in isolation (evenings and weekends only, of course). I show my work to my lover, sometimes to friends, and I respond to their criticisms if, and only if, I think their points make sense. I don't have to change a word of it. Perfect freedom, perfect bliss, and in many ways the opposite of what I do at work. Or is it? You can't spend forty or more hours every week (sometimes more like sixty) working for The Man without some kind of overspill into your own writing. But are all these effects necessarily bad ones?

A workplace where 'good' writing equals that which gets through the system is not designed to inspire self-confidence, or lull anyone into a false sense of security. I've sometimes wondered if I still know what 'good writing' really means. But, if so, is that such a terrible thing? Have all those long ago English lit. classes gone for nothing? Nothing subverts the classically élitist, patriarchal notion of High Art so effectively as time spent in a place where words, designs, photographs, illustrations are all defined as one thing: *product*. And those of us who actually create the stuff are considerably less powerful than the people who go out and market it. (What do you expect? This is late twentieth-century capitalism, and the publishing industry is run by accountants, not by Renaissance princes seeking immortality as patrons of the arts.)

Maybe this cutting-down-to-size is useful – might as well make the best of it, because it isn't going to disappear. If anything, it's a healthy remedy against self-importance, second only to eyestrain as a writer's occupational disease. And if the conditions of my working life have made me cynical, that is probably no bad thing for anyone trying to write feminist fiction.

Sometimes I wonder about this schizophrenia in my writing life. Wouldn't I be better doing something completely different, leaving my mind 'free' for my own creative work? (Not that I'm so employable – I've been working at this one trade for a long time now. . . .) The answer, I've decided, is no. At least for the time being. I've talked about this with several friends who write, but do jobs that have nothing to do with writing. They come home just as tired, just as mentally drained, as I do. Other friends do freelance writing – but they seem to spend so much time hustling work in a tight market that their own projects get put aside for *years*.

Someone asked me recently if I found that working as a daytime 'hack' tended to chase the Muse away. I don't think it does. But it does turn her into a quick-change artist. An enormous gap yawns between the factual writing I do at work and my own fiction. They are separate languages, written in completely different voices (and the more voices a novelist knows how to use, the better). However, in both cases, I use the same way of working – start in longhand, write, cross out, try it a different way, then suddenly, if I'm lucky, the perfect solution appears as if by magic.

The big difference, of course, is the deadline. In the office, we work to tight schedules, and lose sleep at night if we can't meet them. At home, I can take as long as I need. But there's the rub. Whatever I have to do in the way of life-maintenance, cat-feeding, etc., comes out of *my* writing time.

Tight time and limited energy affect the form of my fiction as well as the style and the content. I'm just about hitting my stride at the end of a weekend when I have to put the whole thing aside until the following Friday. No wonder my first novel – and the one just completed – are structured as a series of short, fragmented episodes. The conditions under which they've been written militate against long, intricate, flowing narratives. No wonder it took almost four years after finishing one to start another, which probably took me twice as long to finish as it would have if I had written it full time.

But that, for the moment, is a pipe dream. The ideal fantasy would be to spend all my time writing exactly what I want to, and still earn enough money to live on. Why it's a fantasy would lead into a different, but related paper – about the economics of publishing, the market for lesbian feminist fiction, the ways in which books are promoted and sold.

But that would take time. And time is what I'm jealous of. I'm even angry at myself for agreeing to write this paper, when I know I should be working on my next novel instead. I'm a storyteller, not a political theorist, although I know that feminist conference papers are, *ipso facto*, a Good Thing.

A ray of hope. Maybe feminist fiction will retain, and increase, its edge and bite and energy, because it has been born out of women's struggle to find the time and space and confidence to do it in. A lot of us are trying to support ourselves with one hand, and write with the other. Perhaps the tensions thus generated will lead to a brilliant explosion of wonderful, witty, worldly-wise feminist books. Millions of people will see the light, and all our works will go into endless numbers of reprints and huge mass-market editions. Our hard-pressed feminist publishers will find their pumpkins transformed into golden coaches. Then we can all retire to a life of peaceful creativity on a vine-covered hillside, like the guru-consultant at the beginning of this paper. (He, by the way, writes best-selling cookbooks. That's partly how he does it.) Or – if our politics sustain the shock – we can stay right where we are, and sketch out a few rough drafts for some unputdownable feminist revolutions.

Producing a feminist magazine

Shaila Shah

In retrospect, the doubts and incredulity that met our initial proposals to publish a newspaper by, for, and about women, were inevitable. Our group of five, the 'founding mothers' (as one collective member put it), had little knowledge and even less experience of how to realize our political ambitions. Lacking what many might see as essential professional skills, we gained our strength from our anger at the neglect of issues concerning Black and Third World women, and a determination to be heard. It paid off.

On 8 March 1982, the first issue of *Outwrite Women's Newspaper* appeared, to coincide with International Women's Day. Its publication was heralded by minimum interest from the Establishment media, curiosity from others, and support and encouragement from feminists. Since then, we have met our deadlines against all odds and published an informative newspaper each month that is distributed internationally.

It was at a conference on feminist publications in 1979 that the need for a national feminist newspaper was first aired. It was clear that the Women's Liberation Movement needed a public feminist voice, a forum for agitation, a campaigning newspaper that would not only share and spread news effectively but would also mobilize women. It was almost as if we needed to have a party organ, but without the party. . . .

The following year the idea was revived, but with altered political perspectives, the inevitable outcome of a changing political scenario. A Black Women's Movement was emerging, Black women's projects and centres were getting off the ground, the surprisingly high attendances at the national OWAAD (Organization for Women of Asian & Afro-Caribbean Descent) conferences showed that an autonomous Black Women's Movement was gaining momentum. Militant campaigns against virginity testing and immigration controls, and strike action for improved workplace conditions and the right to unionization had made headlines in the dailies.

Globally, a feminism was emerging in many Third World countries, a feminism that was eschewing Western defined principles and defining its own targets and political strategies. In Britain, links were being forged between Black and immigrant women and their sisters in Third World countries. The racism and White supremacy of the British Women's Movement was being challenged, and no longer wishing to be marginalized or tokenized, Black women had started to organize autonomously. Working-class woman, too, verbalized their anger at the middle-class assumptions, practices, and preoccupations of the Movement and demanded that class be put on the agenda. Third World women questioned the insularity of feminist ideology and its failure to incorporate a critique of Western imperialist policies . . . an overhaul in the Women's Movement was being demanded.

It was in this context that *Outwrite* was born, to provide a platform for those sections of the Movement that had been denied it. Our collective of five (four Black and one White) expanded slowly, and for sixteen months we met twice a week and added to the contents of a bottom drawer in a filing cabinet at A Women's Place, the Central London Women's Centre. During this period we received help of various kinds – in selling advertising, drawing up production schedules, news gathering, and writing – and also had wide ranging discussion.

What would *Outwrite*'s role be? Would it reflect and comment on current debates within the Women's Movement? Would it actively seek to change the direction of the Movement and its priorities? If so, would it have the backing of sections of the Movement to make this possible? Or would it restrict itself to providing information about women's struggles and campaigns? At a time when some Black women's groups were becoming more separatist, would *Outwrite* support this, or seek to build alliances between White and Black women? What was a feminist issue – only those that directly concerned themselves with women's struggles or were all issues of concern to feminists, if the implications for women could be isolated within it? Who would our readers be? Who would *Outwrite* target itself at? Only some of the many questions that it was important to ask.

Through *Outwrite*, we were consciously creating a vehicle for an anti-racist and anti-imperialist feminism, as we felt that both the feminist and the Black presses had displayed an uncommitted and unserious attitude towards Black women's politics. It was clear to us then that *Outwrite* would aim to provide the much needed forum for voicing Black and Third World women's struggles and for campaigns to develop around them. We wanted to establish links between women's oppression and exploitation in different countries, under varying circumstances and political regimes and very importantly, highlight the differences. Methods of organizing, using different tactics and actions, would be learned and exchanged, and thus we hoped solidarity between sisters would invariably develop internationally.

We fulfilled (and continue to) some of our original intentions, the most successful being the provision of information on women's struggles internationally, although coverage of some areas is poor, for example of Africa and Middle Eastern countries.

To date, forty-two issues of *Outwrite* bear testimony to our success. Articles on many issues have appeared: forming working women's co-operatives in Zimbabwe, fighting martial law and fundamentalism in Pakistan, taking action against male violence in Peru, banning dangerous drugs in Bangladesh, Pacific women protesting against the dumping of nuclear waste, speaking out against Zionism, the effects of the Bhopal tragedy on women, sex tourism in SE Asia, Black women in Britain organizing against circumcision, and many others. Differenct faces of feminism have been exposed and the feminist map (certainly for Western readers) redrawn.

Although we have been able to show that it is possible for a women's group posessing few technical skills (initially) to publish a political paper and provide an accessible forum for women to contribute to, the years of publication have not been without difficulty and problems. Briefly, these could be attributed to financial constraints (we have been partly grant-aided for three years by the GLC), cramped working conditions, differing political priorities within the collective, pressured work schedules, the tensions of working collectively, and a degree of naïvety.

We had started with the assumption that *Outwrite* would be a forum which would be both widely and eagerly used, simply because it existed. Another assumption that also proved wrong was that any woman can write and it was mainly the denial of the opportunity that prevented her doing so. Yes, if literate, any woman can write, but writing to make political propaganda does not come easily, and requires skills. Informing and persuading readers, influencing political direction, capturing and sustaining political interest requires not just the strength of ideology to back it up, but also the ability to translate this and offer it in an accessible and readable form. Those skills *can* be learned and absorbed, and this process has occurred within *Outwrite*, too. However, we have been unable to devote the attention necessary to its development, and this has resulted in some articles being difficult to comprehend, using jargon excessively or appearing confused.

Writing for a radical political journal and introducing new and anti-Establishment perspectives that are only held by a minority, requires especially forceful writing. What distinguishes it from mainstream journalism is the concept of the bias. Where mainstream journalism aspires (and pretends) to be objective, balanced, and impartial, radical journalism openly espouses a bias, and more importantly, a bias which is conscious. How this bias is communicated – through life stories, profiles of struggles, interviews with grass roots activists, is then crucial. Attention to detail, style of presentation, and writing clearly and cogently, have often been wrongly dismissed by feminists as being unimportant, bourgeois even, and leading to a questionable professionalism. But thorough research, substantiated facts, clear, logical thinking and presentation contribute to offering a valid political perspective, and therefore one that more women need to fight for. Writing to appeal to anger which consequently urges action is difficult, as often it can appeal to guilt and thereby elicit merely sympathy.

Working effectively, collectively, on material submitted for publication is hard. Editorial meetings at *Outwrite* have functioned as a kind of writers' workshop, but carelessly so. Articles are read out aloud (a method the least conducive to allowing for serious consideration), assessed, and suggestions for change, if any, are made. These are then implemented in consultation with the writer. Adhering to feminist principles and wishing to exercise the minimum amount of power over a contributor's work, *Outwrite* has tried to avoid oppressive editorial practices – too many of us have read garbled or heavily pruned versions of articles submitted to papers and magazines. In reality, however, late submissions, deadlines, disagreements and a number of other factors make it anything but a smooth disciplined process, and again, insufficient attention can result in the publication of obscure and shoddy articles. By this I do not wish to imply that non-hierarchical ways of working or exercising collective editorial control are unworkable. But because collective control necessarily involves several opinions and judgements, all of which must be considered, and which take time (a situation that does not occur when the editor exercises sole judgement), a great degree of discipline, commitment, and organization are crucial to avoid the rush and panic that otherwise result.

As mentioned earlier, *Outwrite*'s assumption that contributions would flood the office was soon proved wrong. The accessibility that we hoped to present to both readers and writers perhaps did not ever really exist, and despite our best intentions, we have been unable to improve the situation much, for example, we only managed to hold one series of readers' meetings in a few cities. We actively invite few contributions and commission even less, and sometimes more by accident than design. We believed, mistakenly, that those women engaged in militant struggles and campaigns would somehow automatically use *Outwrite* (and thereby write for the paper) because of its character and *raison d'être*. This has happened, but only occasionally. The intimidation that one can experience in submitting material for publication, especially the first few times, the constraints of time, the demands that women's lives are overwhelmed by – all contribute to maintaining the silence. It would also be wrong to assume that the activist is necessarily the best writer and therefore the best equipped to express in words the politics that motivate actions.

An intensively supportive and encouraging environment is required to help build confidence in one's ability to write and to see one's writing in print. The confidence goes hand in hand with the development of the strength to accept criticism about one's work, and this process is what I imagine takes place in women's writing workshops. Ideally, although *Outwrite* may have wanted to create such a supportive environment, restrictions and the demands of running a business have made it almost impossible, although editorial meetings for collective members do have the potential to encourage similar processes.

An inability and an unwillingness to pay contributors also accounts for few submissions. The inability is obvious, the unwillingness is controversial. In our early days we did state that since we did not believe that political work should be paid for, writing for a political paper could not be valued in monetary terms either. Ironically enough, most of the collective no longer works on a voluntary basis, so perhaps we need to revise this policy.

A major difficulty for *Outwrite* has been our self-imposed limitations that have defined what we are and what we can be. We started by wanting to be a newspaper, performing some of the functions of a newspaper, and even imagined progressing to becoming fortnightly and then even weekly. Another dashed hope! We now recognize ourselves as being a monthly magazine in newspaper format, containing a blend of news items, interviews, articles, and advertisements. Sustaining ourselves as a news magazine is difficult – lack of access to regular news sources, for example Reuters, and administrative tasks that prevent us from engaging in investigative journalism or even responding quickly to events, has meant a reliance on an uneven flow of material. A combination of original material, press releases, reprints from other magazines, and articles based on information in magazines and newsletters constitute our copy sources. A little help from a friend, well placed in a British daily, also means the occasional arrival of telex news reports – the real thing! Not much of our news is fresh. However, *Outwrite* does have more success in uncovering stories that would otherwise be 'buried', thereby making news that would not receive an audience in this country otherwise; this is especially true of many of our international items. Although the reporting and balance of stories is uneven, with certain issues and news from certain countries far outstripping others, *Outwrite* plays a major part in circulating news within the feminist network worldwide, for example a reprint from an Indian magazine might be reprinted from *Outwrite* by a Canadian one, and so on. The informal feminist network exists and has been gaining strength, but there is an obvious need for an efficient feminist news service to build and sustain international links.

Once the words are written and published, distribution of the paper is then the next hurdle. Any initial hopes of seeing *Outwrite* sold at news-stands were quickly dashed. Agents identified low profit margins for themselves because of our deliberately low cover price and then refused to take us on, and we have declined to be distributed by an agency handling pornography. Today we are distributed by subscription, through a network of wonderful women distributors (in small towns, centres, etc.) and by a left-wing agency to alternative bookshops. Although feminist publishing is enjoying a boom, unfortunately the alternative bookshops are not raking in the profits, as large High Street chains have encroached on the trade, and the resulting financial difficulty that some bookshops have experienced has also been a blow for *Outwrite*. Further, the 'boom' is in the area of fiction. Polemical and theoretical writing are not in demand, and a paper like *Outwrite* now has limited appeal, compared to the reception it received four years ago. Reading patterns are not changing in isolation, a fragmented Women's Movement is perhaps responsible. Only pockets of militancy survive, old networks have disintegrated, many new groups provide services rather than organising in other ways, there is little evidence of interest in theory building, or in discussions about strategies or tactics in the face of increasingly repressive regimes worldwide.

The survival of *Outwrite* is dependent upon the activism and militancy of a Movement, not only to back it, or supply the readership, but to actively feed into it. Where a party organ may be able to steer the political direction of its readers, how far is this possible for us?

Some of us have been rethinking several of our previous positions in relation to the magazine. We have tended to give uneven coverage to many essential issues that we originally existed to reflect and give a voice to, for example issues concerning lesbians, Black women in this country and working-class women. How can we implement changes? Does the present extensive coverage of internationalism and exclusion of more light-hearted material such as humour or reviews, make *Outwrite* a heavy read? Our reluctance to offer material in compartments, for example a lesbian section, home news section, has also meant an unwillingness to consider breaking up the paper in other ways, like introducing an editorial (an extremely useful vehicle through which political pronouncements can be made), features, monthly reviews, comments and so on. For the same reason, the Letters page, an obvious space in which readers can comment, criticize, and introduce points of information, all without having to write a feature length piece, was only introduced a year ago. The questions remain – would a more conventionally packaged paper, which would be easier to read, have greater appeal, or would it mean making a compromise?

Our explorations continue. We are mostly proud of what we have achieved, demonstrating that it is possible, but we still need to constantly question and re-assess our direction.

All the questions do not have answers, but the questions themselves remain crucial. Meanwhile, a business needs to be attended to, and paste-up weekend is again round the corner. With the abolition of the GLC, our future remains a question. Will voluntary input keep *Outwrite* publishing? Our survival cannot depend upon us alone, so how long will it be till *Outwrite*, too, is forced to join the many other feminist magazines that have reluctantly had to take their place in history.

(This paper contains personal opinions and musings, which are in no way attributable to the *Outwrite* collective. A big 'thank you' to Rahila Gupta, Liliane Landor and Sue Stiles for some very useful comments, all of which I was not able to implement.)

They tried to rip me off

Diana Shelley

I used not to believe in copyright. Property, after all, is notoriously theft, and copyright can be seen as a form of property, developed in a society which is capitalistic and patriarchal – all the things we're trying to do away with. We believe in the free flow of information, that ideas should circulate, reaching as many people as we can – don't we? Recently I found myself face to face with a man across a table putting something like these arguments to me. He was explaining how it was that he had taken an article of mine published eleven years earlier, cut it, written a biographical note about me and printed it with other people's articles in a pamphlet – all without a word to me (or any of them) that he was doing it, though he knew where to find me. He told me that 'we in the alternative movement' had always had a practice of reprinting articles without asking. The implication was clear: if I objected, it was I who was out of line.

Ironically, he had chosen the piece because of its feminist content. I found myself with feelings of outrage, feelings which I believe are intrinsically feminist. How did he know that, as a feminist, I was still prepared to publish in a publication containing articles by men (as the original piece had been)? How could he write and publish a biographical note about me without asking whether it was what I wanted to have known about me? How did he know whether I still agreed with the article? And, more than anything else, how could he think it 'politically correct' to deprive me of control over my own work? I realized that my position had completely changed: I believed in copyright.

Not that I'd had no reason to think about it before. Ten years ago the script of a piece of street theatre I was involved in was lifted by a Christian publication, its end altered, and reprinted without any credits. I think I minded more about the change than the lack of credit. A few years later someone, who may have been paid and was certainly credited, took some of my sentences word for word from the *Squatters' Handbook* without saying where they'd come from. We'd always said there was no copyright on it;

after all a handbook is important for its information and we wanted squatting groups to reprint any of it they could use. But there's a world of difference between the people it's meant for *using* information, and other people gaining money or credibility by taking our actual words, and we asked in future *Handbooks* to be credited.

Most recently, an organization which had some involvement – properly credited – in a book of which I am co-author began an application for a grant. They wanted someone else to be paid to write a supplement to it. They didn't trouble themselves to ask either me or the publishers for our permission before they began the application. No doubts there: when I found out, I wrote without hesitation telling them to stop, too angry to risk losing my temper by speaking to any of them. They were trying to take *my* work and make money for themselves from it. For me, it was two and a half years' unpaid work (a year of that full-time). For them, it was something to be exploited.

Like most women who call themselves writers, I don't make a living from my writing, and most of the time I don't get paid at all. Writing may be something I choose to do, but it is still work. It's work, it's what I do, it's a part – an important part – of who I am. As I faced that man across the table I suddenly felt as remote from what he was saying as I now do, a feminist in 1986, from the male-defined 'sexual revolution' of the 1960s and early 1970s. How many times was it assumed that if I were really 'liberated' I would fuck when a man asked? How many times did I assume it, too? For years I believed in being 'free' with my body as the start of that greater freedom we are working for. Now, like many women, I feel that the terms on which I did that were not free, that this was a sexual revolution defined by the patriarchy, heterosexist and exploitative, within which I was not free to discover what I wanted or who I wanted to be.

If, as feminists, we are struggling to drag our bodies from that morass of male-defined sexual practice to claim our own definitions of our sexuality, what about our work? Should that be 'freely' available to anyone who wants to use it or can't we lay claim to control that too? If I now have a right to choose whose bed, if any, I go to and what I do there, haven't I got an equal right to decide which publication, if any, my work lies down in? Isn't 'taking control of our own lives' about our work as much as our bodies, and as intrinsic to any radical politics worth the name as it is to feminism?

After all, for thousands of years men have been appropriating our time, our labour, and our ideas; writing is no different. In the patriarchal view of things, whatever we do is intrinsically without worth and so can be taken and used. Indeed, in that view, it is male use of it which may just confer worth on it. I'm not saying that the idea of copyright can be extended to everything we do: it may be clear when an actual piece of writing has been taken, but what about ideas? Most women must have had the experience at some time of seeing or hearing an idea, a political argument, a plot for a play, an anecdote or a joke which originated from them presented by some man as if it were his own. Often it would be petty to interrupt with 'Hey, that's mine.' But in a world where our work and what we do is constantly put down, that possessive feeling, that sense of being shut off from our work, will continue to be there; and why not? A real solution would lie in a society where women and our work are valued properly, but in the meantime, wherever possible, we need credit. It would be unrealistic to expect credit for all our half-formulated thoughts: ideas are by their nature fluid, unobtrusive, and so subversive, and the way I influence you, the way you influence me, is the way we both grow and change. But when the tangible fruit of our ideas is there, a book, a photograph, a scientific paper, we indubitably need both credit and control.

A further argument against this goes: of course copyright is a protection against commercial interests, but it shouldn't be used between 'like-minded' people or groups. But who, if not me, is to define *who* is like-minded to me? I am active in the peace movement, and the last two groups which have tried to break my copyright are peace organizations. I find them too reformist, incompetent, patriarchal, and irrelevant for me ever to have associated closely with or joined them; to me they are 'like-minded' only in so much as they too are in the peace movement, nothing more. I do not consider them a 'good cause' deserving my unquestioning support, certainly not in relation to other peace organizations. In the case of the pamphlet, though, I went out of my way (in the face of considerable disparagement and rudeness) to minimize their losses on a work already printed by asking for a sticker in the first edition rather than what I would have *liked* for myself – that the entire print run be trashed. Eleven years later, I disagree with the whole basis of the article and it is inevitably out of date; I didn't *want* it republished at all. Even if I had felt happy with it, I'd still have felt angry about having my work taken by an organization I have never respected. Either way, if they'd asked, they would have found out how I felt.

I doubt whether I have to argue this very much to other feminists, and I'm not saying this is just a feminist issue. Men also get ripped off, and shouldn't. But my position now comes from what I have learned in the Women's Movement: that respect for each other and our work is at the heart of really revolutionary change. Keeping control of our work isn't just about deciding who can use it but is also to ensure that *what* we have written is not distorted by clumsy editing, that if a piece must be abbreviated for lack of space it still says what *we* intended it to.

Perhaps it's worth looking at what this control means in practical terms. The copyright position on this article, for instance, is quite straightforward. If you want to reprint all or part of it, please write to the publishers and to me care of the publishers for permission (with the title of the book on the envelope as they probably won't remember me), explaining what you want to use and in what context. If it is so long after publication that the publishers can no longer trace me, try contacting me in the kind of journals I might read (feminist, peace movement). If you really can't find me, please make it clear when republishing that you have tried to, when the article was first published, and whether and how you have in any way altered it. If you must alter it, please do so sensitively, trying to preserve what I meant, not what you think I should mean. The publishers will tell you what they want. If you do find me, please offer me some share of any money you may make (I'll probably still need it as much as I do now), though if you aren't making a profit you'll find my consent won't depend on that. If you simply want to quote a short passage (less than a hundred words is the convention, though I think that in the USA even this is subject to copyright), please give me and the publishers full credits.

I don't own much and I don't earn much and sometimes I feel as if all I really have is my work. If you value it and me, you will find me a reasonable woman. After all, I believe in the free flow of information, in the circulation of ideas and in reaching as many people as we can. As well, of course, as in the destruction of capitalism and patriarchy. That, I believe, starts by taking control of our work, not by letting it go.

Acknowledgements

Thanks for ideas, help and lots of support to my writing group: Michelle Russell, Penny Cloutte and particularly Gail Chester.

Why there's a light-box where my typewriter should be – being a feminist publisher

Joy Pitman

Sometimes, when I'm up till two in the morning doing lay-out, or cycling across the town with a rucksack full of books to post, begging a loan to tide us over a cash-flow crisis, or answering yet another letter of the 'I'm doing research into feminist publishing and I wondered if you'd . . .' variety, I ask myself whether publishing other women's writing isn't all some elaborate mechanism for avoiding getting down to my own.

The two activities are nevertheless intimately connected for me. I first got involved in publishing because I am a writer.

My feminist writers' group had been meeting and discussing each other's work for some time, when in 1979 we finally felt confident enough to follow the example set by the *Licking the Bed Clean* group and set about publishing our own book of poetry. The group had a meeting with a woman involved in book distribution and one experienced in print – both now working full-time with London publishing organizations. Out of that now historic meeting Stramullion – the Scottish feminist publishers – was born and *Hens in the Hay* was eventually published.

My original motivation in helping to set up the co-operative was to put into print the writing from the members of my group which I believed was good and deserved a public. The same motive is vital to me now: belief in the worth of the writing. Without it I certainly wouldn't find myself engaged in any of the sometimes arduous activities which running a small publishing house entails.

At the time, however, I hadn't foreseen just what that apparently simple decision was to get me into. I well remember now the hours spent over the (borrowed) electric typewriter producing a neat manuscript for the grant application to the Scottish Arts Council; having to look critically for the first time at different typefaces because we actually had to choose one; visiting the Heriot Watt Students' typesetters and being fascinated by the mechanical process the woman there demonstrated to me; chatting about feminist art while Diane sketched my portrait for the book; watching Moira bent over her calculator doing sums about printing costs and distribution discounts; folding up paper to see how the imposition instructions from Moss Side Press worked out and put the pages next to each other in the right order. This was a whole new world, with its own terminology and techniques.

What excited me most, though, was the long weekend doing our own paste-up on light-boxes loaned by an Edinburgh cycling magazine. Oh, the delight, fingers sticky with Spray Mount, of shifting bits of typesetting about the page and trying out different arrangements of illustrations with text. 'How does that look?', 'Why not move that verse left a bit?', 'I think this line's a bit squint', and finally, 'Yes, that's it!'

I had never done anything like it before. I was fascinated, delighted, and so absorbed that I almost forgot to eat. It's still the part of the process which gives me the greatest pleasure.

That weekend I recalled my early childhood memories of enjoyable reading which, along with the stories themselves, included the smell and texture of the paper. I realized I had always taken in not only the illustrations, but the appearance of the type and the shape of the spaces around it. Reading for me is a fulfilling sensuous experience: the look and feel of a book as important as its content. And now I saw how I could take part in creating that experience for other readers. It was satisfying and artistically creative in a way which complemented the creativity of writing itself.

Thus did a poor innocent writer become hooked irrevocably on publishing.

Of course we made mistakes. But I don't regret them: I learnt a lot from them. Cutting up minute scraps of typesetting to get the right page numbers for the index to *Hens* taught me that it's much easier to go back to the typesetter and get the index set later on. Having to take a day-trip to Manchester to rearrange half a dozen pages, because we'd misplaced the final section of one of Lorna Mitchell's long poems, taught me why it's important to check these things with the writer! But even that trip had its compensations – I was shown around and got my first inkling of what's involved in camera-work, plate-making and tending a press, all of which help in understanding what it's possible to achieve. Frantic last-minute hassles to get enough bound copies of *Incest* to send out to reviewers before a rival publication on the same topic appeared made me more suspicious of printers' promises, so that we now give them plenty of leeway in our timing schedules. And over 2000 correction stickers later, I'll *never* forget the importance of checking – and rechecking – telephone numbers in a non-fiction work. Even our early idealism about pricing books as low as possible to make them more readily available had to be revised a little, when it became apparent that if we didn't make some profit, we wouldn't be able to afford any more ambitious projects.

Perhaps this all sounds very unprofessional, but it was an important part of learning for ourselves how to do things in our own way. It was the price we paid for having total control over the whole publishing process – something which as women we rarely have, and as writers, almost never. It was worth it.

Sometimes when I'm struggling to make my personal financial ends meet, to fit part-time 'work' for money, time for Stramullion (which at the moment can only afford to repay my expenses and an occasional small fee), time for writing, and some time for a social life, all into the mere twenty-four hours which a day allows, I wonder if I wouldn't prefer to work for a more financially orthodox publishing house. But even this situation has its virtues. I only ever work on a publication *I* really want to, and being short of capital means we have to be damn sure that what we bring out is worth doing. Schedules depend on the time *we* want to put in. When I hear of other women in feminist publishing working long hours every day, or having battles with their financial overlords, I think maybe we're doing it the right way after all. We can grow in our own time, in our own way.

My involvement with Stramullion has been important to me in other respects, too. It has given me an activity in which I am totally self-motivated to learn. No one has imposed this on me – I am learning because I want to.

I went on courses on editing, an evening class on print preparation and, when I was unemployed, I attended the first year of a day-release course in graphic design where I discovered I could enjoy a day over a drawing-board. Most of the learning has been more informal than this, though, and most of it has come through contacts with other women in the book trades and media. Conversations with Mary at Scottish and Northern Book Distribution taught me a lot about the selling end of the process, and I'm even grateful for lessons on how best to pack boxes of books! Sarah Nelson, the author of *Incest*, is a journalist, and gave us invaluable advice on how to write effective press releases. At an Edinburgh Women in Media training conference, I had fun role-playing an incompetent (and subsequently more proficient) interviewee, with the help of a freelance radio interviewer, so that I'm no longer nervous of a microphone. It was at the first Feminist Bookfair that I found the confidence to do some rights selling, knowing that other feminists wouldn't put me down if I admitted some areas of ignorance. I've also been a committee member of the Scottish Young (and incidentally not-so-young) Publishers Society, and despite the occasional puzzled looks and references to 'feminine' publishing, the other 'real' (predominantly male) publishers accepted us as a bona fide presence. Many Scottish small publishers started out as one-person concerns, they understood our problems, and most of them have proved more than willing to be helpful and give advice. Probably here we are in a better position in our relationship with the rest of the publishing world than we might be in the south.

In this way, my initial motivation, belief in the writing, has taken me through a number of different learning processes into a confidence-building situation where I'm even better fitted to learn still more. It's surely no coincidence that my belief in myself as a writer, as someone who *can* do what I want, has grown at the same time.

I think being a writer has made me a different sort of publisher, and vice versa. As a writer, I know only too well that the book is fundamentally the author's creation, and I believe she has a right to be as involved as she wants in the publication process. As a publisher, I find I have my own ideas about typesetting style and design for my own novel, and I would be prepared to insist they were considered. Stramullion's authors have taken part in drafting press releases and cover blurbs. We exercised only minimal editorial control over *Moll Cutpurse*, because as a fellow writer I knew Ellen had already worked on the book in the writers' group when we asked for a little more development of the emotional and sexual scenes, and even requested a meeting with Shakespeare's sister. I knew that one English feminist publisher had praised the meticulous historical research, but didn't like the prose style, while another had loved the style but didn't think it had enough psychological interest, and an agent had suggested rewriting the whole thing and giving it a contemporary setting! These 'expert' opinions differed so widely that they could obviously be ignored; Ellen had written the best book she could at the time; we had faith in it. It could stand as it was. Our best sales record to date, plenty of good reviews, plus offers for American rights and German translation rights have proved that instinctive faith right. As a result I shall trust my instinct more often.

I shall trust my instinct about my own writing too. Yes, I'm always open to helpful criticism and suggestions for improvement, but in the last resort it's *my* writing, and I'm the final judge on whether it's up to my standards. I've seen a fellow writer driven to despair at having to rewrite her initial script beyond recognition, because she was desperate for the money. I would hate ever to put an author in that position, and I'm now a lot less likely to let myself be persuaded by editors to change my writing beyond the point where it remains mine. Hopefully, most feminists would respect this, but those who aren't also writers may not appreciate how important it is.

The most significant thing I have learnt from being a writer who is also a publisher is that the process is a continuous one from notebook and pen right through to bookshop shelves. I believe that ideally this continuity should be maintained as far as possible, whenever possible, and that requires some understanding from both publishers *and* writers. Publishers sometimes need to remind themselves (or be reminded by writers) that a sales record starts life as the creation of an individual woman. A manuscript may represent years of difficult labour: it is a highly personal extension of the writer's self. It deserves as much care at all stages of its treatment as the woman who wrote it. In turn, it wouldn't do writers any harm to realize the constraints under which publishers have to work. Your precious manuscript isn't the one and only wonderful piece of writing which simply must be shown to the world. Publishers have hard choices to make, budgets to keep within, publicity to devise and sanity to maintain.

In an ideal post-revolutionary world, perhaps all writers could learn to be publishers: the means of production could truly be in the hands of the labourer. Until then, we shall have to do the best we can in respecting each other. Writer and publisher are two sides of the one equation. I count myself lucky in being able (just) to encompass both. Despite suffering occasional pain in the stretch that this requires, I wouldn't want it otherwise.

Postscript

Twelve months after writing this article I resigned from Stramullion to concentrate more on my writing.

I am a feminist and a journalist . . .

Susie Innes

I am a feminist and a journalist – and the contradictions that entails are the stuff of my everyday life. Though I can't claim to agonize over every one of them, I have learnt to ignore some of the problems, and I've managed to avoid sharp conflicts.

Being a working, freelance journalist means for me working for the 'straight' press – mainly because they *pay*. But of course one of the things the press is about is promoting images of women, and of the society we live in, which I find neither truthful nor useful, but which bolster the interests of White, western men. (This isn't to deny that the Women's Movement has affected the media. It's also important to distinguish between the 'quality' papers, which do at least some sort of responsible and necessary job, and the gutter press which engages in conscious political manipulation of its readers.)

In day to day work as a journalist, the conflicts between my feminist values and those of the press aren't always apparent. But the contradictions have muddled me, knocked me about, and confused me – and certainly made it more difficult for me to pursue my working life. The arguments are familiar to anyone working in an institution with which they politically disagree but which they see as doing some good. The issues in media are simply sharper, more evident – not different.

What compromises are sensible, what beyond the pale? Is it OK to write about art, but not about fashion? To work for women's magazines – when the pay cheque comes from advertising makeup, sexy underwear, and so on? To quote the director of housing rather than chasing up tenants' groups, because it's quicker? Never to write about prisons because it is intensely difficult to find the facts, and anyway it's more fun to interview novelists? To leave a hundred and one worthwhile stories completely untouched because they'd take so much *time*, and interview the glib Director of Social Work instead? What about reviewing? Is it really on for me to criticize other feminists' work? If I don't, someone else will . . . and that's an argument that has been used to cover a multitude of sins!

The bottom line questions aren't usually about whether the editor thinks a story is too radical (they call it *out of date*, *unsubstantiated*, *too hard*, *too soft*). A first line, almost automatic screening process operates in terms of what I know I can and can't sell to an editor in the first place – is it even a story? Politics or no politics, is it boring? Though the media do push their view of the world through concepts of 'news value' and appropriateness, I still think these basic questions are vital. Good journalism should be clear and entertaining and communicative. If it isn't, no one will read it.

The *real* concerns in any story are with getting it in on time and at the right length, with changing a long word to a short one so you can get all the copy on the page. . . . The (male) editor I mainly work with and I are equally concerned to get a good, neat, lively piece of copy off to the repro house in time to go home and play with our babies. As I juggle journalism with motherhood and my 'other' work as an illustrator and painter, the dominating preoccupation is with *time*. So that, for example, a fact about a store's refusal to distribute a book about lesbians is sacrificed because it takes four phone calls to establish. The story that needs to be written about conditions for children in long-stay mental hospitals is never written, while one about another group, which can hand you information on a plate, is. (The other main reason many a good and worthwhile story never makes it into print is that *people won't talk to you*. NHS cuts and nurses on the dole? No one wants to stick out her neck to complain, and theories and rhetoric come easy but facts are rare. And when the story turns out not to be true, it's *me* with egg on my face . . .)

It is certainly easier to become a successful journalist if you don't believe in anything very much or very conspicuous (except your own prosperity and getting to the pub at lunchtime). Though I think there's less of a pretence these days that journalists can be objective, the beliefs of the White, male middle class are still seen as 'reality' – and commitment is still a dirty word around newspapers. You have to be exceptionally able and confident to circumvent the prejudices, whether or not your politics appear in the stories you submit.

And if they do, editors and producers may be reluctant to employ you. When I was first a journalist (eleven years ago) topics like Reclaim the Night marches were seen as wildly radical, getting me a reputation as highly subversive! I'm pretty sure that I suffered in one instance from sex discrimination, meaning that I lost a job (and a lot of self-confidence) – but there's no way I can prove it. And since journalism is one area in which women have made relatively great inroads and a few women have become very successful, to talk of discrimination can easily seem like whining, like an excuse for your own inadequacies.

Nevertheless, women in journalism suffer the same sorts of discrimination as in other areas of work – with the added hassle of a particularly macho ethic of the hard-drinking, cynical, porn-loving journalist, and, curiously, the fact that there are a lot of women journalists! 'I don't know what you keep going on about,' said my editor, when I mentioned this article, 'you've won.' (The only reason I'm not in his chair is his skill, sheer talent, and experience, and my lack of it, of course.) Women now make up half the entrants to journalism, but twice as many women as men fail to continue as journalists after the training period; women dominate the lower paid book, magazine, and weekly paper sectors but only 300 of the 3000-plus Fleet Street journalists are women, and women in senior editorial positions in newspapers remain unusual – 8.8 per cent, and that includes women's page editors. Only 20 per cent of news specialist writers are women, and they are usually at the 'soft' (and less respected) end of social services, education, and consumer affairs; only 1.6 per cent of sports writers and 2.3 per cent of newspaper photographers are women (NUJ figures). (One picture editor told a woman photographer I know that he would not have used her photograph – which he did, on the front page – if he had known it was taken by a woman, because women can't use cameras.)

Women journalists are encouraged into the women's pages and magazine work – most insidiously by the automatic assumption that they always have and always will. Once safely ensconced in the ghetto, they are rarely taken seriously or seen as fully professional. The woman who has the confidence to persist in writing about nuclear power or local authority housing is unusual; too often, there are reasons to take the path of least resistance. And more fundamentally, as a feminist, it can be difficult to carve out a career writing about mainstream issues – my analysis of *why* nuclear power is promoted against all sane evidence is so different from the conventional liberal/left analysis, let alone the pro-nuclear lobby's thinking, as to present me with real communication problems. At press conferences I have sometimes had the embarrassing experience of not having my questions understood; I tend to think this is because I'm stupid, but sometimes it has been because I am simply coming from somewhere else.

And thinking about stories I've worked on recently, I notice that my approach has necessarily been different from the approach of an 'ordinary' male journalist. For example, a story on the threatened closure of a small hospital used mainly by women and children – *of course* I see it differently from someone who will never need a hysterectomy or an abortion. And it's a real fight to make a piece which is 'unbiased' enough to be published, *and* which won't sell short the campaigners' efforts to keep the hospital open. An interview I did recently with the author of a new book about being gay dealt at some length with her experience as a lesbian. It was cut to hell. Even the word *lesbian* was edited out, which brought an angry attack from one lesbian reader. You can't win in this game. . . .

After enough of this kind of experience – spending hours taping and editing in order to help an inarticulate person make an important point, only to have a bored radio editor cut half of it; spending a week working on a piece about the reality of having no electricity and four kids in a dump housing estate, only to see it rejected out of hand – you learn to become protective. You also become more indifferent to badly cut work, and care less what anyone thinks about the piece. More and more, however, I try to write on issues which don't involve my feelings or feminism, and struggle not to let the conflicts affect me more than they have to.

And that's mainly because journalism is about earning my living. One way in which, in retrospect, I see my feminism affecting my work is that, in collusion with my conventional upbringing, it reinforced the idea that work isn't a priority. Your mother, your 'alternative' friends, *and* your consciousness-raising group, all told you ambition was unacceptable – 'unfeminine', 'materialist', or 'male-identified'. Some of this has some truth to it, but it leaves me financially totally insecure, and with a sense of frustrated potential.

Money is still a taboo subject. It is an essentially middle-class game to pretend it isn't important. Freelance journalists are less well paid and seen as marginal – it isn't surprising that women make up a higher percentage of freelance NUJ members than they do of staff members. (That's also because of the myth that freelancing is easy to fit in alongside child-care. It isn't.) Freelance journalists are engaged in a perpetual fight, through our union, for our work to be properly paid for – and we're perpetually undercut by people for whom it is both a hobby and a source of prestige to appear in print. At the time of writing, a new feminist magazine, *Everywoman*, has started up on the basis of not paying contributors; *Spare Rib* once had the same policy, and so do many other publishers who see it as the first saving in a tight budget. These same people go out on picket lines to fight for a miner's right to work. I've never heard of anyone planning not to pay the printers – who are overwhelmingly male, strongly unionized, and wouldn't *dream* of working for free, ever.

Taking myself seriously as a journalist meant very quickly stopping writing for free or for low fees – this article is a dangerous exception. People are always asking me to, for *their* good cause. And it is very difficult to value your writing, and time, enough to be tough on this one. Meantime, most editors and publishers are a deal better off than most writers.

And, of course, the economics of running small circulation magazines are tough, but let it be said loud and clear that any publication which expects women to work for free or for low rates is exploiting those women. And it's also excluding time-consuming, investigative, and well-crafted writing, and usually, working-class women, mothers, and anyone else without time to give away. (OK, you can write on the dole, but you shouldn't have to.) So much for access to the means of expression. . . .

As a feminist and a journalist I sometimes think you have the worst of both worlds – mistrusted as a journalist by feminists and as a feminist by journalists. To be a successful freelance journalist you have to be very tough, persistent, and energetic, and either very good or very well-connected. I'm not particularly successful in terms of income or status, but there are other definitions of success, and to do work which is varied, stimulating and occasionally useful is certainly OK! There's the wonderful feeling of having finished a difficult piece – and the despair when the editor tells you to rewrite it. There's the sheer interest of interviewing, having the right to ask all those questions. And you learn new skills – like typing with one hand and balancing a windy baby on your shoulder with the other . . . then comes the draggy feeling of realizing it's eleven at night, you're tired, still have the ironing to do, but must also find some sort of ending to an article . . . like this one, right now . . .

Would it be so very terrible to simply, unprofessionally and inelegantly, *stop*?

Translating as a feminist

Ros Schwartz

Why should feminists, as writers, readers, or publishers, be concerned about translation as an issue? What are the connections between feminism and translation?

As readers, we buy books which are made available by publishers. If we are literate only in the English language, the only books available to us are those written in English or those published in translation in Britain; so, unless you can read one or several foreign languages, the vast majority of writing remains 'a closed book'. This should concern feminists because it is hard to be aware of what is happening to women and to feminist movements in other countries if we cannot exchange notes. This unavailability of writings originating in other languages amounts to a form of silencing. As feminists, it should be our concern that the work of many women authors is being denied to us. If we feel it is important to explore the differences between ourselves and women from other cultures and are aiming towards greater understanding and combating racism and intolerance, it is vital that we should be able to read about the experiences of women from other cultures. It is up to us all to find ways of opposing this passive silencing.

UK publishers give various reasons for being reluctant to bring out translations. Firstly, there is additional expense involved in what is already a costly business; secondly, unless the editors themselves are fluent in another language, they find themselves having to make editorial decisions based on somebody else's recommendation, and thirdly, they claim that there isn't the demand for books in translation, that the readership is resistant to foreign works.

It is fair enough to raise the problem of additional cost, but there are ways round it. After all, this does not deter publishers in other countries from publishing works in translation, notably the French, who have a voracious appetite for works by foreign writers. There are a number of countries, including France and Scandinavia, which offer grants to help foreign publishers with translation costs. Then again, British and American publishers could bring out a co-edition and share the costs, as could paperback and hardback houses. There are other ways of getting over the cost hurdle than asking the translator to work for a minimal fee, which is what often happens when publishers do not have a clearly defined policy about translation.

The editors' language problem is a very real one. The long-term answer to that is that commissioning editors should make it their business to learn one (or more) languages and meanwhile they should find readers in other languages whom they can trust and who are sufficiently briefed in their requirements to ferret out possible works for them to publish. This is how publishers in other European countries operate. I feel that at the root of the whole problem is the legendary insularity of the British and their general resistance to things foreign. Publishers frequently commission a work in English on the basis of a synopsis and sample chapters, so they are on shaky ground when they refuse a book in translation because they don't fully comprehend its contents. It is quite feasible to make some amendments when translating, especially in consultation with living authors.

As for the claim that translations don't sell, perhaps we should ask why? What makes any book sell? Although there are no hard and fast rules, and it is often something of a mystery, one thing that helps is publicity. Publishers are selective in the books they choose to hype, and perhaps money invested in publicizing previously unheard-of foreign writers won't pay off, but if you don't try, you'll never know. *The Name of the Rose* by Umberto Eco was refused by a number of publishers for the sort of reasons I have mentioned, but when Picador, in association with Secker and Warburg, had the guts to 'take the risk' it paid off handsomely as the book became a best-seller. There are risks involved in any publishing and large sums of money can be lost if a wrong decision is made, but selling books is not very different from selling soap powder or any other product. People have to know about them. Sales forces have to be briefed to get the books into the bookshops, the media have to be made to take notice. There's no point just publishing a book by a foreign author and hoping it will sell, saying: it cost enough just to publish it, we can't afford to promote it as well.

Translation is not always straightforward: language is inextricably bound up with culture and experience, and there is not always an equivalent word, expression, or concept in another language. I am sure many people have seen foreign films subtitled into contemporary American slang which ignores the content of the film, and, even without being linguists, have felt the choice of language inappropriate. In books, take the example of Alice Walker or Toni Cade Bambara whose fiction records the experience of Black Americans. Their use of language may have no equivalent in German or Spanish. The problem that arises is how to convey the content faithfully. To use literary Spanish would detract from these writers' innovative use of language, while to use Mexican or Puerto Rican idioms would equally betray the tone of the writing.

But that should not be a reason for not translating the work of 'difficult' writers, for it can easily become an excuse for excluding anyone experimental or anyone from an ethnic minority. On the other hand, Alice Walker may prove no more difficult for the right translator than Frederick Forsyth might be to someone outside his cultural context. It is a problem the translator must be aware of and seek to resolve, preferably in close consultation with the author, if she is living. This is an important step towards a feminist approach to translating contemporary writers. In a way, translation dispossesses authors of their text. The translator creates a different text which should respect the original as far as possible, but is inevitably an interpretation of it. It is only when translating that I become aware of the constant ambiguities underlying words, and make choices which I hope are closest to the author's intentions. Authors have already been dispossessed of their text once, in signing away rights to agents or publishers. They may have titles changed, jacket designs imposed – at least the translator can ensure that she has rendered the work as faithfully as possible by confronting issues of language creatively, with the author.

It may be appropriate to include a glossary or footnote to make some words more accessible to a readership from a different culture. Sembène Ousmane, whose novels are set in Senegal, writes in French, but includes a lot of words in Wolof. In the Heinemann African Writers Series translation, by Clive Wake, of Ousmane's book *The Money Order* (1972), these words are kept in and a glossary is provided at the back. The narrative retains its African 'flavour' without mystifying the western reader. A different approach to this problem is taken by Salman Rushdie, who writes in his book *Shame* (Jonathan Cape, 1983), 'To unlock a society, look at its untranslatable words.' He deals with these untranslatable words by keeping them in Urdu and incorporating an explanation for the western reader into the text. He thus preserves the concept embodied in the word and makes readers aware of something outside their own cultural experience.

It is important to be aware that what is currently available limits and distorts our perception of the world. Reading Manny Shirazi's novel, *Javady*

Alley (The Women's Press, 1984), which gives English-speaking readers an insight into the experience of a girl growing up in Iran, made me wonder how many other women all over the world have experiences to recount, so different from my own, that I will never read because they do not write in or are not translated into a language I know. Unless we can gain a greater understanding of other cultures, there is a danger of cultural imperialism within the Women's Movement as well as outside it. Western feminists are often tempted to prescribe solutions which do not take into account the very different cultural backgrounds of other women. This ignorance can only be dispelled by the wider availability of writings by women from all cultures, both within Britain and from the rest of the world.

The dearth of documentation and literature in translation is a serious issue in that it maintains ignorance, and it is that ignorance which fosters prejudice. Britain is increasingly cut off from the non-English-speaking world and tends to identify more and more with the USA because it publishes books in English. This form of cultural imperialism pushes Britain further away from Europe. Britain is part of Europe, not America, but there is a communications gulf which is much wider than the Channel. The exchange of ideas which has always flowed between European capitals is bypassing Britain. This can only reinforce the deeply rooted mistrust between us and our closest neighbours. Our history, culture, and political philosophy is bound up with the rest of Europe, yet so little is known of contemporary European writing, let alone works from the rest of the world. This is as true for feminist theory as it is for anything else. The USA tends to feature too prominently, deploying not only missiles but also 'culture'. Britain should be reinforcing links with the rest of Europe, and the British Women's Liberation Movement should be aware of theory that is being developed in the Women's Movement in the countries closest to us, not just in the USA.

Translation itself is something of a paradox: a good translation should be invisible, i.e. it should read as if it had been written in that language. The translator, rather like the housewife whose house is always clean, is invisible. Only when the translation is clumsy (when the house is dirty) does the translator become visible to take the blame. There are many women translators (no one knows the figures as they tend to be isolated and invisible). It is work that can be done at home, fitting in with having children and doing housework, and is generally badly paid. Translators are vulnerable because of their isolation. They seldom receive credit, either from critics or, sometimes, even from the publisher. Translators in Britain do not generally receive royalties from book sales, unlike their European and American counterparts. If a translator is dissatisfied, there are plenty of others who will accept the most dreadful conditions and the publisher can pick and choose. And yet translators have the power to contribute to the success or failure of a work.

Power is an important issue facing translators: where does the translator's responsibility begin and end? How does a translator deal with sexism or racism in the original work? There is one school of thought which says that translators are not responsible for the text, they are merely vehicles for conveying what is there. But I think it is the responsibility of a feminist translator to be vigilant over language and eliminate sexist and racist expressions while keeping to the spirit of the original text. To give an example: in several European languages, the word 'black' is used with negative connotations, as in English. These expressions can be translated in a way which preserves the intention without causing offence to any group of people. 'The blackest day of my life' can equally well be expressed as 'the worst day of my life' and feminist translators ought to make those changes and inform the publisher that they intend to do so. Similarly, translators must confront the s/he issue, making choices and taking the responsibility for those choices.

Translators have a part to play in the introduction of works by foreign authors. We can make it our business to seek out books in foreign languages that deserve translating and bring them to the attention of publishers. Thus we can play an active role in the selection of books for publication, rather than passively waiting until asked to translate something of little interest to us as women and feminists.

Feminist publishers can help remedy this appalling chauvinism by making a conscious commitment to print works in translation (as some are now starting to).

Readers can make their wishes felt by voicing a demand for more works from writers of different nationalities and cultures and convincing publishers that the readership for books in translation *does* exist.

What the hell is feminist editing?

Marsaili Cameron

Many people are unsure of the nature and scope of feminism; and perhaps equally many would furrow their brows if asked what an editor's job involved. Nearly everybody, I suspect, would throw in the towel if required to conjure up the daily round of a person who saw her task as that of feminist editing.

If debate has raged over this subject, then it has raged at some distance from my desk. From time to time articles on sexist and non-sexist language have appeared (mainly, it seems, in American publications); and several books now offer analysis of the sexist bias of the English language along with suggestions on how to counter this. The 1981 appearance of one of these, the British edition of *The Handbook of Non-sexist Writing* by the American authors, Casey Miller and Kate Swift, caused a mild bout of soul-searching in the trade press of the publishing industry; but, several years on, it's all still a bit of a hoot really – or, worst sin of all, positively *passé*.

The non-sexist writing issue has constituted the spearhead of feminism's assault on writers and editors; and progress has been disappointingly, but perhaps not surprisingly, slow. However, this issue is by no means the only one involved in a serious consideration of feminist editing. Indeed, from some points of view, it can be seen to have received a disproportionate amount of attention.

So what else *is* involved in this whole mysterious business? I shrink from any formal definition of either editing or – even more noticeable shrink here – feminism. But I hope that by using some personal notes I can uncover a few issues and questions of more general significance.

First of all, let me make clear the kind of editing I'm talking about. Mine is not the *grand* kind of editing where timid authors proffer their heart's blood, dried, and typed in double spacing, to a capricious and awesome deity with the power of literary life and death (will they publish? won't they? will they? won't they?) No, my work starts after the grand gestures have been made and the manuscript (usually a book, non-fiction) has been accepted for publication.

In the early days of my career (in the early 1970s), I was employed as a publisher's copy-editor and my job involved such things as checking the consistency of style, putting spelling mistakes right, unravelling obscurities of sense (in collaboration with the author) and marking up the manuscript in such a way that the printer knew which typefaces were to be used where, and so on. Any major editorial decisions on the book's structure, balance, content, and tone were generally the province of the commissioning editor.

Nowadays, I work for myself and make my living by writing rather than editing. When I do take on an editing job, it's generally because that particular project truly interests me; and I undertake what you might call 'structural editing' rather than the nuts, bolts, and commas of copy preparation. This means that I'm now allowed (and it's quite a relief) to concern myself with questions of structure, content, balance, and tone.

Some brows may be showing signs of wrinkling at this point. 'How come,' you may ask, 'important things can still be decided *after* a manuscript has been accepted for publication? Surely it's up to the author to sort out all these things for herself?' To which I could only reply, 'It all depends.' It depends on who the author is; it depends on how the book came to be written; it depends on what readership is envisaged for the book. It's unlikely, for example (though it has been known to happen), that the work of a professional writer will need substantial editorial attention. Why should it? Such authors are familiar with the tools they're using: they know (or should know) how to achieve the effects they want.

But take the case of a person who is in no sense a professional writer, but who has something of such importance to say that she feels only a book can meet the case. Now, how the hell do you write a book? How do you start? How do you finish? How do you decide what order to put things in? Well, you don't really know: you've never paid much attention to these things before. But you're driven by a great need to get this book written and you do it, somehow; and, what's more, a publisher says, yes, great stuff, we'll take it.

And then comes a very hard part. An editor springs from behind the friendly publisher and she says things like, 'I found the chapter on maize cultivation fascinating . . . but I couldn't quite catch its relevance to your main theme of women and architecture,' or, 'Very interesting, that short section on middle-class philanthropists . . . so interesting in fact that I think many readers would welcome a fair bit of background information.' And she goes on to ask things like, 'Why did you put X before Y? Do you think that readers might find it helpful to learn about Y first?'

Your head is ringing; your stomach is churning: after all, you thought that at last your part was finished. But it's likely too that, after the first fine flush of loathing, you acknowledge that this person may have a point – or half a one, anyway. You know, deep in your heart of hearts, that you struggled so long and so hard with the *content* of your book that you did sometimes forget about those mysterious people who might one day read it.

Now, leaving our author to her bitter thoughts for a moment, does it seem to you, as it does to me, that this second type of writer is very important indeed to the feminist reading public; that her voice has been heard far too little in the past and should be heard far more loudly in the future? If you do share this view, then I shall offer you a further thought to chew over: that a writer of this kind deserves the best editorial care and help that can possibly be given.

Good editing is about the facilitating of communication. Editors stand on the borderline between author and reader; good editors know both countries well and can interpret signals coming from either side. The editorial skills lie in ensuring that, as far as possible, the messages being sent are likely to be received and understood. They may be rejected, of course, or scorned or yawned at – the messages are the author's own, in no way the editor's responsibility – but if the editor has succeeded in her task of helping the author, then when the book is read, messages will be understood clearly which might otherwise have been missed. It seems to me right that women should offer each other such help.

It so happened that I discovered editing and feminism at about the same time. At that time, certainly, there seemed very few bridging points between the two. During the day I worked for a medical publisher, tiptoeing round frequently monstrous medical male egos and trying to make sure that X-rays appeared the right way up. The few women authors I met were matrons of the old school; I always felt that they thought it a reprehensible matter that I had been given no uniform. During the evenings I attended meetings of women's liberationists and lesbians – quite separately, I must add: in those early days the two groups hadn't quite come to terms with each other's existence. And so it was that what I was learning to practise by day – diplomacy, tact, patience, perseverance – was soundly rejected in the evenings when rebellion, spontaneity, assertiveness, and boldness were hailed as the only way forward. I can't say that the contrast struck me much at the time: the whole world was confusing, myself most of all, and, anyway, a job was only about earning a living – and what did it matter how you did that?

But, some thirteen years on, several things now strike me quite hard. One is the quintessentially *feminine* role of the editor. Here is the nurturer, the carer, the Invisible One; unobtrusively, she guides, she supports, she listens, she advises, she responds. The other, complementary, thing that strikes me now is that this composite baby shouldn't be thrown out with the rest of the 'feminine' bathwater. Women's lives are not of one texture; we live, work, think, and feel in myriad ways. And so the task of communicating, one to the other, can never be a simple one. It seems to me that we still need our guides, our intermediaries, our listeners, our advisers; and it seems to me too that the qualities and skills involved in such activities are noble ones.

It's perhaps clear by this point that I don't regard editing (though I suspect many people do) as a process of stifling, of dulling the authorial voice, of imposing arbitrary rules and constraints in the interests of better consumer packaging. Certainly, things can go wrong between editor and author; after all, they're working together in a minefield of insecurities, vanities, suspicions, fears – and one or other of these things can explode at any time. It's rather more difficult, in fact, to describe how this minefield can be successfully traversed, how the relationship between author and editor can work well. But let me try.

Towards the end of 1983 I was approached by a feminist publishing house, the Women's Press, and was asked to read, with a view to editing, a manuscript which they had recently received. The women at the Press were very excited to have received this particular manuscript and had almost immediately made the decision to publish it. The manuscript had been written by Ellen Kuzwayo, a community leader in Soweto, the Black township outside Johannesburg, and it told of many things: the history of Soweto, present conditions in the township, the author's own life, the courage and strength displayed over the years by South Africa's Black women. Ellen Kuzwayo had spent the best part of two years working on the manuscript; she had never written a book before.

The story that I read engrossed me, horrified me, dazzled me, haunted me; clearly, the book *had* to be published. But I also realized – as had the publisher – that, were the book to be published just as it was, the messages which Ellen Kuzwayo was so determined to get across would be lost on most of her potential readers. This manuscript was the product of a lifetime's working, thinking, feeling, struggling: Ellen Kuzwayo had so much to say

– and so much to say of great importance – that she had, as it were, quite overwhelmed her pages. She wanted to say everything, and she wanted to say everything all at once: no reader unfamiliar with the South African situation could have processed what was being said.

For me, the manuscript represented the greatest editorial challenge I had ever faced – and far and away the most important one. I began to think of ways in which the book might be structured so that the author could successfully achieve her goal of telling many different stories – and so that the reader could follow her every step of the way.

At this point Ellen came to London from South Africa in order to work on the book and to play an important part in the making of a film, *Tsiamelo: a Place of Goodness*, based on her life. I felt very nervous about the prospect of meeting her. From experience I knew all the usual pitfalls and difficulties that can attend the editor-author relationship; and, in this case, I was also acutely aware of the differences in background, experience, colour (I'm White) and age (nearly 40 years) between this author and myself. For our collaboration to be successful, I knew that Ellen Kuzwayo had to trust me; but would she be able to do this? After all, why should she?

I liked her as soon as I met her. She has great natural warmth, as well as long experience of putting people at their ease. The hard part came later in the meeting when I had to explain to her why I believed that the manuscript still needed a considerable amount of attention. She listened to me in silence, her face still; I felt that I understood something of what she must be feeling – she had worked so hard and so long and now she was being told that the work must continue. I gave her a paper outlining some structural suggestions and asked her to look at it quietly for a few minutes, then tell me how she felt about the suggestions.

She took the paper and sat reading it at a table at the far side of the room. All I could see was a back of military straightness. My heart went out to her; I held my breath. After a minute or two, she turned to face me and said, 'I've listened to what you have to say. I agree with most of your suggestions. When do we start work? Tomorrow? Can you come at 8.30 or 9?' All the qualities so apparent in the manuscript – her courage, her determination, her clear-sightedness – sat there facing me at that moment.

For the next week, we worked intensively together on the manuscript. I asked questions, made suggestions; she answered me fully, thought about what I had said, and at times got up at 4 a.m. to write so that she could give me material when I arrived for the next day's work. If ever I said, 'Ellen, I'm sorry, what you're saying in this paragraph isn't clear to me', she replied, 'If it's not clear, then we must re-write it. What's important is that what I've got to say is *heard*.' No author had ever said that to me before. Usually (and to some extent I can understand why), an author will work on the assumption that if the editor/reader doesn't understand, then, tough turkey, they're pretty dim.

After a week, she returned to Soweto and we continued our work by post. My part of the task was made infinitely easier by the fact that I had met and worked with her. As I worked on the manuscript, alone, I could hear her voice in my head; I knew almost by feel what she wanted to say, how, and why. That week for me had been almost like a love affair, where you're tuned so closely to another's thoughts and feelings that you almost lose yourself in their being. As the work progressed, back and forth between us, I could feel the different loyalties involved for me – to the author, to the reader, to the publisher, to the book itself – settling down together in harmony.

'All right,' you may say, 'that's editing. But where does feminism come into it?' Well, feminism comes in in a variety of ways, too many for me to describe here. But let me give you two examples. First, I believe that no publishing house but a feminist one would have allocated to this project the time and resources it required. Secondly, there is the issue of selection of contents. From the start, Ellen had been determined that her book should not be a simple autobiography. 'There are so many stories,' she would say, 'so many lives, so much courage. And all these unrecorded, unrecognized, unnoticed. I want to change that; I want to tell these stories.'

There was not, of course, enough room in this one book; selection, sadly, had to happen. For one of the chapters, I suggested to Ellen that the lives of four particular women should be described in detail: two were world renowned, one was famous within South Africa and one was in no way a public figure. My reasons for choosing these four women were simple enough and had little to do with ideology of any kind. Admiration and warm affection suffused Ellen's descriptions of these women's lives and gave her writing the glow of life.

When I made my suggestions as to which names to include, Ellen looked at me with amazement. 'Yes,' she said, 'I'm more than happy with that list. But what I can't understand is why you chose the last name in the list. I would have thought that European readers would have wanted to know about the famous women only.' I pointed out that her own writing had guided me in the choice of names. When she wrote of the fourth woman, Mrs Nthaelone Manthata, whose son had been imprisoned and tortured for his activities on behalf of the Black community, her narrative brimmed over with compassion and admiration. No one could read it and remain unmoved.

As far as I was concerned, this incident represented the closing of the circle. I was crystallizing for Ellen those things that were most important to her, things to do with women's experience of the world; the editing of the book was a truly shared project.

However, author and editor did not subsequently ride off together into the sunset. The publishing charger on which we were mounted carried a great variety of other people with other professional concerns. There were those interested in production issues; those concerned with promotion; those fighting for sales. In editorial terms, much detailed tidying-up work remained to be done; and editorial hands other than mine gave patient and painstaking attention to this aspect of the task.

In 1985 the Women's Press published the book under the title *Call Me Woman*.

PART THREE WRITING ABOUT OURSELVES

T. S. Eliot never called himself a clerk

Berta Freistadt

How was it that I took so long to call myself a writer? The desire to express myself in words came early and strong. At 7 I wrote my first poem and at 10 a play. Between the ages of 14 and 16 I'd attempted six or seven more plays, a verse drama, a pantomime, and was imitating Chaucer for the school magazine. When I left school I began a body of poetry that has grown to become one of the most important things I do. As a teacher in the 60s I wrote magazine articles and several plays for my students. And yet it was only about four years ago that I began to call myself a writer.

Somehow the writing I did was either part of my job or so intimately connected with my private life as to be invisible not only to others but also to myself. In those days there were men who showed me their poetry but I don't remember them looking at mine. Their work was of course the real stuff, mine was a copy. Perhaps this attitude that I had to my work and myself can be traced to my 1950s girls' grammar school roots. I was a slow learner and somehow couldn't understand the world I lived in, nor make any sense of the framework for living that existed around me. I simply couldn't read the signals. Added to which my spelling was erratic, and though I could write ten-page stories, my total and fairly continual lack of understanding of the structure and analysis of sentence construction did nothing for my academic reputation. This parsing, as it was called, seemed a root base for an understanding of more subjects than Eng. Lang. and how I managed to get away with as little knowledge as I did remains a mystery to this day. I am still ignorant of the difference between pluperfects and past participles and have often felt that I'd have been better off at the top end of a secondary modern than at the nail clinging, cliff edge position I maintained during what was euphemistically termed my school 'career' at the grammar.

I wonder now if I was so different from my peers – it certainly felt like it at the time. Starting from the bottom stream my ambitious mother, occasionally even doing the work for me, and I, managed to scramble up into a better stream. Not the top, but at least in sight of those glorious creatures who *all* went to Oxford, Cambridge, Bristol, and Manchester. Later I also saw those cities but from the front line of the chorus, not as a student. But alas, at least my headmistress had me sussed. She told my mother that I'd never get A levels. She was actually wrong, but right in theory. A levels implied a certain kind of brain, a certain kind of learning and thinking which I didn't have. I did get A levels, English and Art; but that only seemed to confirm her judgement of me and this lack of understanding and encouragement, or rather her complete understanding and appreciation of my lack of academic talent, marked me for life. I took it as a truth that I wasn't academic, since proof if I needed it was all around in the shape of those who were. It was the days of existentialism; I read Sartre and Camus with little real understanding and longed to be an intellectual. Realizing that I wasn't came as a bitter blow. I wasn't so stupid that I didn't sense that I was missing something. I was like a child in a cot hearing her parents whisper across a dark room – I knew something was going on but I couldn't quite catch what it was. I was very sad discovering that I wasn't an intellectual (especially as I had the long hair and the long jumper to go with it!) but of course now I can see that I was mistaken; my writing is as often to do with ideas as with feelings and I daily inhabit a world full of signs and symbols which I am perfectly capable of interpreting. But in the late 50s I didn't know what I *was*, only what I *wasn't*. And of course what I wasn't was a male intellectual or even the next best thing – a female, male intellectual. Nor were there writers' groups to give support, nor women-only workshops to encourage the first scribblings. Most people, it seemed to me, learnt at university or at least by copying established writers. Forgive me if the tone of this is developing a bitter edge. But as yet, the personal was far from acceptable, let alone political, and so it never occurred to me that I should/could/would be a writer.

A few years ago at a women's writing weekend someone described how she had come to call herself a writer. It was when she was filling in an application for a new passport. Coming to the dotted line marked 'Profession' and realizing that she would have to live with the description she was about to write she stopped. What was she? A mother? Yes. A housewife? Yes. A teacher? Yes that too. (Bus conductor, secretary, brain surgeon, bee-keeper!) She decided there and then that her writings made her a writer. And that is what is in her passport to this day. I was much impressed with her story. And her confidence. Soon after this, on certain occasions, I too started to call myself a writer. At first I felt that I was claiming too much and that I'd certainly better justify the claim. Though truth to tell in those days it was part defiance. I felt I was taking a stand not just for me but for other women too. I had a reputation as a loud mouth so I might as well put it to good use. It was important that though I might look as though I was unemployed, or worked in the bakers, what I was actually was a writer. After all, we can be fairly sure that T. S. Eliot never called himself a clerk. Having taken that step I began to remember all that I'd written, and I was flabbergasted. Finally I accepted that there has never been a period in my life when I didn't do some sort of creative writing. Then the name became mine and less of a political statement. It is still hard to say; sometimes it feels pretentious, and sometimes I feel an enormous prejudice and resistance from others when I use the term 'writer' about myself.

Once having started I saw that it was a question of taking myself (yourself, ourselves) seriously. And in the course of this I learnt several tricks, or shall I call them techniques? You'd be amazed how important/serious a poem looks once it's typed in the middle of a fresh sheet of paper. Rough scribbles and drafts in biro are the worst thing for confidence: they are psychologically as though unwritten, invisible. Typed, a poem becomes real. Maybe good maybe not so good, but real: work, craft, art. And I began to carry a notebook with me to rescue the words and lines that might arrive out of the blue. I ceased to let myself forget those small and uninvited inspirations that push themselves forward like naughty elves at the most inappropriate times. I decided that I was showing myself scant respect when often I would have a good idea and later only remember that: that I'd had a good idea and not what it was. The laughable thing about all these notes is of course that they need – a filing system all of their own. Sometimes they're used straight away but often they and their books languish for years unappreciated, turning up often as a piece of my past to remind me of some long dead enthusiasm. Sometimes such an enthusiasm becomes an obsession and will spread itself in note form over several years. Then I'll find as I gather the notes of one particular 'family' together that I've a stronger and more detailed idea than I had imagined. And sometimes the notes for one idea can slip years later quite happily into something totally different.

I am often asked how I came to write plays rather than novels and I never quite know how to reply. I can only suppose that having been connected with the theatre since a child, either as audience or as a reader of plays and later as an actor and a stage manager, that it is the form, being most familiar, that comes most easily to me. As a writer I enjoy the very restricted structure that a play offers. The thought of ten or twenty chapters to fill makes me sweat a little. But the challenge of fitting into two or three acts all that needs to be seen and done and said is like an extremely satisfying puzzle. And then there's the visual dimension, which seems to me, when compared to that of the novel, like the difference between a game of snakes and ladders and mental arithmetic, and you can imagine which I prefer. There is also a communality about the theatre which suits me too. Not only can you never be alone as a playwright, what with the director, the actors, the administrator and the stage manager, but often there's a feeling of shared responsibility which can be really reassuring. Reading a novel is a very private activity. If I were to write one I feel that I would never be able to know what my reader felt. But in the theatre the response is instant and multi-dimensional; between the actor and her part, between the actors and the audience, and often between the audience and the play itself. To be a part of this is very energizing.

But if I've overcome one set of problems, it's only to find that there are others. Most difficult of all was and is finding the time to write. Is it another cliché that only men have wives, mothers, and secretaries to do all the things I must do before I can sit at the desk? The washing, the shopping, the cooking, the letters, the dentist, the cleaning, the lesson preparation, the tyre puncture, the tax returns . . . oh dear, this is so predictable for a woman. If I'm lucky I can usually find, on average, in a good week, when there's nothing else to do, five hours a week to write. It probably means that I'm not as serious about it all as I think I am. Somerset Maugham is said to have written two hours a day every day of the year whether he was working on something or not. He 'worked' at his writing. But we live in a world where the idea of work is very restricted. It usually means that which you'd rather not be doing. If you're lucky it sometimes pays you enough to live on and, whatever your class, usually involves doing business, service or labour of some kind outside the home. If we don't do that sort of work, whether by choice or not, we can be seen even by radical or liberal eyes as dossing around. Together with mothers and the unemployed, producers of ideas, words, and art, dancers, painters, and writers, are all labelled lazy, work-shy, and self-indulgent, and usually middle class. We don't do any 'real' work. Is it any wonder that most of us women have to do the laundry before we can sit down to write? And there is a stigma particular to women that must be overcome, which is the ban on doing things either for ourselves or doing those things that we enjoy. Such women are branded selfish. Not only do many of us, whether we are Black or White, middle class or working class, struggle in our many differing ways with the 'I can' but all of us also have the 'ought not' to deal with. I am making some headway not only with the writing but also with my head. I can and do find the time to write. I have organized my life working in a part-time job which I can drop whenever I need to. And since 1981 I've had several plays produced and a few poems and stories published. Recently, though, I've felt a great sense of desolation and exhaustion after spending the best part of nine months trying to 'put my work about'. A thankless task, but as I see it, still part of the job. Having named myself a writer I've no intention of dying before I've had my say. I want my words heard now. And I want a wide audience. This means approaching agents, directors, theatres, publishers. And a new in-tray for the rejection slips! As I said, a thankless task, but none the less one that seems a natural progression from those days long ago when I'd forgotten the poems I used to write.

Naming yourself a writer feels a lot like having a child. You're not sure what you're letting yourself in for when you start and you do most of it with little help and a lot of criticism from others. You feel responsible most of the time for what you produce turning out well and being approved of, knowing at the same time that you've had to compromise and conciliate. But having said all that I doubt now that I could give it up. Apart from a childish compulsion I have to record what happens to me in the hope, I suppose, that recording the ordinary will elevate it somehow, writing as a way of life, a way of being, perceiving, reacting and relating is like a vice – I'd need another one to be able to kick it. I think it's with me for ever now. Like the albatross.

Acknowledgements

Thanks to Eve, Kate, and Elaine for advice and criticism on the original 1983 article, and to Gail for her ditto on this draft. And to Annabel for the typing.

Writing for my mother

Pearlie McNeill

I have often said that I write for my mother. In saying this I mean that if, years ago, my mother could have read the sort of material that I strive to write, then maybe her life and mine might have been less painful.

As it is, my mother has been lost to her conditioning, but there are countless numbers of mothers and daughters who may not be lost and, knowing the language, experience, and impact of working-class life, it is from here that I begin my craft.

I am a writer.

I am a woman writer.

I am a feminist lesbian writer.

I am a working-class writer.

But there is a paradox here and I am acutely aware of it. Because of feminism, my lifestyle has changed dramatically. More and more I learn, slowly and often painfully, how to bring that life into my own control, and in so doing, I am able to write about and resolve whole chunks of the past – things like growing up with a violent father and recovering from depression and mental breakdown, despite the dubious skills of the medical profession. Indeed, feminism has provided me with a framework from which I can evaluate my life and society in general. Feminism has also given me an education which has been more than just reading or listening to feminist debates. I have received valuable support. I have also received a great deal of challenging criticism, and in attempting to evaluate that criticism, rather than fighting it off, I have struggled with my own fears head on. I have discovered more in me that is capable of change than I would ever have believed possible. However, from within this process has come another truth. The more I change, the more I learn, the more freedom I gain, and the more my choices widen, the further I am removed from the deprivation and isolation which my life seemed to be all about.

In effect, it could be said that feminism has, in so many ways, removed me from my working-class origins. Yet the fact remains that I am shaped and somehow still defined by that working-class background and I have no wish to demolish that shape or cast off that definition, for to do so would be to reject who I have been, to deny working-class experience, and to diminish the positives that I did gain from my childhood, my background, and my environment.

I was in my second year at high school when I wrote my first play. It was lousy. What was important about the experience was that I readily accepted the discipline necessary to write it. Throughout my teen years I wrote fiction and poetry, but by the time I was 20 I'd stopped writing altogether.

Thirteen years passed.

I'd married, moved to the suburbs, had two children and one long mental breakdown, and struggled to find a reason for living.

Then my marriage broke up.

Through visits to a women's health centre, I was introduced to feminist ideas.

It was no easy victory but, as many of us know, feminism often prefers a gradual takeover.

Now, years later, the commitment is a way of life.

I began writing again in 1975.

I joined a writing class in Sydney's western suburbs, led by a feminist. So lacking in confidence was I in those first weeks, that when asked to write a description of a living room in centuries past, I dug out my copy of *Forever Amber* and stole three paragraphs of description verbatim. The class continued, and slowly I developed a little confidence. I chose to think of myself as beginning an apprenticeship. The apprenticeship will probably never finish, but the strength gained from adopting this approach has encouraged a sense of identity to emerge.

Whilst we all have perceptions of what being a woman and a feminist mean to us as individuals, it is less clear what role feminism should play in our craft, or what constitutes a definition of feminist writing. Similarly, it can be difficult to define what is meant when I say I am a working-class writer. But the challenge in this article is for me to attempt that definition.

To date I have written several short stories, articles, a novel, a radio-play, and co-edited two anthologies of feminist writings. Most of my characters are women. These fictional women work at home or in factories, maybe they are shop assistants or even cleaners. For the most part they have been exposed to rows in the home, possibly violence, and they speak in a language that doesn't mince words and is probably of a sort you'd be as likely to hear in the back streets of Liverpool, London, or Leeds as in Sydney, Melbourne, or Brisbane.

I've yet to invent a character who's, say, been to university, earns a healthy income, teaches for a living, or who could boast of holidays abroad. If the golden rule of writing is that we should write about that which we know best, then I am more than well equipped to write about working-class experience and I would be foolish to pretend otherwise.

Wherever possible, I show my characters as women possessing tremendous spirit and gutsy determination. This too has a connection with my mother. She was a very important role model for me. Throughout my childhood years I watched her stand up to that bully of a man who was my father. Without surprise, I can now understand how it was that I could jump in when a fight started and attempt to defend her from his blows, even though my efforts were puny and quite unsuccessful.

As an avid reader of popular fiction in the 1950s and 1960s, I often felt that there was a division between the writer and myself that could not be bridged. This division, I now realize, had to do with class. The publishing tradition has largely reflected middle-class values, and it is therefore not surprising that a *them* and *us* situation can occur, if readers are unable to relate to the subject matter and/or the way it is written about.

When a character's life story in a novel, for example, is resolved by either money or privilege, it has little meaning for a working-class reader who has neither. A bit like watching Shirley Temple movies many years ago. You can't believe it could ever happen to you. Shirley's adventures always ended with what could be called a middle-class resolution. The significance for children like me was as far away as the hope that I might get a pair of Shirley Temple boots for my birthday.

Many feminist writers, despite their purpose and vision, have been imbued with certain standards and values through learning institutions, particularly universities, and much of what I read in the 1970s was re-creating this *them* and *us* reality which I was more aware of than what the writer was saying. I couldn't go to university, so the resolution offered in Marilyn French's novel, *The Women's Room*, was another Shirley Temple story. Early feminist non-fiction books produced in Australia, usually of the history-of-women category, were so hard to read I was reminded of the school text books we're all used to, when all I was aware of was the enormous effort needed to finish the task. There were writers who did make an effort, though, and is it merely coincidence that they were often women known for their poetry?

Adrienne Rich's book, *Of Woman Born*, was like coming home, so too was the novel, *Woman on the Edge of Time*, written by Marge Piercey.

I'm not suggesting that a book, article, short story, play, or poem has to be written using simple language, oversimplified concepts and so on. What I do want to stress is the importance of developing an ability to create a comfortable rapport between writer and reader – a rapport that makes it possible to cut across distinctions of class.

It is a myth that women from working-class backgrounds are unable to grasp difficult concepts and complicated language. It is the presentation of concepts and language that needs more and more thought. We also need to see more and more women from working-class backgrounds in print. There is a lot these women have to tell us and I'm convinced that there are many, many women eager to read what they have to say.

As a working-class writer, committed to working within a feminist tradition, there are moments of negativity (fortunately decreasing in number) when I feel uncomfortable, even inferior, within the embrace of the Women's Movement. This, in part, is what it means to be working-class: to feel a conditioned inferiority to those around us who have had more opportunities, better jobs, and so on. Accepting those feelings as part of the process of growth has offered me a way forward, even if I still admit to that class cringe from time to time.

The fact that I now have time and opportunity to write, and that I live my life with more choice and direction than my mother ever had, or her mother before her ever had, is an indication of how far I have travelled from my working-class origins. Yet it is from these origins, and my struggles to understand what those origins mean, that my material for writing is drawn. My feelings always reflect my present stage in those struggles, and I've long since passed the point where I would choose to go back, even if I acknowledge (on bad days and in bad moods) that the going can be tough, sometimes too tough, for me to deal with.

So I now choose to create and/or reinforce credible role models that I hope a working-class woman (my mother?) could identify with, while injecting my work with a brand of humour that could be labelled sardonic, and is as familiar to me as the World War II songs my mother sang whilst doing the washing up.

The task of creating a feminist tradition of literature is no mean challenge and must include a consciousness of class within it. More and more feminist writers are taking up this challenge and breaking away from male publishing standards and traditions, exploring, experimenting, and evolving new ways of expressing themselves. Ten years ago it would have been hard to set up a bookshop selling only books written by feminists. Now there is a continuous stream of these books appearing on more and more bookshelves. Some enterprising women are publishing their own material or working collectively to produce material written by writing groups. Whilst applauding this groundswell, I still find it saddening that so few books I read speak of working-class life or inform me of a wider range of experience than that which I know from the past ten years.

In truth, it is still largely middle-class experience and middle-class writers who have given us most of the ideas, theories, and stories that we have learned from so far. I do not want to condemn or ignore that truth. I want to widen it. If the task of creating a feminist tradition is no mean challenge, then creating a working-class context within that tradition is an even greater challenge and one I want to be a part of.

Feminists have stressed the importance of creating new words and of reclaiming and/or redefining existing words, in an effort to overcome the restrictions that a sexist language has placed on women. We must also try to bear this in mind when thinking about the restrictions class has placed on women and how this is reflected in language.

For many women writing is therapy: a means of finding answers and resolution. The importance of keeping a journal or a notebook may be a woman's first step towards writing as a craft or it may remain a private way of helping herself to understand and extend her own powerfulness elsewhere in her life. In using writing as a means of understanding ourselves and what happens to us, we are using a valuable resource. It is in this area of insight, awareness, and resolution that our integrity and emotional honesty can be used to great advantage and if, however subtly/unconsciously, we exclude working-class women from that process, we are denying them access to an important tool of liberation.

These qualities of integrity, honesty, etc., coupled with an ability to meet a subject head on, has meant that many women writers, through the years, have refused the temptation to write objectively. By this I mean that they have allowed their personal feelings to inform their writings. This truth is often reflected in the manner of written expression a woman writer chooses, for example letters, diaries, stream of consciousness and so on. In resisting that temptation to be objective (as male writers have insisted *they* are), women writers have struggled to provide new approaches to old problems. As feminist writers, no matter what our class background, we each play a part in the continuation of that struggle.

On being a late starter

Rosemary Manning

When I was asked to write a paper for this collection, I felt rather a fraud, for I have no feminist writing to my name. Indeed, I only became interested in feminism in the early 80s. This was after I had taken part in some ITV programmes about gay life and had come out as a lesbian. I was 70. The programme brought me into contact for the first time with lesbians and feminists, many of whom were writers or in some other field of the creative arts. It was a turning point for me, and I realized that I had a lot of catching up to do.

Looking back on my upbringing and family life, I cannot think why I wasn't a militant feminist in my teens. Except for my mother and myself, the family were all males: my father and three brothers, all much older than myself, together with several extra brothers, boys whose parents were abroad. Perhaps it was hard for me when I was small to feel the masculine pressures around me as anything but agreeable. Ten years or more younger than any of those boys, I was of course a kind of toy or pet. I was a curly-haired, rather pretty little girl in those days and they enjoyed playing with me. It wasn't until I was in my teens that things changed. The boys were then in their 20s. I was a lumpish teenager and merely a nuisance to them. One of my brothers coined an expression which ought to have made me a feminist of the deepest dye. It was 'HLAW' which stood for 'How like a woman!' and he shouted the term at me whenever I said or did anything that he thought foolish or ignorant. But I never questioned the patriarchal layout of my family, still less of society, and although 'HLAW' may have made me feel hurt and inferior, I accepted it as part of the awfulness of family life in general. At least my father, whom I adored, valued me more, it seemed, than his sons. I was given a university education and that was more than many daughters acquired in the 30s. Only one of my brothers was given it.

Although I didn't question patriarchal values and attitudes, I certainly questioned the status of marriage. In many ways a conformer, I was at any rate roused to rebellion at the idea of getting married, which of course my whole family expected me to do. From my early teens I resolved that I would never marry and I held to this resolve passionately and publicly. 'Publicly' meant at boarding-school, since once I was away from home I was too out of touch with my family to express any kind of views to them. With a dawning glimmer of feminist values, I condemned marriage as slavery, and when I was about 16 I wrote a furious play on the subject. The central character was Clytemnestra who murdered her husband, King Agamemnon, with an axe, a deed of which I thoroughly approved. Although the murder was really in revenge for the sacrifice by the king of his daughter, Iphigeneia, to induce the gods to send favourable winds to assist the Greek fleet on its way to Troy, I slanted my play rather differently. Clytemnestra was given some stirring speeches on free love and its superiority over the bonds of marriage. But Clytemnestra's 'free love' was a liaison with Agamemnon's cousin, Aegisthus. I was influenced more by Shelley than Radclyffe Hall, and it would never have occurred to me to twist the story to give Clytemnestra a lesbian lover, even though I was beginning to realize privately that I was attracted by my own sex. When I was in my 40s and beginning to write novels, I still wrote in heterosexual terms, though for a far more conscious reason. By this time I was teaching. It would have been virtually impossible for me to write in any other way. Not until I wrote the autobiographical book, *A Time and a Time*, did I write openly as a lesbian. It was brought out under the assumed name of Sarah Davys. I was now the headmistress of a girls' school. How could I have admitted that I was a lesbian?

'Admit' is an important word in this context, carrying as it does the implication that homosexuality is not a natural state but an aberration to be kept under covers. Some young lesbians with whom I talk today find it hard to understand that such a defensive and secretive attitude could really have existed as late as the 60s. Nor can they always comprehend my apparent lack of conviction about my lesbianism. But there are lesbians and gays who even now in the 80s find it hard to come out, especially in their homes. Although I recognized from my teens the attraction that my own sex had for me, I had sought no explanation, for the climate of the times, the hints in the press and the theatre, and in half-heard conversations, embarrassed or sniggering, told me, in so far as I was told anything, that my predilection was *abnormal*. I did not want to be thought abnormal. Who does?

My first really happy love affair set me on the road to realizing that I was *not* abnormal. The breakup of that affair when I was just on 50 led to my attempted suicide, described fully in *A Time and a Time*. This book was written to clarify my mind as to why the affair had ended and how I was to face the future. It was still threaded through with the self-hatred that had fuelled my act of self-destruction, but it was an honest attempt to look at myself and my life. It was several years later, when I embarked on a richly rewarding, long relationship with another woman, that I began to escape from self-destructive attitudes. After many years, this relationship ended, but this time I reacted quite differently to loss. I became outward-going. I have written in a new autobiography about the distance I have come since *A Time and a Time* was published in 1971. This new book is the first of my writing which can be said to be influenced by feminism.

I am not a joiner and do not think I shall ever be an active lesbian feminist. I do not want to be labelled a lesbian writer or a feminist writer. I am simply a writer. But I do support the basic tenets of feminism as I interpret them, and though I am not active in the Women's Movement, there is nevertheless one subject on which I will take every opportunity to speak and write, believing as I do that we writers have a responsibility. The years of Thatcherism have destroyed many of the gains made by the Women's Movement. It is essential for women to support each other and hold together, but what knowledge of feminism I have acquired leads me to suspect that this may be difficult.

There is a wide spectrum of opinion within feminism. Can women of such disparate ideas work together at least on a broad basis? We cannot afford to quarrel among ourselves. Almost worse than outright bloodletting is cold separatism, the splitting up of the movement into factions too stiff-necked to communicate with each other. I foresee a long period of erosion of women's rights, a process that is well under way with rate-capping. We are all in danger and I believe that in the future we are going to be increasingly under attack: feminists, lesbians, gays, Black and Asian communities, Jews, the poor, the disadvantaged, the disabled.

I think a book about feminist writing is the place to emphasize our responsibility. We must be the voice of the inarticulate, of those who will be shouted down, beaten back, and if possible silenced. Our present rulers make no effort to conceal the principle they find so efficacious: divide and rule.

I will end by quoting some words of Angela Davis, taken from an article she wrote for the American feminist paper, *Sojourner:*

> Those who are our adversaries would pit us against each other. . . . The differences between us pale in comparison to the differences between us and our opponents.

Writing as a lesbian mother

Caeia March

Silence is *not* golden when it is imposed by others.

Finding my voice, rhythm, and images as a writer of fiction and of poetry, is, for me, a process of recognizing myself as a woman, a feminist, a lesbian, and a mother.

The process of writing fiction and poetry began for me in the spring of 1980 while I was still married. For the first time since I was 18 I began to write about my feelings. I was 33 and never called myself a writer, although I earned £800 a year from a sociology book that I had published with another woman for use in schools, when I was 26. Since then I'd written and edited for socialist education journals, for a series of books for schools, for social science teachers' journals, and for *Spare Rib*, about becoming a feminist teacher. (For that I used the name Kate Elliott or I'd have risked losing my job.)

Writing was something I did every day. But it was about others, about schools, about the system, and occasionally, about revolution. It was about the reality outside me, until in the spring of 1980 I began my autobiography, to try to find out why I was so unhappy. My contract, researching into youth unemployment in Hackney, finished in May. I will always remember that summer, because every day I took an old folding table that had been grandma's out into the garden, and I wrote.

The peonies fatbudded, then revealed themselves the colour of pink sugar mice: the colour of northern Christmases in the 50s, when my Gaelic grandmother lived with us in a mining town near Sheffield.

She lived there in that garden, with me again, that summer. I moved open with the peonies, allowing the feelings through like petals, fold upon fold.

In June, I joined a consciousness-raising group, and also a feminist writers' class at the City Lit. In the CR group, I found some of the words I needed. My politics became centred in my uterus with an urgent need to reclaim myself as a woman-identified woman. I wrote it all down.

For the writers' class we were asked to bring some dialogue. Once started, I couldn't stop. I wrote sixty hours a week, increasing to eighty then ninety. No one could come near me.

In the evenings, I brought grandma's table indoors and continued writing. I hid in the pages, wrapped my body with the words. I discovered a tape recorder inside my skull, just behind my left ear. It played at me without a pause. Eventually I had four days of high dose Valium to turn it off while I slept. I slept. I wept. When I woke up I started writing again. If I didn't write, I couldn't sleep.

I didn't know that I was writing my way out of compulsory heterosexuality.

In all the years of marriage, I never knew a time when I was not under continuous sexual pressure. All in the name of the sexual revolution. My husband read the Kinsey report and the Hite report and every other report, and *Playboy* and *Mayfair* and *Cosmopolitan*. And pressurized me to do the same.

I experienced it all as threat and violence but I didn't know that because I didn't have those words. All I had words for was having thrush all the time and being unhappy at other times and sexually delighted sometimes, which confused me. Although I had done a year at a London medical school when I first came to London, before rejecting the dissecting room and switching to sociology, I didn't have a word for my own clitoris either. In medical school it was four lines in a 700 page textbook which said it was a vestigial penis. I had a child before I knew I had a pleasure organ called a clitoris. I had a miscarriage and another child before I met my first feminists and fell in love with one of them. I didn't even have the words for describing that falling in love. So I called her my dearest friend and stayed hours in her company whenever I could, and was married and despairing and monogamous for many more years.

In July, I wrote a section on pornography. I was shocked to find that my words were staccato. Sharp off the pages they spiked me. I tore up those pages, ashamed that I had ever given into the pressure to read porn, and afraid that I wouldn't be able to interact at all with my husband if I wrote any more like that. I returned to the comfortable phrases and sentences. It was to be another four years before I wrote 'Photographs', a short story of my experience of porn.

That summer I fell in love all over the place with women, but said nothing to any of them. There was nothing for me in the house, so I wrote and ate in the narrow garden. I'd have slept out there if I could, but I couldn't escape a double bed with a kind man, the father of my sons, so easily.

In my writing I recognized later that my emerging lesbian sexuality was censored out. My awakening anger and despair, joy and hope, were muffled. Like bright sea-washed pebbles embedded lost and hidden in feather pillows. It wasn't just that it takes a long apprenticeship to learn the craft and discipline of creative writing. It was much deeper. I did not know who I was or what I really wanted. I had been trained not to know.

By August, I had written five variations of my autobiography, *A Limited Wedge of Sky*, but the descriptions were not clear enough; the words given to the characters, not angry enough; the emotions too even, without the ups and downs of life as I lived it. (As a child I was hellish angry, often. My family was the sort you could lie side by side with, in a field in a thunderstorm. They'd keep you safe, but you'd still find the storm exhausting. I swung from high to low and mother would say 'I don't know what to do with you. One minute you're up and the next you're down. Oh, for a bit of peace and quiet.' She still longs for that. It's not likely, now that she's a mother of a lesbian mother.)

I am now aware of the process of that summer: that my writing played a central part in my self-awareness and my political understanding.

On 2 October 1980, I left my marriage and my children.

Two summers later, I distilled some of those pages of my autobiography into a short story for the Sheba collection, *Everyday Matters, vol I*. The story showed my coming out process. It was not bland. The writing had exploded into all my emotions. It was full of pictures, colours, questions and risks. There was room for anger and politics as well as fun and joy. It was large enough for a whole woman to search for her new creativity inside it.

I became apprenticed to myself. To find in myself and in my writing the parts of me that I'd censored; uncovering the thoughts and ideas that had been stifled; facing the hostility that lies in wait for women who challenge heterosexuality.

At first I called myself a lesbian who left her children. I tried to forget they existed. Then my body went on strike, forcing me to let out the distress and anger through glandular fever. On the days when I could sit up, I wrote about it in terms of a healing process, not a disease. I came through with more self-knowledge as a mother. A year and a half later, I dared to go to groups saying that I was a lesbian mother of male children and I was also a writer, and that these parts of me could not be artificially separated.

While I was a het mother I was intimidated when women called themselves poets and I didn't know how to read their words or talk to them. But in the process of coming out I began to write poetry again and to read theirs. I am sure that this is linked with class as well as gender and heterosexism. Those of us in our northern working-class grammar school who wanted poetry were systematically eased away from an understanding of ourselves as poets. If we wanted poetry, we were taught to go outside ourselves to the accepted ways of the male middle-class literary tradition.

During the first year of living on my own, I began to meet other working-class lesbians, and to identify with the struggles around class in the present Women's Liberation Movement. This brought me closer to my mother and dad, who raised me working class and stayed working class, and didn't in their wildest imaginings think of me becoming a lesbian. Their feelings have had to do somersaults to face it, with all its effects on them, their Christianity, their grandchildren and their daughter. It has been one hell of a family struggle. A high of fury and a deep of resentment; a width of charity and a length of hope.

My mother always said she was 'a bit of a feminist really'. In her later years she's taken to writing rhyming poems and has always kept in touch with me by letters. She is proud of the fact that working-class women like her, with no formal education beyond 16, can and do communicate in writing. My dad loves words. They are both staunch Labour voters, aware that working-class people have a long history of challenge to people in power. They both see writing as part of that. Dad writes plays and has written one novel, but he's been unsuccessful with publishing. They encourage me, but I ache for both of them to be recognized.

Finding my own rhythm and images has also been about the childhood images of earth, sea, and sky; and bone marrow memories of Gaelic words and voices. Mother was always so proud of not being English. Her family are Manx. So with my grandma informing me that she was descended from the Vikings, and from the Celts before the Vikings, I grew up with a sense of time past, and the knowledge that it is people who make the present into the future.

My children have their own future, to make for themselves. They have suffered the trauma of my changes, but now they know me again.

Now I call myself a dyke. I stand on flat sand, toes in the ocean, within sight of the moon, and I am my own ebb and flow. I stand. A dyke by the sea, arms raised to the sky with the land behind me, and the silver moon sea night in front of me. And I am less afraid.

> But where are my children and how do I name them?
> I name them as my contradictions whom I claim
> and face and love.
> I name them as mine though I left them
> with their father.
> They know who I am and how and when
> to name me.
> They know that I love them and that
> where they are concerned
> my survival and theirs depends
> on the honesty with which we dare
> to share with one another
> our thoughts and feelings.
> They may grow up to be gay or het
> but I am their mother a woman
> and they can never grow up to be women.
> Neither of them has made this society
> in which they were birthed
> out of my body.
> And if they are to survive
> they must like themselves and
> love themselves for there are enough of them already
> who live by hate.

My children are boys. I will not impose them on other women. And I won't have them imposed on myself. But neither do I risk their feelings by exposing them to women who might damage them. So, when they are with me, the places I can go are limited; the conversations I can have are curtailed; and the isolation is extreme. The exception is my supportive lover-relationship, but if we want to go out some place where *boys* are not welcome, then one of us must stay behind to childsit with them.

In the isolation for me as a mother, there is also the isolation as a writer. I can overcome this in the times when my sons are not with me, but for full-time mothers everything competes against the creative process which requires time, energy and money.

Lesbian mothers are all classes, all races, and all cultures; and we all have a story. But if we publish *we pay* for every word through the lives of our children. Some of us have children by self-insemination, so that there is not the immediate threat of loss of custody or access. However for most of us, who had children before we were lesbians, the whole of life can be a custody case. Every time we meet the institutions of our society: schools, clinics, hospitals, GP surgeries, the DHSS, and financial places such as banks and the post office, our relationship with our children can be called into question. We have our strategies and tactics sorted out beforehand. This is basic survival, for us.

Survival is not only about facing the contradictions and living through them, but also about communicating to others. I have been told that I am not a real feminist because I have boys; not a real lesbian because I have children; and not a real mother because my children are not with me full time. But I want neither to lose my identity as a mother by denying my contradictions, nor to lose my identity as a writer by being totally oppressed within the mothering that is part of me.

As I write this (autumn 1984), my sons are almost 13 and almost 11. This summer we three went to the Isle of Man to visit my parents, who now live there again. My mother still writes about it in her letters. Her relief that they are what she calls normal seeps through the handwriting.

Some things about the visit were difficult. We all found the island racist (it is) and traditional in every way. (It is.) We all live in a multi-racial society and we missed that. There were hours when we longed for home. And it was so dykeless there too. On the island, I wrote a short story called 'Time Warp' about the changes in all our lives: my need to be a mother to my sons in spite of my rejection of the power of men, and of the ways in which men expect to find women to do their emotional work for them, long after they have grown into adults who are old enough to do it for themselves. We three talked about that. That night when they were asleep, I wrote it down.

To be a lesbian writer is a basic definition for me – to work with other lesbian writers to re-make the language, asking ourselves again and again, how to recognize, challenge, and overcome the male middle-class racist tradition in publishing, taking the risks which are necessary.

As a mother and as a working-class lesbian it is hard to find the time for writing. I wrote non-stop while I was unemployed for two years, but now that I am a clerical worker, full time, I'm falling asleep over my typewriter by 9 p.m. On access weekends I want to write and be with my sons. This leaves a few nights a week and some weekends. Hardly enough time to write my answer to Radclyffe Hall.

Writing imposes demands on my lover as well as my children. While I'm typing this she's making the tea, finding scissors and glue for the editing, working out how she can get to a photocopier, and whether she can hand deliver this in time to meet the deadline. She knows this pattern inside out and backwards way on. She also writes. I did this for her all last weekend. It's a sexual relationship not a romantic friendship . . . when the writing and the child-care give us the time!!

The commitment of lesbian mothers to our lesbian selves and sisters is profound, because of what we've had to go through, both as mothers and as lesbians.

In court I'd have been sliced up and pasted in between the lines of the statute books. Men like their parallel lines. They use them to vent their hatred of wives, women, lesbians. They line women up/separate us out/fence us off from each other, whenever they can however they can.

They will box us inside their categories. With never an overlap such as Black suffragette, or working-class woman writer, or lesbian mother. They will use their man-made phrases and their male-dominated history books.

Yet women have always resisted, rebelled, revolted. As mothers, as wives, as lesbians. Revolted against the male words; the iron railings; the metal bars of the prison windows; the gilded bars of the sweet scented suburban canary cages; and the parallel ridges of corrugated iron on the boarded-up tenement windows.

Dykes have chained themselves next to their women lovers on the same railings, while the history books called them friends. Dykes have survived, some of them, solitary imprisonment all over the world. The history books call them – people. Dykes have struggled out of rural and urban and suburban cages. The history books call them – housewives.

We are struggling to write, claiming rights for children and grand-children. Claiming the right to be published, as lesbian writers. Claiming identity. Naming ourselves in terms, our own terms, of race, class, culture, disability. Demanding the commitment by publishers to the writing which reflects the complexities of lesbian lives. And which celebrates our naming as well as describing our contradictions, prices, and problems. And, since there are so many ways of being a mother, lesbians as mothers are demanding a published literature which shows us to our friends, lovers, and mothers, as an alternative to compulsory heterosexuality. The words are being written. They should be published.

In the room where I type I now have a shelf full of pebbles. I put them under water sometimes to see the veins of the amethysts sparkle. Sometimes I dry them again, if the intensity is too bright. But I shall never put them back into pillows.

Words are weapons

Pratibha Parmar

Someone famous once said, 'Words are weapons for liberation' and if I had to encapsulate all the reasons why I write, then it has to be because I, too, believe that writing is a crucial form of action. Writing has always been a powerful means of protest and change for subjugated people all over the world. For as the Egyptian writer, Nawal El Sadawi says: 'Writing is like killing, because it takes a lot of courage, the same courage as when you kill, because you are killing ideas, you are killing injustices, you are killing systems that oppress you. Sometimes it is better to kill the outside world and not kill yourself.' While writing can not always be a substitute for action, words are nevertheless powerful weapons in the struggle against imprisonment, exclusion and invisibility.

Neglect, absences and distortions about Black and Third World people are common features in much European writings. As a Black woman who is a product of the Asian diaspora, words offer me a means of channelling my diverse emotional and intellectual energies into a creative form. I write for many reasons. I want to change ideas and idealogies that only serve the interests of a dominant majority. I wish to document histories and her stories that far too often fall victim to a deliberate amnesia. I want to reflect our realities and help create spaces where it is possible to offer an ever changing imagery of ourselves.

There has been a long and somewhat painful journey to this point from where I confidently and self-consciously identify myself as a writer. As far back as I can remember, I never had a childhood yearning to be a writer. I never wrote secretly in my room, like Anais Nin at the age of 7, partly because I shared a room with my two brothers and a sister, but also because I was too interested in roaming the streets and climbing trees. Even now, at the age of 30, I don't carry a notebook around with me to jot down any sudden inspirations while travelling on the bus or doing the shopping. But I call myself a writer. Notice I prefix that statement with a 'but'. There is a story behind that.

Until two years ago, even though I had written numerous articles in magazines and journals, and co-written a book, I had never entertained the idea that I was a writer. It was only when a Black sister encouraged me to recognize that what I had been doing in the last few years was writing that I slowly built up the confidence to name myself a writer. It was during that slow and painful process of accepting and proclaiming an identity as a writer that I simultaneously began to question the widely accepted definition of what a writer is.

One of the things that struck me was that my reluctance to name myself as a writer was partly to do with the tyranny of fiction and poetry as the only 'legitimate' form of writing. It seemed to me that even amongst the feminist community you were only allowed to call yourself a writer if you wrote novels, short stories, plays or, better still, poetry. And until recently I have only written non-fiction; articles, political essays, and theoretical treatises didn't count as proper writing.

The hegemony of fiction over non-fiction wasn't the only reason for my reluctance, and it wasn't only the lack of images of Asian women as writers which undermined my confidence. I also had a powerful image of who and what a writer was: he was a White man, probably bearded, sitting at his typewriter with a cigarette hanging from his mouth and drinking endless cups of coffe, and when his imagination got stuck, drinking neat Scotch or going for long solitary walks in the dead of night. This image captured my growing perception that you had to have white middle-class male privilege to call yourself a writer.

While the ghosts of such images may sometimes fleetingly come back to haunt me while I am trying to write, I have persisted in exorcizing them. To understand my persistence with writing I need to go back to my roots and examine my personal and political history to see *how* I began to write.

I was born in Nairobi, Kenya, and I learned to speak and write English at the age of 8. Three years later my family migrated to England, by which time I could read and write textbook English which made me the butt of many racist jokes at school. I learned to survive very quickly by picking up a North London cockney accent. Sometimes I am surprised when I remember that English is not my first language and here I am, writing all these things in English. It also helps me to understand why my sentence structures are often considered by editors to be the 'wrong way around'. Writing this, I have realized that I have never given much significance to the fact that I can speak three other languages apart from English, but also that Gujarati, the language that I grew up to speak for the first eight years of my life, had been rendered inaudible, except within the close confines of my family. A common legacy of British colonialism is that many of us may speak our mother tongue, but we are unable to read or write it; this is the price of learning English.

As a young woman I read voraciously, I read absolutely everything I could lay my hands on. In Kenya, I read all the Enid Blyton books, as these were the only English books available to me. In England, I read everything from Spiderman and Superman comics to Mills and Boon romances, and later still, E. M. Forster and Balzac. At college I set myself the task of reading through all the Penguin modern classics series, going through one book a week. I also remember reading *War and Peace* in three days, staying up late at night totally engrossed and absorbed in the lives and worlds conjured up by the words on those pages.

I was the first one in the history of my family to go to university. I worked to go there, because at that time it was the only respectable and the least traumatic way in which I could leave home. My first year at university was a nightmare. I felt lost, friendless, and was painfully shy. Going to university meant many things, but most importantly, it meant that I was thrust into a totally White, middle-class, and articulate environment. I felt that everyone expected me to talk and behave like them. I felt I could barely articulate two sentences, and as to my opinions on anything, I had no confidence, nor did I imagine that I had anything valuable to contribute.

I took a year off before finishing my final year at university and went to India – my first visit. I worked and travelled around India for a year, working in women's projects in villages. It was in India that my hitherto liberal and humanitarian ideas about poverty and inequality in the world got grounded and shaped into concrete understandings, framed into a systematic analysis by a few wonderful and committed women and men who talked to me about Marxism and about their struggle to change their society and fight poverty. I was fired by their energy and enthusiasm. What they said made so much sense and really helped me to understand not only what I had been seeing and experiencing in India, but also what I had not been able to understand about living in England.

I became politicized about being Black in England. Not that I didn't understand this before – I couldn't fail to know this, seeing that I came to England a year before Enoch Powell's 'rivers of blood' speech, while in my school there were gangs of skinhead girls and boys who used to go around 'Paki' bashing. I had learnt to survive all this, with bitterness and anger, but there was nothing that helped me to understand it all, until I went away from England.

I had gone to India, naïve and full of many unacknowleged emotions and stirrings, and a need to find an identity. I came back feeling strongly grounded as an Indian woman, but more so, totally identifying myself as part of the Black struggle in England.

Once started, there seemed to be no stemming this process of change and development. Feminism and anti-racist politics became the major foci in my life. As my understanding of the world became clearer and my awareness of my history grew, so did my wish to write about these issues. I joined a local Black group which produced a magazine. They asked me to write a letter about the local anti-racist group, and without a second thought, I sat down and wrote a fiery letter which was the first bit of political writing that I had ever done. After that it seemed that there was no end of things to write about. But above all, who I was dictated, in many ways, what these things were.

Being an Asian woman meant that I wrote about being Asian, being a woman. Taking the raw material of my experiences, I fashioned them into analytical and polemical articles. I protested about racism and Black people's struggles through these writings. Most of my writing was 'academic' and factual, while being also polemical and journalistic. Being at university and looking in the sociology textbooks for explanations for the existence of racism and about the relationship of Black people to British society, all I found were books written by White academics explaining our cultures, and putting forward theories about Black people's lives. I was angered by most of these books, especially when I looked for books about Asian women. These were often written by White women who were more interested in furthering their careers than representing the interests of the people they theorized about.

I wanted to record the life of my mother, who was a home worker as far back as I can remember, whose whirring of the heavy industrial sewing machine could be heard in the early hours of the morning. I also knew that she was not the only one, that there were hundreds of other Asian women like her. At the time, the only way to begin to do this was within an academic setting, to do factual and systematic research which would give validity to the deeply emotional and angry response I had.

It is only in recent years, after having written articles about the lives of Asian women, young and old, when Asian women students seek me out and say how important it has been for them to read what I have written, that I realize the very real need for us as Asian women to be able to create our own theories and explanations of the world. These will, of necessity, be grounded in our experiences and strengthened through our individual and collective perceptions.

There has been, and still exists, a tendency in the Women's Movement to criticize academic and analytical writings on the grounds that it is inaccessible and uses specialist language that only a few people can understand. Such writings are inevitably dismissed as the 'left man in our heads' or we are told that it is all patriarchal thinking. Yes, it is true that most academic writings are inaccessible, even when they don't need to be, but to castigate women who attempt to write theoretically and analytically is short-sighted and prejudiced. For me, writing has required me to call upon many of my cultural resources, particular perceptions, and specific experiences. Just as writing a short story or a novel requires the writer to research and organize her thoughts and perceptions in a particular pattern, so does academic and journalistic writing. Analytical thinking and writing play a crucial role in the creation of ideologies, and it is important for Black people to be part of this creation. Not to do so is to allow White academics, male and female, to continue to use our oppression to theorize about from their perspectives.

There should be no hierarchy of 'correct' forms of writing. In recent years, the sudden discovery of the Black woman writer by White feminist publishers has created a fashion for our creative writing. Undoubtedly fiction demands a different kind of emotional response from other forms of writing, and I believe it can often be the most powerful means of arousing hidden emotions and senses. But for some people, reading a theoretical article can be an intensely emotional experience too, through finding challenging and new ways of interpreting the world. I have a friend who waxes lyrical when she had read a theoretical article which might fire her imagination, and I can see the bright light in her eyes as she explains and talks to me about what she has just read, making connections with the lives of Black people around her.

For me as a Black woman it is vital that our histories and our struggles are documented. It is vital, too, that we become visible in ways we can control. Writing is one way of doing this, where we can create images of ourselves through our visions and imaginations, as well as challenge existing stereotypes. We must speak through whatever means are available to us, or we will be condemned to silence, misrepresentation and invisibility.

Leaving it 'til later

Maggie Iles

Let me introduce myself. A child, a mere babe in arms in terms of feminism, a toddler, hardly managing to keep her balance in the first few faltering steps towards *being* a writer.

I've had precisely 52 years and 9 days of being a woman. And I've been a writer since I was 4. Inside my head, I mean. I had a teddy bear, I recall, who had one ear and an arm stitched on by the grannie who brought me up. This dear old lady refused to believe my story – she called it a story, I knew it to be the truth – that Ted had a mother who lived at the bottom of our garden, and that we were all invited to tea on Tuesdays and Fridays.

No one believed my stories then. Later, when I discovered there was a moon in June, and a little house, covered in tea roses, where the at-last-united pair would go after the honeymoon, no one wanted my version of that scenario, either. Fortunately.

And that was when I began looking in mirrors. And smiling. Out of habit. If I wasn't going to find fame as the local teller of tales, at least I could be good-tempered. They liked that. It went down well. Here was someone to be relied on. To say, 'Of course you're right. You're always right.' To anyone!

The longing was still there, and the stories were still alive and growing. But I waited until I had done all the things that had been my most cherished excuses. I brought up the family, and took a paid job to keep my daughter at university. Instead of writing. Then there was my handicapped son, who needed hours of training. Just to learn to cross the road. And when he was more or less independent, capable of making a life for himself. . . . Hurray! The opportunity to sit down and. . . . But no. A senile father, once hard-working and caring, and his sister who shared his home, needed help. And if you're an only child. . . .

That took another two years. I never questioned that I should do these things. But there was no possibility of writing at the same time. I acted out the role of loving parent and dutiful daughter with a zest that would have delighted previous generations of females who had done as much, and more, all the way up and down our family tree.

But did I do these things with love? Perhaps . . . perhaps. . . . But if I had *chosen* to do them, not felt compelled to take them on, it might have been different. I might have been filled with an energy that would have spilled over. And proved more than enough to allow me to create something for myself.

I'll never know. But afterwards, after all the restrictions and the loss, I was free! As free as air. And I erupted, like a champagne cork out of a bottle! *Now I could write!* Now, at last I had it within my grasp. Dear God, if you are up there, thank you. *I am about to be a writer!*

The day after the funeral I accompanied my son on his last visit to his doctor. She was the person responsible for the housing of the mentally handicapped in the area. The individual who had the power to sign those forms. To confirm that James was ready to take on the big, beautiful world out there.

I was exhausted. James infuriating. Anxious, tense. Not himself at all. We could both have been coming down with colds. The doctor kept us waiting for an hour. When we got inside she asked the usual tedious questions. The answers were all in the file. This woman was a fool. All these people were fools.

The room was choc-a-bloc with students. Social workers, nurses in the making. All doing their apprenticeships. Practising on us. The doctor spoke quietly. 'Good morning, my dears!' She was pleased with herself. James was sixth on the list. The last client this session. It had been a successful day. We shook hands. She said, 'You've stopped smiling! Good!' I looked around. She was addressing me!

She added, 'I've always seen you as one of the angriest women I have ever met!' The room went black. And now I'm searching for the phrases to tell what happened. The wall was breached? My cover was blown? Clichés all. But it's easy to tell you the rest. I screamed, I shouted, and I yelled. I hurled abuse at her. At fate. At being a woman. And being taught by a series of other women, to *care*.

Years of repression about everything, about nothing. Tears that had lain dormant for a lifetime formed themselves into explosive, violent words. They fell over each other, no longer suppressed by a smile. I had let go!

I wanted to make the grand gesture. Take a taxi home. But I'd left my purse on the bus. One of the social workers, embarrassed, I imagined, because of my display, gave me a lift in his ancient mini. On my doorstep, he looked at me. And he laughed. He actually laughed! He said, 'Good on yer girl! I shouldn't say it. But I've been waiting for years. Just for those few minutes back there. You've given me hope. A new lease of life. . . .'

I didn't have time to work it out. Maybe she'd had a plan. Today was to be Maggie's watershed . . . who knows. It was all too complicated for a simple soul to comprehend. Besides, I was too busy. Getting to grips with my miracle. Because it had happened.

I looked in the mirror once more. And I gritted my teeth. I glared at the reflection staring back at me. 'And up yours!' I said to the world. 'Knickers! To the lot of you!'

The family agreed I had made their lives easier. It must have been a strain living with all that good nature. And they responded very well to my new occupation.

'Ssshhh! Mum's working', they said in hushed and reverent tones. The man in my life fetched and carried. He took the lid off the typewriter every morning. And covered it. Like the budgie, at night.

Tell me, you experts. Is this how feminism is born? Now why didn't you let me in on it before? 'Pick that up!' I said. And 'Put that back where it belongs.' 'I think I'll take up cigars!' I smiled sometimes, on the odd occasion. When they deserved it. I could do anything, be anything. The power, I confess, went to my head. Friends, acquaintances were shocked, defensive, and then fell over backwards to please.

I typed. The air was filled with the sounds of the furious pressing of keys. Heavenly music. I inscribed yards of the stuff. I used sufficient computer print-out paper to decorate the Albert Hall. There could have been a phrase here and there that was passable. And a hint of poetry around page 53.

I typed out thousands of words, short stories, articles, poems, and three chapters of a novel, and a plot for another. Far too many words. The experience of a certain sort of life. Perhaps my anger about the past had to be got over, though I never considered that I had an angry nature! I have to see life through love, and I wanted to write with love. And humour, especially kindly, ironic humour.

What a task.

Somehow, I had to learn to get it into shape. 'You must join a group' – our local librarian was delighted to hear that there was one other creative soul in the district. 'That's the way to become a writer,' she said, 'you can't just *do* it!' And my luck was in. It was September. The culture-seekers' bonanza was about to begin.

I enrolled with twenty-two mixed students. Mixed in age, sex, and experience. The males left after the second week. The younger women soon after. We were on our own. A menopausal crowd. We wore our pearls, I remember. One of us, who shall be nameless, actually wore . . . dare I say it? Jeans!

The writing when we began was alive, vibrant, painful. Towards the end it became disciplined. It had a shape, and it had a form. It was almost sellable. But it had little soul. And almost no spark. Why did they leave, those young people with their fresh, direct ideas? Did they have less sticking-power as the tutor suggested? Were they frightened off by us 'older women' and our collectively awesome approach?

Or had they simply dipped their toes into the water, and found that there were more pressing things to be done? Maybe they had decided that the writing could wait. I hope not. I hope they found a space where their thoughts could flow, and form into something worthwhile.

But I had learnt the basics of the craft. Where to get the right equipment. And I knew the rules of the game. No exclamation marks and a limited use of the dot . . . ! All I needed now was a theme. I had to work out the necessary number of peaks and troughs. I needed a heroine with whom I could identify, and who the reader would love.

For I needed my reader. More than anything I yearned to have one. Of my very own. Who would understand these characters of mine.

My heroine could be less than perfect. She could make mistakes. Trip over, fall flat on her face. Then pick herself up and start all over again. She could swear if she felt like it. And kick the cat. If that was what she wanted to do. Of course, she didn't. But she became real. Flesh and blood. And because she was human, the characters around her became more believable. Their relationships, complicated and sometimes destructive, became the structure of the book.

I was weaving a tapestry. And it was to be full of light. And colour. It had its own flavour, its distinctive smell. I thought I might forget the rules, but they were there, being obeyed without my realizing it. Oh it was such fun to do! So absorbing! Fulfilling, and wonderful, and yes, often painful and torturing . . . a world on its own, that I could re-enter merely by picking up a pen.

And what was going to be said in this epic? Did I think I could change the world? Influence one person towards seeing the humour and the joy in just *being?* Surely it was possible to do that with conviction. And without preaching. But I got no answer from whichever inner voice I was challenging.

Until the thought came, 'Maybe . . . maybe you have to just tell it. As it is.'

So I had to settle for the best I could do. As I typed, the words seemed fresh and funny. Two months later they stood out, black and unfamiliar, like a foreign newspaper, in a language I'd never learnt.

The apprenticeship continued. With no one but the editor who hands out the rejection slips to tell me how I was doing. Would I know when I was fully qualified? Would I have missed the boat by inches or miles? There is no degree of rejection, no fair, promising, poor, awful.

So what was my real aim? I didn't want to waste precious time churning out rubbish that might be sellable, and add to the mighty pile of writing that leads women to feel that they have no option but to be used by life, that they have no choice other than the search for the best-looking doctor in St Barnabus. The converted are there, waiting for the novel that is going to reinforce what they already appreciate and know. But the unconverted, who want to be amused and entertained, and to find escape from the monotony of the factory floor, the bedpans and the drudgery. What of those? Could I reach them? Was I being hopelessly, unrealistically, senselessly idealistic?

A year and a half later, 45,000 words retyped three times . . . and it was done. Will it be successful? Who knows? But the completion of the task is reward in itself. Can my experience help anyone else who is longing to write, struggling to get ideas down on paper between the other tasks that fill our days? Honestly, I don't know.

All I can say is that I am sorry I didn't try harder to make time work for me, instead of the other way around. And now that I can do as I will . . . what next? The ideas are falling over each other. There is so much that is new to try. A conversation overheard on a bus sparks off an idea for a play. A table companion in a local café has this wonderful and fascinating story. They are all possibilities. To be laid down, stored in the warm, dark cellars of the mind. Insurance against the day when inspiration might run dry.

But forgive me. I must fly. The third chapter of novel number two has just hit me. And there's not even time for another cup of coffee. . . .

An apology

Or, Why I haven't written about 'My Night at the Chibalos', or even a piece on 'Why I haven't written "My Night at the Chibalos" '

Penny Cloutte

June 1982

I knew the Chibalos, a Zimbabwean family, in London for several years, while the war for liberation was on. Johnathan worked for one of the movements; Ebba got what work she could, in the intervals of keeping house, having and bringing up several children, and providing hospitality and support for various Zimbabwean comrades and kinsmen passing through London. At Independence they went home – he first, to a government job, leaving her to pack up and follow. We lost touch. Then, this January, I went to Zimbabwe myself and found them again. Johnathan had left his government job and was working for a mining company, the most senior African employed there. I went to visit them on their remote mining settlement, in the huge posh bungalow where they were the only African family for several streets. . . . Ever since then I've wanted to write about them, about our relationship, about what the freedom struggle was like for women, and what it has resulted in for Ebba. About my role as a member of the imperialist power and how that struggle has influenced my life, all the things it has meant to me . . . and perhaps even more, my questions about what right I have to write about it at all, how to do it in a way that will not perpetuate imperialist cultural domination. . . .

But I haven't written it . . . I can't write it. . . . I can't write it because I'm six months pregnant. . . . I can't write it because I'm moving house this day week. . . . (Today the removal men delivered the boxes and packing cases; I've started to dismantle my home, and I've nowhere to sit.)

I can't write it because I've got backache from typing for my living all day.

I can't write it because I've got only two more earning weeks before my maternity allowance starts, and I have no savings. I never know when I get up each morning whether I will earn this day, or not.

I can't write it because I'm starting to be a therapy workshop leader, and I am to lead my first workshop in three days' time.

I haven't even written to the Chibalos to thank them for having me. . . . So how can I write about them, when I haven't even written *to* them?

I only wrote this because my writing group strongly insisted that I did so, in fact gave me pencil and paper and made me go off and do it on the spot. . . .

Further apologies, December 1985

It's now over two years later and I still haven't written *it*. And I'm in a panic about this piece. I've missed my third deadline by two weeks – but Gail hasn't been on to me about it, does this mean that her life is in crisis too? How much energy it takes just to keep going as a woman, even without a husband or kids – even with my fmaous (*sic*) eighteen child-free hours a week.

I can't even type any more! (Lack of parctise [*sic*]) . . . .

I haven't even got as far as sitting at my desk for weeks, though I do now have one. It is my stress indicator – when things are bad I bury it in papers, books, sometimes even clothes, and can't get near it, or my typewriter. This morning I have got as far as excavating my typewriter, and am writing this with a precarious pile of unsorted miscellaneous papers towering over us, threatening to fall in on us at any moment.

No, I'm not entirely serious.

Why won't I be entirely serious, and just get on with *it?*

So what would *it* have been like? My conception was to tell the story of what went through my head as I travelled towards the Chibalos' probable address, found them, spent an evening and a night with them and then left for the capital. Nothing dramatic happened, i.e. no sex or violence or moments of truth or personal confrontations; but those few hours I spent with them were so rich in memories of both events and aspirations that they and I had known and shared and not shared during the years of the liberation war, that I felt for me they encapsulated a lot of the triumph, the contradictions and the hints of betrayal of life in post-Independence Zimbabwe. It was an ambitious project, a 'stream-of-consciousness' short story, with political points being made sharply but obliquely. Eventually it would be part of a series of pieces, to be entitled 'Some memories of a liberation struggle', about my involvement as a woman in UK solidarity work with the Zimbabwe liberation struggle.

So why haven't I written *it?* Well, there have been a few practical difficulties, and a lot of life-events: losing my father, becoming a mother, living with and then separating from my daughter's father, changing continents, seasons and houses several times, changing jobs and then back in London on thc SS. For ten months of last year we were in Mozambique, a war zone, and a difficult place to look after an infant. An even more difficult place in which to try and write: no women's presses or autonomous organizations, no writing group, no other women writers except journalists and academics. Perhaps they were there, but as I was still not out of my scribbler's closet I couldn't find them.

But no, the problem was not just the practical difficulties, because I did do some writing there – about childbirth – even in the midst of water shortages and power cuts. It was the internal obstacles that stopped me. I felt invisible, powerless, alienated. I had no economic connection to the place, other than as an employer of domestic labour, and as a consumer. I felt guilty about my economic privileges, which enabled me to do my thing and sit at my typewriter writing about, say, childbirth, while people were starving not that far away from me. On the other hand I couldn't think of anything I could do to alleviate the economic crisis the country was in, so why not write? I've spent too much of my life thinking all the time about others, putting my needs second.

All the same, there were these inner voices: 'Independent Zimbabwe has had a very bad press already, don't add to it. . . . Too many racist books have been published about Africa already – leave it to Black women. . . . You're only a White woman, only a housewife, anyway. . . .'

That last voice reminds me of my father's, from way back in my life: 'Who wants to hear your opinion, anyway? Who cares what a little inky schoolgirl thinks? If you work hard at school, and go to university and get a good degree, and become someone of importance in the world, *then* perhaps people might be interested in your opinions. . . .'

Well, I did work hard at school, go to university and get a good degree; but have I become a person of importance in the world? Even to myself?

My father's dearest wish was that I should become a writer. That's one reason why I haven't (yet) – he's only been dead two years.

I have been stuck on this paper several times, and had a series of thick, cotton-wool-between-the-ears, mental-activity-impossible colds. In an attempt to get unstuck I wrote a piece called 'Silences in my life', which ended up being all about my father. I got a cold after writing it, and a few weeks later when I read it out in my writing group, I got ill again. I was too frightened to even think about it for weeks after that. I have come to realize that my fear is that these illnesses are but the tip of the iceberg, minor indicators of the power of whatever deity it is that I am offending. Keep this up, it is saying, and you'll get something worse next time – cancer, or a stroke, or. . . .

'Writing about her body – a necessary, a freeing subject for a woman writer' says Tillie Olsen. Yes, I know, that's me talking in quotations, just like my father. We are very alike, you see, that's what's so terrifying. It felt such a relief when he died.

And suddenly, as I write this, I remember a poem I wrote recently about my relationship, as a teenager, with my father when we were still friends on the surface, though underneath I felt he was a greedy monster waiting to devour anything I produced. He encouraged me to write poems, got them typed up by 'the girls in the office' and pushed me – ordered me – to send them off to the *New Statesman* and such. I hated this overwhelming exposure before I was ready, but didn't dare say 'No!' I just stopped writing poems, or anything else.

I think this is the crunch for me: I still feel unentitled to have my voice heard, about Zimbabwe or anything else, because of unfinished business with my father. So perhaps my next writing project had better be my Daddy and me. Indeed, how better to confront patriarchy than to start with my own father?

I have got started again; I do write poems sometimes; I am still scribbling away in my closet. But it's taken a long time – twenty-one years since I left home. And it's taken the Women's Movement too: feminist organizing, a women's political presence in art, literature, politics; feminist publishers, writers; and for me, personally, a writing group and years of feminist therapy. But what actually got me started on writing again was a week of 'Amazon Activities' in Leeds, organized by some radical feminists. We were welcomed by a notice saying, 'You beautiful, wonderful women, *welcome!* This week is for you.' I did body-painting, had massages or cuddles whenever I needed them, led my first dream group. We read poetry; made music without speaking; practised collective child-care in the bar, taken over for this purpose; made goddesses out of wood, out of dough, out of ourselves. . . . It was a magic time.

Another breakthrough was when I was doing a twelve-week workshop on sexuality, which involved spending a lot of time giving care and attention to my body, and especially to my genitals. Writing a letter to myself about 'who you are, sexually' suddenly freed me to write about the fact that I was unemployed, and this was the conception of what my writing group calls my 'ovarial work on Work' – still unwritten.

Now I have another fear around writing – that of *not* doing it! Unused creative energy is a deadly force, as I have had ample opportunity to observe. If I don't manage to get it out, channel it, I could end up taking a chainsaw to someone's head, like the woman in Alice Walker's short story, 'Really, doesn't crime pay?' (in *In Love and Trouble* (The Women's Press, 1984)). Being me, I am more likely to take it out on myself, as depression or cancer. But my adult self is determined to find another way. The day will come soon when I have the courage to discard the closet scribbler self-image, and say 'I am a writer' – to make for myself the time and space to write, to clear that desk at last! Tell my father's ghost to go to hell! I will believe in my writing, my work, my self!

NO MORE APOLOGIES!!!

Writing as an Irish woman in England

Moya Roddy

I don't write as an Irish woman in England: I found myself writing here and fell into a category.

There's a mirror lying on my desk: I pick it up and look at my face. All it shows me is what I already know. I write to find out what I don't know. Or refuse to acknowledge.

That's why I find writing fascinating. And frightening.

Category of course is the wrong word – it's too weak – I fell into history: my own personal history; the history of my country and its relationship to England; and the history of language.

All these feed into one another and cause contradictions. And tears, fears, fights, and an awful lot of energy wasting.

But out of contradictions comes chaos (or chasis as we called it where I come from) and out of chasis a new world or in my case, hopefully, a new word.

To get on with it.

I came to England the wrong way round. I was on my way home from a rather extended visit to Italy (about two and a half years) but I had only enough money to get as far as London. At least I've told that story so often it's the one I believe in. (If I ever become famous it'll go into my biography: so only tell the stories you want to hear repeated.)

That was eleven years ago. Since then I've worked as a community worker, been unemployed, got a degree in media studies and now work freelance in television. In between jobs I try and write. (And try to write.) What have I told you about myself? Nothing.

'Whar are ye gonnta be when ye grow up Loretta?' Jo asked her friend.

'Dunno, whar are you gonnta be?'

'I'm not gonnta get married, that's for sure.' After a minute she added, 'I'd like to be a teacher like Miss Kearns.'

Seeing a glitter in Loretta's eyes she hurried on, 'Or a secretary or something.'

She hoped that put her off the scent, she didn't want her to guess she'd sent Miss Kearns a Christmas card. She could hear her:

'Teacher's pet, teacher's pet, Teacher's pet with her knickers wet.'

'I gonnta get married and have loads of babies.'

I left Ireland because of a broken heart and because the man I would have had babies with didn't love me. But I am not Loretta. The baby I made from that aborted love took nine years to gestate. When the umbilical cord was cut I knew only the Irish Sea could have washed away the blood, sweat and tears. England was the midwife and I was grateful for small mercies.

When I was younger I wanted to be a painter. In fact I wanted to be anything that would haul me out of the poverty-stricken background I was born into. (I knew nothing about fighting to change things then, only of finding ways out.) I went to evening classes but my mind was really on meeting someone with talent, not developing my own, so I learned very little. ('How's the talent?' we'd ask each other at parties.) But I remember the teacher showing us the spectrum. If you spun it fast enough all the colours would merge to form white. It was like magic. As it slowed down the colours would all return to their respective segments. Each giving colour to its own bit of the world.

During the day I gave advice to those who were losing their homes, having their social security stopped, being forced to leave the country or being battered by men. In the evenings I went to political meetings and spent endless hours discussing politics with friends. And fighting and arguing.

In bed, away from it all, I read Mary Daly. My spirits soared into a world where language danced to a woman's tune and energy spurted from the gaping holes left in old words.

Of course there were problems. She was re-inventing language, re-creating history, but Woman – raceless – classless – was the protagonist.

Unidentifiable Woman.

In my own writing there were gaping holes too. My country was looking over my shoulder and shaking its head. I watched with horror what was going on in the north of Ireland while my characters worried about their sexual politics or whether to have babies or pursue careers.

Maeve turned over in bed smiling. It was only yesterday she'd got confirmation from her doctor. She touched her belly. It didn't look different, but it felt just a tiny bit harder.

'There should be no problems, although you're older than usual for a first.' The doctor glanced at the file in front of her: '30, still you're healthy. Are you going to keep on working?'

I desperately wanted Maeve to jump up and demand an abortion because she couldn't possibly carry on her political work otherwise. But Maeve insisted on worrying only about her friend's attitude to her pregnancy and what sisterhood had done to motherhood.

But I was Irish, living in London, didn't I have a duty to write about the North, to make the English aware of their role, their responsibilities? I wrote a letter to Mary Daly.

She didn't reply.

Writing for me is a bit like trying to find the light switch in the dark. You grope round, trying to feel your way, bump your nose, stub your toe. Then you switch on the light and for a split second the position of everything in the room is blazingly clear to you.

After a few minutes you realize what you bumped into was the enormous old cupboard in the corner, language. You never liked its shape, it was handed down to you, and you've always intended to get rid of it as soon as you find something to replace it with. Worst of all, there were strict instructions in the will as to what you could do with it.

Would anyone like to buy a second-hand cupboard, in remarkably good condition and with impeccable credentials? I don't need it anymore . . . .

Twenty-two years in Ireland, eleven in England. Two languages. Irish English and English English. Both with completely different sets of assumptions, historical realities, attitudes, touchstones, etc., etc., etc.

When I was growing up they used to say 'The best English is spoken in Dublin.' I never knew what they meant. I was always warned by my parents 'not to speak like Dublin kids'. Coming from the country they had an inbuilt suspicion of everything the city offered. Coming to London I had the same.

Now I look for the gaps between the two languages in order to escape.

Class conflicts

Jo Stanley *with* Billie Hunter, Margaret Quigley, and Jennifer Wallace

The women who worked on this paper were members of Hackney Women Writers' Group, which came together at different stages in 1982. About ten of us gravitated towards this new grouping at Centerprise, the community publishing project and bookshop in north-east London. Most of us had done little creative writing before. A few had a lot of doubts about their grammar.

We all came from working-class families of various grades. One woman's dad was a clerk with the coal board; another was a general labourer. Mine was an insurance man. None of us had been brought up to think of writing as a thing to take seriously, let alone as a career. We'd been expected to do helpful jobs like dentist's receptionist, nurse, primary school teacher.

In summer 1983 I heard about the Feminist Writers' Conference, and that papers were wanted for it. So I suggested to our group that we do one on working-class writing. It was then that we all got a shock, discovering our enormous differences over class. Because the Hackney group met at Centerprise, which is part of the Federation of Worker Writers and Community Publishers, I had assumed that 'working-class' was implicit in its title. I only found that this was not the case, and that the women at the group did not feel that it was class that united them, when four of us sat down to discuss this paper. The discovery opened up an important process by raising questions of how we defined ourselves.

Because I write for a living (as a journalist) I wrote this paper. I did so after a number of meetings, though not all with the same women each time. Following up issues raised at these meetings, I posted round a paper containing these points and questions which would expand them. Each of the women named as contributors wrote lengthy comments on this, a bit like a game of consequences. This final paper raises as many questions about our assumptions as any of the preliminary discussions about class did. And it in no way represents a consensus – more of a hodge-podge of four-and-twenty blackbirds that I have stuck into a pie, with great trepidation at this handling of others' ingredients on their behalf.

One of the first surprises when we started discussing the whole topic was that two of us had firmly taken for granted that class was at the basis of the group, and two others hadn't seen it as working class and didn't want it to be specifically so. Nor did they believe that it was our (approximately) shared class background that made the group gel so well.

Jenny, who was unwaged at that time, argued that lumping ourselves together as a particular class meant forsaking ourselves as individuals and giving ourselves up to generalities. I argued that we should always keep that background in our minds, but not let it get in the way. Margaret, a community worker, said 'Our backgrounds can't be denied – they are crucial to us. But I can't help thinking there's more to it than class.' Billie, a midwife, thought that, for her, being a woman was more important than her class background. And it became important to work out the balance: was our class equally, more, or less important than our gender?

We spent a lot of time trying to decide whether we were 'really' working class too. It led to a lot of discussions, both inside and outside the group. We phoned each other up to talk about this nagging difficulty. It went on for months and re-emerged each time we got together to discuss this blasted paper – both before and after the Feminist Writers' Conference. Though it felt important for me to define my class, the others got increasingly pissed off with the whole debate and didn't feel like carrying on with this paper. Some felt it didn't justify the amount of energy being expended on it, that it simply wasn't relevant. Others thought that questioning the class basis of the group was disrupting the unity of purpose of the group, which was to create the means to write in a supportive environment.

I think we all felt strongly allied to the sort of writing that comes from the non-lit-crit world: the personal testimony now emerging from feminist and community publishers. When we first started at the group, we were more familiar with accepted 'mainstream' writing. Some of us had read a lot of 'good' literature (Dickens, Forster, 'A' level stuff). But we were looking for things that expressed the realities we know as women. Some had looked at little current and genuine working-class writing. OK, there isn't much around, but why hadn't we grasped what was under our noses? The group met in a room directly above Centerprise bookshop, which is the best place in London to get such books. Yet we didn't go and get them.

Betty, one of the older women in the group who had just had her autobiography published by Centerprise, gets very impatient with some working-class writing. She said that because she was so familiar with the life of hardship which (especially older) people describe in their autobiographies, it was boring. It took me ages to start reading Pat Barker's *Union Street*, no matter how much and how often I tried. And I know other women of my background who have had the same difficulty. It confirmed my suspicion that middle-class people might write about working-class people and topics but still not produce 'working-class writing'. *Union Street* didn't read as if it was written by someone who lived in that street, but by someone who appeared to think that if you lived in a street full of terraces, then your life must be stuffed with dreadful episodes.

The novels of working-class life that emerged in the late '50s, such as Stan Barstow's *A Kind of Loving* and Alan Sillitoe's *Saturday Night and Sunday Morning*, were equally disappointing to me. They neither represented my class reality, nor portrayed women as I knew them. A lot of so-called working-class writing is written by people who are now middle class and looking back: Catherine Cookson and John Braine could be seen as this. Mainstream publishing seems often to equate working-class experience with the past, characterizing it as something like the Hovis adverts: cobbled streets and mother always waiting at home to give the lovable lad in droopy trousers his tea. I feel this is done, perhaps even unconsciously, to neutralize working-class culture, to consolidate the myth that all the bad times are behind us: 'Everyone's middle-class now.' It's too dangerous for the status quo to acknowledge the extent to which deprivation is still a reality in this country.

None of us working on this paper wanted to be trapped by our own or other people's stereotyped ideas of working-class. You don't exactly think of people fulfilling their full potential when you think of working class. The myth is strong that you can't be working class and intelligent, or working class and interesting. Certainly not working class and a good writer. Traditional, negative images of working-class people abound. For example, that they all live in council houses and lead boring lives. These images have reinforced the doubts of some of our group members about whether we could write interestingly about an objectively boring life – say, doing a very repetitive job in a factory. All the stories I wrote as a girl were about beautiful young women who lived in grand mansions, travelled alone to exotic places and always had scores of rich, besotted, and handsome young men waiting to satisfy their every whim. My heroines had double-barrelled surnames, fascinatingly convoluted ancestry, and never had to eat tapioca at school. It was inconceivable to me that I could offer a reflection of the real world I knew, in my fiction.

But some of us feel as if we have now become the privileged people we once only heard about. Further education and the choices we have made have changed our lives. For example, another member of the group, Sue, took herself travelling a lot, and played in a women's band. We have become different from the working-class women we worked with. According to some definitions, we might have to label ourselves middle class. So some of us feel like neither chalk nor cheese.

Billie, whose dad became a financial director, made the class change quite early on. 'I never had any sense of being working class until my parents became middle class – and then I felt like a fish out of water. The situations I liked about my childhood were to do with warmth, honesty, a matter-of-fact approach to life. But when we changed, I can't deny that I really got into having more money, nice clothes, ballet lessons, wine on Sundays. I didn't reject "posh" at all, I'm afraid. Material possessions and comfort seemed really desirable.'

We would never consciously try to produce working-class writing in the group. It just wouldn't occur to us to write differently from how we felt impelled at a particular moment. No one in the group ever thought, 'God, that's really working class', nor could anyone have thought it – with either approval or disapproval – when hearing another woman read her work out. But we realized that our backgrounds came out strongly in our writing. The topics we chose and the people we described were what other people might call working class. Stories have been about women waiting at tables for a living, working in factories, being in unions, living in bad conditions, not having work or much money, being isolated and unconfident. Margaret has written a piece about a woman's anger with an arrogant doctor – a battle that she won. I based a play on our estate.

Another thing our writing usually has in common is its straightforward style. We feel angry with writers who choose difficult terms, using words which are beyond the understanding of most ordinary people. Margaret valued the information in Marina Warner's *Joan of Arc*, but only after she'd battled through the language to reach the interesting ideas. The awful thing was, she thought her mother, who is interested in history, would like to read the book. But she was annoyed that the inaccessible way it was written would prohibit this.

No one in the group would make up for early educational disadvantage by littering work with the most impressive words that could be found in the dictionary. However, because of the changes in our initial class backgrounds, several of us were concerned that we might have lost some of the straight-forwardness of working-class expressions; not the vocabulary but the nail-on-the-head directness, after getting used to moving in a more élite world where pussy-footing can be the norm.

We realized that it was literary floaty writing that had put some of us off writing when we were at school. Jenny said, 'Emphasis was placed on how you expressed things, rather that what you expressed. Little value was placed on describing our own life, and a lot was put on that of the more privileged world.'

Billie, however, had an English teacher who helped her through all the doubts about language and grammar: 'I used to find some pieces of writing made me feel things, even if I didn't understand the words. And she helped me see that that was what should be happening, and that I shouldn't get hung up on the actual language.' She felt that the struggle to write was so great 'because you have to grow through, past, all the rules set by other people that have made you feel useless previously'. Jenny's first complete piece of writing went well, but she struggled to set it out so that it was understandable: 'I don't think I'll ever really conquer the struggle of thinking and expressing clearly. The complexity of everything will always demand this.' Yet she agreed with Billie that the struggle was as bad for non-working-class people, and added, 'Even if you have a large vocabulary, certain things are always difficult to understand and express.'

Why do we write? Because we want to, of course. Jenny thought she had initially started writing to do something that was different from normal family activities. I wanted to create other, better worlds. And I believe that working-class writing is a blow struck back in the class battle. It shows us, as well as our oppressors, that we have equally valid, real lives and voices. That blow is important to our confidence. It feels vital. Margaret emphasized, 'It's important that working-class women share their experience, in writing, and so find that people are interested in what they have to say, and that they are just as valuable as anyone else.' We all felt it crucial that working-class women write, and are seen to write. So much needs to be told.

We weren't sure if there is a particularly working-class tradition of women telling stories. Uncles and dads talked a lot, told tales of 'work' and the war which were full of 'adventure' and action: the world outside. But women told stories on a different level, more personal and domestic. It was a level that we probably didn't value enough in childhood, and perhaps still don't value enough.

'Women seem to talk a lot among themselves,' said Jenny, 'often about emotional and physical things that children traditionally aren't supposed to even hear – birth stories, "old wives' tales", gossip are always put down by men.' Billie agreed: 'At school, we were always told off for "gossiping". It implied something malicious. My reaction was eventually to reject it as "girls' talk" and head for intellectual discussion with the boys.' Margaret remembered that she was always subtly taught that men's affairs and talk were more important than women's.

Talking in the bar after the Feminist Writers' Conference, we found ourselves telling stories of our own and other peoples' experiences of sexual harassment: 'gossipy' stories. One of us asked why we never wrote stories about these things – as if there were two separate worlds, the talking one and the writing one. But Billie thought we did write about these experiences: 'These "gossip" stories are the fuel for everything we write, even if they aren't in the original form exactly.' Jenny wondered if there were areas, or just occasions, which we could not talk about to other women and so wrote about instead – either as a safe way of broaching a difficult subject or just out of the need to have a chat to something/someone.

We were all very clear about the importance of talking a lot with other women, both because of the way this can sustain us in our belief in ourselves as writers, and just because of the pleasure of swapping common experiences.

All four of us who wrote this final paper would call ourselves feminists. And I, for one, would no more want class to get in the way of this than I would want feminism to get in the way of class allegiance. Liverpool writer Jimmy McGovern has argued in *Voices*, the journal of the Worker Writers' Federation, that if you're a feminist group then you must be middle class. He opposed a feminist group joining the federation on these grounds. But most members of our group feel very strongly that this is rubbish. Of course you can be feminist and working class. Our class roots and our feminism usually only feel incompatible at times if we're with really middle-class women whose brand of feminism seems to exclude us.

And we feel it is important that solutions be found to the problems that stop working-class women writing: lack of time and facilities; family hostility at stepping outside of traditional roles; above all, the self-doubts about merit that stop us validating our experience on paper.

To different extents, the four of us who finished this paper have reduced those self-doubts to more manageable proportions. Billie, Jenny, and Margaret have not done much writing lately, but that is more because of their circumstances (first baby, becoming a mature student, and having a demanding new job, respectively) than writing doubts. I am writing almost full time. We don't often meet at the group, which still continues, because of our changed priorities. But we go drinking and dancing together, hire holiday cottages *en masse*, and lovingly value what we have gained by the ways we worked together and helped each other during the early days. And this extends to the other members of the group too, who were there at the start.

Young, gifted and getting there

Rosemarie Ademulegun

My parents arrived in London from Nigeria back in the mid 60s. Like most happy couples, they had plans and dreams about this city paved with gold which all fell through. When I was born, it drew my parents together for a short while, mainly because I was an over-active child. Then my father decided to leave my mother to bring up my brother and me. Labelled an evil child by my mother, I had a tendency to cut up her new curtains or tie a bone to my brother's ankle and then allow our dog to chase after him.

I am 20 years of age, but because of the way my life has developed, I spent my time among women in their late 20s and early 30s when I was only 17 or 18. This made me grow up mentally a lot faster than I might have done otherwise, and at college, I got into a group of people who were active around feminism and anti-apartheid. Recently I have been spending more time recovering my youth by mixing with women who are between 15 and 18. To communicate at first with these women, I must admit, I found very difficult; but at the same time, it helped me stretch my imagination more than if I'd stuck entirely with my own age group.

Like all school children, I began to write the very moment I could read and write. Instead of staring out of the window day-dreaming during long-winded maths lessons, I lost myself in the fantasies of writing. And in the fifth form I really needed to escape from studying, so I invented a character who ran away from school to find adventures that I could never dream of doing. In many ways the character was based upon myself, and the people she met up with were the women from my commerce group. In my writing, I would always have something clever to reply to women who picked on me; women who were boring became blown into really exciting characters, though I kept the loud-mouthed ones as they were, but funnier. I was manipulating people as characters and when my class mates read it, they were shocked. But I only wanted to do it on paper, as I couldn't and wouldn't do it in reality.

I worked as an assistant Saturday librarian for three years, mainly for the money, but also to satisfy my lust for good reading. I love being surrounded by books; it's a way of learning. It doesn't matter whether I actually manage to read them all, just as long as they're around me.

In 1984, my eye caught an advert in the library for *Patience and Sarah*, a play about lesbianism being shown at the Oval House Theatre, which I immediately went to see. The play did little for my lost interest in writing at that point (lost just before I left school), but it did a lot to help me confront my own sexuality, which I had been avoiding up to that moment. If they could get it together in the nineteenth century, I must be able to do it now, I reckoned.

Oval House is a community arts centre as well as a fringe theatre. A week later I returned to the Oval to try my hand at anything they had to offer. For an entire year and a half my whole life was engrossed with dancing, singing, instrumental music, and acting. I believed that my vocation lay within one of the arts, but I had to try them all out to find out which suited me best. I enjoyed acting to a certain extent, but I realized that although I enjoyed it, my whole heart wasn't in it. Being the same repetitive character during a fortnight of performances made me very bored, and I couldn't stand it when I was acting and we had to stop when someone forgot their lines, whereas I soon realized that writing is something you can take at your own pace.

With writing, I am in control. I can do it when I want, but also I have total control over my characters. I now appreciate the art of writing more, having tried all the other things and found that it was what I really liked doing all the time. I was very depressed whilst at the Oval and I started writing poetry when I wanted to get my feelings down on paper fast. But I found I couldn't write poems in any other sort of mood. Then a friend advised me (quite kindly) to leave poems to those who are gifted. (I did.) I accepted the advice with relief and now concentrate on what I really love – fiction writing.

My first completed play *Aveu* started out with three very close firends of mine plus myself. I placed them in a room with a topic thrown in, and waited to see what came out at the end of the day. Looking back on the first draft, it was weak and feeble, nothing solid, merely a bunch of women avoiding answering any real questions. So after leaving it for a year, then working on it for another nine months, I managed to change the characters and the topic so much it became a plot in its own right, a play with a message, life, and action. Here is an extract which shows something of the characters of the friends:

Josephine is the host of the party and Gemma plus Patricia are waiting for the arrival of Sylvia.

Sylvia: Hello darlings, have I kept you all waiting long?
Patricia: No, we haven't been waiting long; but tell me Sylvia, when did you decide to start wearing dead animals on your back?
Sylvia: Patricia, darling, I know that you must be jealous, so I will ignore that horrid remark. Gemma, I wasn't expecting you here, I thought you would be chained to the kitchen sink with snotty Wendy at your feet.
Gemma: My child's name is Mandy, she is neither snotty nor around my feet *and* I'm never chained to the kitchen sink.
Josephine: That's enough Sylvia, I want this night to be very pleasurable.

Being a feminist writer, it is terribly important for me to try and write about the type of women many male authors would like to believe don't exist. Such women, married or single, always tackle life head on, with strength and love, for example, the housewife bringing up child/ren on her own, struggling on to win without the aid of a man.

Male authers so often portray females in a very unrealistic light. For example, Wilkie Collins, in his book *The Woman in White*, writes about two women, sisters. One is strong and forceful, but to compensate for that he makes her ugly. The other sister is weak and shy, which seems to be the only sort of woman men make beautiful, or like Joan Collins, who is strong and sexy, but at the end of the day, still longing for a man; otherwise they are shown as ugly so that it doesn't matter, or a raving diesel dyke. I haven't got time to wait for male attitudes to change.

All my characters, so far, have been women, either lesbians or straight, who get on with living their own life. Sylvia, one of the characters in my play, wouldn't see herself as a feminist, but she is the managing director of her own company, she doesn't allow men to rule her life. She didn't even want custody of her own child when she got divorced, but she thinks feminism is about 'women who burn their bras and cut their hair'.

The main reason why I get cross is that people presume that because I am a Black lesbian I'm only interested in writing Black lesbian stories. I see myself as a feminist writer *full stop*. To think that I must continuously create Black lesbians in my writing just because there aren't enough in the bookshops would seriously damage my imaginative growth.

Imprisoning vision: towards a non-visualist language

Kirsten Hearn

Through talking to women and having greater access to their writings in the last couple of years, I have begun to regain the confidence I used to have in communicating and entertaining with the written and spoken word. In the last twelve years since I became blind, I hardly wrote anything except letters and diary entries. Although these were important in themselves, I did not think they were 'good enough' for public consumption. In coming out as disabled in 1980, I felt the need to express myself and my opinions and experiences in our society.

The aesthetic loss in not being able to see colours or objects around me has to be separated from the practical and political disadvantages of being blind.No political movement could ever restore my sight, but this does not mean that the rest of you who struggle for political change can avoid responsibility for helping me to participate fully in making that change. For example, not being able to read print means that I don't have access to a lot of literature, but it is possible for the producers of printed information to make it available by taping it.

In attempting to express my experience of the world in writing, two major factors hampered my progress. Firstly, the practical difficulties were immense. I needed to use machines, be they typewriters, tape recorders, or braillers, or to rely upon another person to help me write things down. Whichever method I selected, I found I lost spontaneity in the mistressing of the machinery, or the exertion of my will over another person's style and habit of expressing themselves. Perhaps if I had been a fluent braillist, accustomed to that mode of communication, I would not have found it so hard. It is difficult to edit and rearrange braille text when my reading speed is so slow, difficult to review and control the words on a tape, and impossible with the use of ink print.

Secondly, I felt the need to describe not only the activities of my life, but my understanding and experience of the world. As a tactile artist I was keenly aware of what my four remaining senses told me about my surroundings. (A tactile artist is someone who makes sculptures primarily for appreciation by touch. All of my pieces are accompanied by an audio tape of me reading poetry related to the structure.) I found no difficulty in communicating this experience in three-dimensional form. The problem arose when I wanted to describe a particular experience in a fictionalized, imaginative manner. Although there are a number of descriptive words using the aspects of sound, taste, smell, shapes, textures, atmospheres, and vibrations, when I used them for my purposes they felt out of place with the language I was accustomed to use. They did not adequately describe a particular experience and moreover, they had already been usurped by sighted describers for their own purposes. I also found entrenched in the orthodox use of language negative values attaching to physical attributes, e.g. the words 'blind', 'deaf', 'paralysed'. They made me feel uncomfortable. They reinforced my personal feelings and experience that I was not welcomed and was considered an intruder in our community because of my physical difference.

In choosing to write about myself and my disability I felt I was taking both a political and personal decision. I needed to shatter the myths surrounding the lives and experiences of people with disabilities, so that I could re-establish our culture. Having taken that decision I had to be continuously careful and rigorous in my portrayal of life as non-sighted. Immediately I fell foul of the visual dominance of our language. For example, in expressing opinions I found myself wanting to 'hold a point of view'. In comprehending arguments and attitudes I wanted to 'see what they meant'. I found myself, through habit, continuing to say that I 'watched television' and would 'see someone tomorrow'. I found I could not make positive statements about my surroundings because I had to use phrases like 'feels like', 'seems like'. These gave an air of hesitancy to my work.

At this point, I decided to reclaim the word 'blind'. When my sight was diminishing, I had taken to myself certain euphemisms describing non-visual states. I would call myself alternately 'visually handicapped', 'visually disabled', 'visually impaired', 'person with a visual disability', etc. All of these words suggested a negative experience through the prefixes 'im' or 'dis'. I was reluctant to use the word 'blind' because it seemed so very final, and because of its associations with wilful ignorance in the traditional use of language.

The word 'blind' in our visually-orientated and dominated language means, according to dictionary definition:

Adjective: blind, non-sighted, without mental or moral discernment. Blind to; cannot appreciate; blind forces, not ruled by purpose.
Adverb: blindly, recklessly, without seeing.

The above quoted dictionary definitions do not merely refer to physical sight, but also attribute to blindness the concept of lack of understanding, and connect it with wilful ignorance, recklessness, and folly. By implication, therefore, people who are termed blind because of a physical condition cannot escape this slur upon their character and personality. To avoid this slur either I must not use the word at all, or I have to reclaim it from its handicappist, blind-person-hating associations. I have chosen to do the latter.

Our language is riddled with words like this, which are descriptions of particular physical conditions that are at present used derogatively. The present colloquial use of 'spastic' or 'spazzy' is a commonly used term of abuse arising out of a hatred and fear of people with cerebral palsy. It shows the way that our language develops. The fact that it is not at present defined that way in the dictionary may be because people with cerebral palsy did not tend to live long before this century, whereas blind people did.

Think about how these words are used: myopic, short-sighted, tunnel vision, paralysed, lame, deformed, deaf, dumb, cripple; plus the whole plethora of words associated with mentally handicapped or mentally ill people: mentally defective, idiot, moron, imbecile, mad, schizoid, manic, and so on. These words describe mental or physical difference, and are commandeered by able-bodied people and used negatively to describe actions, strategies, or personalities that they disagree with. We, as disabled people, are made responsible for our deviation from the able-bodied norm. By association with the negative values of these words, it is implied that we do not understand, are wilfully ignorant, or lesser. Our aspirations and abilities are distorted and our needs ignored.

In the early years of my blindness I stoically resisted any attempts on the part of my friends and family to change the language that they used. I feared that by doing this they would continuously draw attention to my disability and, by implication, my difference or abnormality from the so-called norm. I felt that this would lead to the unwelcome expressions of sympathy and sorrow which embarrassed me and made me feel even more alienated and left out. Although conscious of the visual dominance in language and the wider community, I was at that time unwilling or unable to express pride in myself as a human being. I did not feel proud to be blind. Who would, in a world where we are excluded so completely from everyday activities? I had not yet explored and unearthed the positive aspect of my disability.

One 'compensatory' remark that was made to me whilst in the process of losing my sight was concerning the 'magical' sixth sense that all blind people are supposed to develop. This rather bat-like sense could supposedly do anything from saving you from a yawning chasm, to telling you what colour your friend's jumper was. As I opened my eyes after the operation and emerged into a world yellow-stained and blurred, and was pronounced 'registered blind', the halo of the sixth sense did not suddenly descend about my ears, as I thought it was meant to. Twelve years on, it still hasn't descended, but what I have learnt through numerous encounters with lamp-posts and flights of stairs that miraculously appeared whenever I moved, is to use the other four senses that were left to me – four senses whose combination now makes up a world of precise and intimate vibrations, sounds, smells, tastes, and textures, which will still not tell me what colour my best friend's jumper is, but which do give me an acute awareness of all that is around me. It is not just the sniffing of the air on a breezy spring morning as I stand at the bus stop near Hyde Park, or the sound of the wind rustling the trees nearby, but a much more precise awareness of the shapes left by bodies moving in the bus queue, the dancing of vibrations surrounding the bus, as it shudders to a halt beside me. It is the subtle appreciation of my fingers hardly touching and still-ly caressing the folds of my friend's duffle coat, aware of the proximity of her arm and the rest of her body. This world I inhabit, that seems so blank and void of stimulus to sighted people, has much more to offer me in terms of aesthetic pleasure than the bareness of the four senses taken at face value, mere sound, taste, smell, and touch, as sighted people perceive them.

At the time I lost my sight, my overwhelming desire was to be 'normal', to be 'accepted' as a valuable member of the community. I wanted to 'integrate', but did not understand then, as I do now, that to do this and be accepted, I had to accept the able-bodied version of it, which is assimilation. This meant that I had to reject my 'condition' as in any way positive. I must ignore my needs arising out of my physical difference, because, in asserting them, I made people feel uncomfortable, and reminded them of their responsibility for the world being so unwelcoming to me. As I began to learn that 'integration' and 'acceptance' were only valid on their terms, I had to keep asserting my physical difference in order to remind people that my needs were different from theirs, and had a right to be met.

Part of asserting my needs was to remind people through my particular use of language. Thus, I felt it was correct to remark to a male blind delegate at a conference we were both attending, as he hovered towards me, bent on attracting my attention, 'Fred, I can feel you there – what do you want?' My heart sank, as his snicker told me that my harmless little remark had been taken sexually. It comes to something when the language of your life experience is taken by someone who, in some ways, shares it, to mean what all men think it means. After all, I did *feel* him coming across the room, I could feel him standing there. Vibrations and sound particles, plus his habitual clearing of the throat, told me that this blob was, in fact, Fred, and he wanted to talk to me. I suppose I could have said, 'Fred, I *hear* you', as indeed I did, but for me, touch and sound, in that mixture of vibration and noise that made up the blob at my elbow, were united in his appearance – dammit, where's the *Roget's?*

The problem is that it's not just to do with the more shallow forms of speaking to people in commonplace interactions, it also crops up all the time when I am trying to describe my more intimate reactions to the world around me in my writings. Trying to be non-oppressive and realistic in communicating my experiences prevented my creativity from flowing and intimidated me into not being able to write. I did not think my poetic writings possessed the fertile flow of words which, by able-bodied standards, were both meaningful and acceptable. It seemed as if my verbal gymnastics were impenetrable to traditionalists or, at the best, baffling in incorrect use of language. At last, motivated by discussions with tutors at college and in the disabled writers' group, I decided upon finding new forms and uses of words.

Extract from 'Convocation Jive'

1
Through the chaos of the rasping thumping incessant rhythm
The atmosphere jolts and heaves
Obliterating the space.
I am standing, uncertain,
Vulnerable amongst the heaving mass of bodies
Which from time to time is moved by a wave pulse ricocheting
As my body makes contact with the sticky fleshy jolting dancers.

2
External impulses wriggle and slither their way inside me
Through the barriers' ever-filtering experiences.
Vibrations present in the hollows, bouncing in and out

Between the hard brittle structures,
The stringy sinewy fibres
And the dense flabby matter.
A responding, ever-moving, ever-present reminder,
A reference point of shape and scale through which my every experience is measured.

3
The jerking speech pattern of my neighbour
Split by the obliterating rhythm
Their unrecognizable tones throw me into confusion
As the sound splutters, bouncing against my eardrums.

4
Through lengths of differently-shaped chambers, hollows and tubes,
Patterns gulp, expanding and contracting.
Bumping, bouncing, pushing rhythmically the air
Intertwining and mingling with the beat
Even yet stagger-pulsing,
Seeping through longer, thinner chambers.

5
I wriggle away, my body searches for air-space,
Firm familiar structures of walls and furniture.
I edge about the perimeter of the space,
Seeking the recognizable landmarks.

6
External impulses wriggle and slither their way inside
To the barriers' ever-filtering experiences.
Vibrations present in the hollows, bouncing in and out
Between the hard brittle structures,
The stringy sinewy fibres
And the dense flabby matter.
A responding, moving, ever-present reminder,
A reference point of shape and scale
Through which every experience is measured.

The next stage in my thinking was to take formerly visual statements and refuse them. I found myself having to explain all the time what was meant, which was very frustrating and time-consuming. I wasn't being an effective communicator. In the piece 'Convocation Jive', which accompanies an installation made up of two 5 foot square, ⅛ inch thick pieces of industrial felt, draped to form two chambers, I describe the experience of crawling into the larger of them:

> The air densifies and thickens
> Tactilely blackens
> Rolling, rough felt
> Pressing against my body,
> Slowly, half-deliberately,
> Its curves and cavities
> Weaving, re-arranging and moving again.

I wanted to explain the particular experience of just how the atmosphere changed when I crawled under the felt. It seemed to shut out sound, whilst encasing more subtle vibrations, very much as a cloud suddenly shuts off the sunlight and the air becomes more dense. My awareness of the presence of the cloud is not only in the absence of warmth from the sun, but in the way that its action seems to lower the sky.

The arguments I had with people were mostly about the negative connotations of the word 'blackens' in the phrase 'tactilely blackens', as well as about the attachment of an obviously visual word to one about touch, disputing my ability to feel darkness. Another example, which caused me to bow to pressure from my tutor and leave out what I thought was a key descriptive word from my final version, because he insisted it was visual, was my use of the word 'pirouette' in an installation about going to Greenham:

> My arms are captured and pinned back by my neighbours,
> And as the human chain completes itself,
> Arpeggios of voices pirouette,
> Rising into the still air.

For me, the use of the word 'pirouette' completely captured the way in which women's voices spanned above us as we linked arms around the base. I really *felt* our voices making that whirling movement, as though I was standing on one leg and spinning round. My tutor said that I was bowing to the visual experience of *watching* a pirouette, allowing old sighted memories to transform the auditory experience. He said the visual connotation flashed into his mind when I used that word. I knew he would pick it up in my assessment (it was a piece for my final degree) if I continued to use the word. I did not want to have to spend hours explaining what I meant to the examining board, when it was perfectly clear to me.

In talking to other women, I discovered that having to explain our use of language and images to men is a common experience. I began equating my struggle to explain my use of language and images to able-bodied people with that of my struggle as a woman dealing with sexist language. This made it easier for me to demonstrate my position in society to able-bodied women and their role as my oppressors.

The guardians of the language are naturally horrified by our efforts to retrieve it from its sexist, homophobic, ableist and racist shackles. I have already experienced and will, no doubt, continue to experience protestations and accusations that, by avoiding ableist words and usages, I am defiling and mutilating 'the Queen's English'. We need to use our skills as writers in order to redetermine and define words. In doing so we must maintain for ourselves the communicative and fluid poetic beauty of language.

Acknowledgements

Thanks to Gail Chester for all her work in helping me get this piece together, and to Penny Cloutte for typing the final version.

PART FOUR SUPPORT AND COMMUNICATION

Making connections: the collective working experience

The Common Thread working-class women's anthology group

This article is the result of a taped discussion between women from the Common Thread working-class women's anthology group. Sue transcribed the tape, Linda and Julie edited it, and June and Julie typed it. It is just part of an ongoing discussion about our writing and the way we work.

We are a group of working-class women aiming to publish a collection of working-class women's writings by late 1986 or early 1987. At the time of writing there are nine women in the collective. These include lesbians, lesbian mothers, heterosexual women, Black women and white women, Jewish women, and women with disabilities, aged between 20 and 70. Some of us are writers, and some of us are just committed to the idea of getting working-class women's writing into print.

Although being working class has meant different things to different women, this anthology aims to explore what we have in common, as well as celebrate our differences. We are not all the same: we reject the Hilda Ogden/Alf Garnett stereotypes, and the best way our book can demonstrate this is to reflect our variety. This means that the collective and the book must represent as wide a variety of working-class experience as possible.

The Common Thread collective came into being in 1984. An initial meeting was organized in 1983, on the strength of a £500 donation made to one of the present collective, who then advertised in *Wires* newsletter for working-class women who would be interested in taking part in a conference and ultimately become involved in producing a book about, by, and for working-class women. The administrative group of twelve that emerged from this first meeting was composed mainly of White, able-bodied, gentile women.

We felt that the collective as it stood could not produce the kind of book we wanted – we needed input from women with a wider range of experience. We spent a lot of time compiling an extensive mailing list. We advertised in local newspapers (throughout England), the *Voice*, the *Caribbean Times*, the *Asian Times*, *Spare Rib*, *Jewish Chronicle*, *Outwrite*, mainstream women's magazines such as *Cosmopolitan*, women's newsletters, *City Limits*, *Time Out*. We mailed Women's Aid, trades unions, MIND, women's groups, girls' groups, WEA Adult Education, women's centres, health centres, lesbian groups, disability organizations, the National Union of Students, bookshops, and libraries – anywhere we could reach working-class women. We also held open meetings and tried to arrange meetings with groups of women who were underrepresented on the collective. Individual contact with women at social or writing events helped to spread the word. Encouraging each other to write and convincing each woman of her ability to contribute to the book proved to be very important. We, as working-class women, have such a poor opinion of our capabilities, especially those among us who are multiply oppressed. Equally, working-class women have not been a happy, homogeneous group. The deep divisions of racism, anti-lesbianism, able-bodied chauvinism, etc., have made it difficult to build up enough trust for women to feel it worthwhile putting effort into such a mixed collective.

It seems hard to measure the success rate of any one method of recruitment. Women have joined the collective as a result of meetings, advertisements in magazines and newspapers, referrals from publishers, word of mouth, and through attending 'Shooting Our Mouths Off' reading events, organized by the Common Thread as a forum for working-class women's work. Overall, it is the consistent effort of making yourselves and your politics known to women in a variety of ways over a long period of time, that works.

Linda: Trouble is, there are so few books published by working-class women, that we're trying to make up for it. It is only one book, it can't be everything for everyone and we can only tend in that direction.

Jeanne: It's about getting as much input as possible. Having collective meetings around the country was one way of doing this – but with the best will in the world, lack of money has meant it was ridiculous to transport women up to Leeds and Liverpool, when most of us were living in the South. So, most meetings are in London, but we have always been clear about paying fares for all women, no matter where they live.

Linda: Nobody has priority over anybody else. If we don't have the money, we are not going to make the decision that somebody can't come.

Jeanne: The only thing we could do if we ran out of money is to set up a holding operation. Really one of two things, if we thought we had money definitely coming in – we could organize a loan, or we could get together in London to raise funds specifically to continue the work we are doing. But there would be no question of continuing without women from outside London, any more than we could go on without paying for child-care, or a signer, or a cab for anyone who needs it.

Phoebe: Getting a disabled cab paid, or a lift from Jeanne makes all the difference. When you're dependent on Mrs Thatcher, it's tight going.

Jeanne: But despite our commitment, there are still problems, as women don't feel that their fares are justified.

Julie: It's unusual for groups to pay for such things as travelling and child-care, signers and so on. So some women feel guilty about what they think of as eating into our funds. They tend to feel that we're doing them a favour.

Linda: It's so typical of women to feel guilty about everything – of taking up any time or space.

A large part of the discussion centred on why we, individually, joined the collective.

Jeanne: Well, I got involved with this because I didn't want to be an individual working-class woman who was always having to answer questions about how oppressed you are as a working-class woman. I wanted that to be collectively answered, and I thought a collection of writings would do that.

June: I wanted to get involved primarily because it sounded like a bloody good idea. It sounded to me like something I would be proud to take part in – I couldn't believe there was a group of working-class women. I thought you'd call yourselves working class, but in fact would turn out to be posh London types, talking above my head. Most women's groups do unfortunately get taken over by articulate middle-class women. I find it difficult to relate to them as their experience of life isn't mine. I thought it would be great to be with a set of working-class women who openly declared themselves working class and weren't frightened of it. I thought how proud and pleased I'd be to be part of something which got working-class women into print.

Kate: Same here, with a certain amount of self-interest.

Sue: When I started off with this group I wanted stuff published. I was writing then, and women were saying, 'Why don't you send it away?' and this was the only response I got from a group that I liked. Then the group became something else for me, it became more important that it was a book of working-class women's writings, and I sort of forgot the bit about getting my stuff published.

Julie: I wanted to meet other working-class feminists. I had the idea that the Women's Movement was middle class, which intimidated me. But I also liked the idea of getting involved with a publishing project. I felt that there must be a lot of interesting stories 'out there' that weren't being told.

Linda: It was as if I didn't exist. Books either ignored you, made a caricature of you, or at best dismissed you as 'Nellie the parlourmaid tended the fire.' I felt desperate for a vision of the world that wasn't White and middle class. I wanted one which included me. I felt I had more in common with the Black working-class writing in *This Bridge Called My Back* and *Home Girls* (both published by Kitchen Table Press in the USA) than with any books published in Britain. I gobbled them up.

Carole: Yes, every time I pick up a book, I find it's been written by and for the middle classes. I walked into my local library and asked for the *Spare Rib* book and was told, 'You should pick another book, you won't understand it.' That was in 1976, and nothing has changed. I want to read books by working-class women who have suffered the same as myself.

Susie: I joined the Common Thread as this is a working-class women's group. I'm a proud working-class woman, proud to be a lesbian, a woman and working class. This is a chance for us to take a stand and shout, 'Look world, here we are and you ain't going to overlook us anymore.' A chance to change the role that people see us in, to put the record straight. I was glad to be involved. Forty years ago a woman of my age would have been thought of as past it. It's right that working-class women should have their say.

The first job was to meet with feminist publishers. This we did in small groups. All of them expressed a serious interest in the book, but were not prepared to back it up with an advance until we had a chunk of manuscript to show them. So we are back to square one, trying to fund-raise to meet day-to-day running costs of about £100 a month and trying to publicize the book and the collective. Over and above this, we are trying to raise £2000 to subsidize a print run, so that more women will be able to afford the book. We also want to pay contributors £30 each, and not the measly £5 which was suggested by one of the women's presses.

Fund-raising efforts have included benefits at clubs and discos, and sponsored events. A lot of time and effort has been put into applying to councils, charities, and regional arts bodies. Benefits and discos raise about £100 a go; they can take a lot of organizing, so the fuss involved must be kept to a minimum. Sponsored events can be lucrative and take little work to organize. At our last sponsored event one woman raised £200. And these types of events are also good publicity. Hackney Council gave us £500. We have had a good response from charities – the Sarah Robbins Trust gave us £250, and Rowntree has promised £750 towards subsidizing the print run. Greater London Arts have subsidized a 'Shooting Our Mouths Off' reading to the tune of £100, and might also contribute towards the print run. Having said that, fund-raising takes up a lot of time and can sometimes obscure the work we are doing – but it is something that we cannot afford to neglect.

Working collectively can be much harder than operating in a traditional hierarchy. It is important that we should all have an equal say in creating our working environment. It is much better to work as equals, as we all learn from each other and thus contribute more to any given situation. Of course it can be difficult, and it is certainly more time-consuming, but it is also more satisfying to have your say and then co-operate with a compromise, rather than having to go along with decisions made on high.

Other groups have major problems working this way, but we don't find it impossible. We all agree on the basic ideas guiding the group; it's the details we tend to get picky about. And we all seem to get on fairly well.

We work differently from the majority of groups in this country, so why are we working like this?

Julie: I hadn't really thought of working any other way.

All: Hmmmmm!

Kate: Well I think that working in a hierarchy is oppressive.

Jeanne: The other alternative is having two editors, but then there is the problem of limiting ourselves, when we want to reflect a variety of lives in the book. The political responsibility would be too much, there's no way we could get the diversity we want.

Linda: Yes, we've tried to get as much input as possible by having a large collective, having open meetings and so on, so it's not just two editors or one group of women running the show. We're trying to make the whole business more democratic by opening out.

Julie: From a practical point of view, two editors are normally in a position where they are on a publisher's commission. Two trying to do this job without backing would be impossible. It would be a full-time job, and the fund-raising would be an enormous task.

Jeanne: It's also about skill-sharing. Women in this group have many skills. I didn't feel I had any knowledge of publishing, and I was quite relieved when I found out that Joolz was working in that field. It was really important to find women who . . . .

Kate: You're such a creep!

(Laughter)

Jeanne: Well it seemed like a mystery world, and for some reason I thought you lot in London would know all about it.

Linda: The first time I went to a publisher I was quaking at the knees. All that art. I just hoped they were more scared of us than. . . .

Julie: They were terrified.

Linda: We went in looking very burly, furiously chewing our gum.

Jeanne: Oh God, yeah, you two and Sandra. Good god, how daunting!

Julie: Death squad!

Kate: Did any of you smile?

Linda: No, I was just chewing my gum.

Jeanne: Oh my God, with that big black leather coat, and Julie hiding behind billows of smoke.

Kate: So that's one of the advantages of being a big group – we can terrorize publishers.

Jeanne: Yeah, the more of us the better. We always realized we would have to do a lot of publicity right from the start, because we wanted this to be more than one book in isolation.

Linda: That's right – it's not just about publishing a book, it's having readings, getting the idea of working-class women's writing taken seriously.

Jeanne: That's right.

Linda: It's like when I went to the Feminist Bookfair in Liverpool. There was a woman who said that it was really good that all these working-class women were learning how to write about themselves in essays. The fact that they could string a few words together was enough. She actually said that they would never get published, being published was not up to them. How patronizing can you get? It's an idea which still holds a lot of water, especially with adult education. We need to get away from all that.

June: Then there was the story about the literature panel turning down an application from working-class women because they felt that working-class writing was not 'Literature'.

Julie: Which makes D. H. Lawrence look like a bit of an arsehole.

Sue: It's so blatant.

Julie: We haven't decided yet whose contributions are going in, but I feel reasonably confident that quite a few women in this group will submit work.

Linda: When I first started in this group, I wasn't even confident enough to read anything out, let alone be published, but as things have gone along, I've become more confident. I don't feel that what I've written is particularly political, but then again that isn't true, as recently I've written some political stuff that I might put in as a contribution.

Jeanne: I see some of the stuff that you and Sue have written as being exactly what I want in the book.

Linda: What sort of stuff do you mean?

Jeanne: Well, that stuff you did about your dad and disability, and the stuff you read me about your experiences when you were at college. You know how difficult it is to explain what you want in the book, because if you say you want it political, people think 'heavy' – I mean political, not polemical.

Julie: Publishers seem to have caught on that feminist writing is a good commercial proposition, but even though there's been an expansion in women's work being published, working-class women have been excluded – apart from the odd story about 'My life at the mill a hundred years ago'. No new working-class women writers get to see the light of day.

Jeanne: Well, when this book eventually gets out, it will be of benefit to me – I'll be able to whizz it all over the place, instead of answering questions about being working class. And to be honest, there's a secret side of me that thinks, you never know, I might actually get it together and do some writing. That's the other thing about this process – it makes me think that I might be able to write.

Writer/worker/feminist

Sara Maitland

I am a full-time, professional writer, who earns a small but living wage, putting words down on bits of paper and having them printed and distributed. I don't want to sound arrogant or whinging, but I do want to plead a case, based on my own experience as worker and as feminist, that there is an unacknowledged tension between paid and unpaid writers within the Women's Movement. These tensions are dividing women who ought to have a good deal to share – and they come out of our own confused ideas of what writing is and how we can use it.

I think that there is sometimes a comforting belief that it is not possible for feminists to be commercially viable writers: that our culture is so thorougly male-dominated that the feminist text will never see print for long. There is an element of truth in this, but it is also a consoling myth: if we're certain to fail, we don't have to try, even when we can see several women whose work is treated as feminist, both by the women's community and elsewhere who are at least getting by.

Instead, I, and other professional writers I've spoken to, often feel excluded and uneasy at feminist writers' conferences as if we were seen as a threat to that comforting myth of automatic failure. My feminism has been called into question – too often, I feel, just for doing something that many other feminists there would like to be doing too.

The British Women's Movement has always been ambivalent about success. This is not necessarily wrong, but in the case of writers, we should discuss just what sort of success we are talking about, and how the existing situation might be improved.

As a published writer of course my concerns are not always the same as those of women who are not yet published. Even being at a conference may be 'work' to professional writers and 'recreation' to other writers. To raise my working problems about contracts, rates of pay, the way writers are treated by reviewers and by publishers, by women's publishing houses, and so on, always seems selfish among women whose concern is often that they have no contracts, no pay, and no publisher to be ripped off by. But this is a false division – partly because the ways in which books are produced affects us all as *readers*, and partly because we should all be concerned about the working conditions of other women, and especially perhaps those in a job that we might hope to enter, at least part-time. Nor can we make a simple split between these concerns and those of 'pure' writing. Content and form themselves may be, or may feel, different for paid and unpaid writers. I have to make particular choices: about how I will spend my time, how I will balance needs and desires. For example, I have published my three longest books with 'straight' publishers, mainly for financial reasons; but I do believe that the publisher, the presentation, and the distribution of a book affects the way it will be read, so I have to ask questions like, what, if anything, do I owe to the Women's Movement, or it to me? Shall I write this or that next? Whom shall I talk to about this idea before I start working on it? Do I want a commission, which implies writing with constraints, although some payment will be assured? If not, how am I going to finance this project? These seem to me to be proper questions about my economic viability, not the 'selling out' of some artistic purity. In our present society, no one works without compromises of many sorts, and it seems unreasonable to expect writers both to do a decent job and to preserve a fantasy perfection of intent. Textile workers and teachers do not get slated for working in imperfect conditions, only for failing to attempt to change them: I do not see why writers should be regarded differently. These concerns are social and should be shared.

I think we have to acknowledge the reality of work. Either writing is work, in which case its conditions – in some ways similar to the conditions of all out-workers and piece-workers – should be the concern of all feminists who are interested in women's work issues; or it is not work at all, in which case we should stop being indulged, whether we earn money by it or not. Like most workers, I do not have full enough control over my own means of production. Nor can I negotiate better work conditions on my own. Like most home workers, writers are notoriously difficult to organize. This difficulty is especially extreme in the case of writers, because we are socially valued as 'individualists' and are perceived – and too often perceive ourselves – as middle-class, special-status, socially exempted 'artists'.

If writing were regarded as work, properly, this would undercut much of the dangerous mythology with which bourgeois culture has surrounded the artist. The social context ofwriting, a manufacturing industry with its capitalists and workers like any other, is hidden in the curious cultural myth of the joyful agony and solitary genius of the writer, who is served by the publisher for the 'good' of the community. This is a dangerous delusion: it disguises the reality that cultural privilege is in the hands of the dominant social group (White middle-class men); and it supports the ideology of 'vocation' (a divinely appointed mission of virtue somehow placed above economic realities – which leads directly to exploitation, lousy wages and appalling working conditions). It is not just 'The Capitalists' who exploit feminist writers: I have been called 'unsisterly' for saying I was unable to travel to another part of the country to do a reading if the organizers could not even offer expenses: that is, to give up two days of work and pay for the privilege myself. It is not good feminism to exploit other women's labour. Of course women can and do offer their services for free, but this should never be allowed to undermine the right of other women to say they cannot or do not want to do so.

The bulk of writing is not about inspiration at all – it is about copy-typing, administrating, small-business managing and debt collecting, much like any other self-employment.

Even the 'creativity' is socially formed and nourished. Within the Movement we have not done enough to make this clear – all books grow out of a social and political context, which must ultimately include such considerations as the level of literacy, or the availability of after working-hours lighting in a society, and if we took the social context of writing seriously enough, we would indeed start to produce radically different sorts of books. For instance, I have never produced a piece of writing which has not been improved by editing, by sharing the work with someone else. Yet editors are nearly always regarded by writers as the Enemy, who wants to steal away the individual's own text and dilute it, claim it, manipulate it. (Yes this happens too; but not that often.) If writers and readers (producers and consumers) took a more active interest in the process of production, a more real recognition of the shared collective product, the book, would emerge. The text is not magical; it exists only when it is set down, for example, on paper, which someone, somewhere made. I find it bitterly difficult myself, this true collectivizing of consciousness; it means breaking and remaking some of my dearest and most self-consoling notions of individualism – but I know it is a crucial feminist project.

I have spent part of the last year attempting with Michelene Wandor to write a 'collective novel' (to be published in 1987 as *Arky Types* by Methuen). It was difficult and extremely exciting, but whatever it is, it is certainly different from any other sustained prose fiction I have ever read.

Although we talk a great deal about 'the new feminist forms' we are not really doing enough to create new ways of writing and producing books, and I think this is because we are stuck with the myth of the isolation and individualism of the artist. I was fascinated, for example, by Judy Chicago's presentation of *The Dinner Party*. She seemed to have made a conscious effort to create a feminist communal artefact, but finally she, like the rest of us, seems caught within the trap of the individual creative soul, who delegates her vision to the inferior 'craftswoman'. This was reflected both in the *form* of her production – it was other individuals, especially inspired women, who were invited to sit at her banquet – and in the way she referred to the project's co-workers in her presentation material; there seemed to be no acknowledgement that the craft skills pre-dated and *created* the possibility of her own work. Without a centuries-long tradition of skill and creativity she could never have imagined an art project based on needle-work.

We must acknowledge and implement more collective ways of writing. This must happen at many levels; and indeed some of it already is. The feminist publishing success in getting anthologies – fiction, non-fiction, and most recently the differing-view-points-on-one-theme book – more widely read and enjoyed is culturally important; so is the effort to find ways of recording and producing writing from groups who have not had proper access to print.

Whether we like it or not, we have structured a movement which is presently heavily dependent on books and other printed material. As well as being a writer I am also a reader, who needs more and better published material. We can only achieve this if the women who are producing this material are nourished within the Women's Movement, so that they in turn can share their knowledge with other women, thus producing books within our community and also books that will reach out and invite women to join the political transformation in which we are meant to be engaged. But this cannot happen if the women who produce them are cut off from the Movement, and regarded either as special heroines (as happens in the USA) or as rather dubious and suspect sell-outs (which I think happens here).

I do not feel a victim of the Women's Movement. I do like being a writer. I know that I am privileged by birth, education, good friends, good health, and the proverbial 'room of my own'. I acknowledge too that these privileges can be misused – even by feminists. The International Feminist Book Fair in 1984 produced some alarming performances, for example, Mary Daly's behaviour at the ICA. She refused to share a platform with Hester Eisentein, despite having said she would, and refused to give her audience any explanation of her decision, while blandly announcing that she felt no obligation ever to converse with other women. This was a classic instance of how women can use their 'success' to oppress their less well-known sisters, to make anti-social and anti-egalitarian demands, to monopolize space and time, and most signifcantly, to silence alternative opinion. Published feminist writers including myself may, on occasion, be arrogant, noisy, class and race élitist, competitive, jealous, and unsupportive, but this does not remove the political necessity to re-stress the community of all feminist writers in a way that neither denies the importance of work and economics nor promotes destructive and untrue myths.

Not chance but a community: women and élitism in poetry

Sally Evans

> I've rumbled poetry, twigged what follows on
> because of chance in meeting other writers
> and then discovering there was no chance
> but a community outstripping mention . . . .

Traditionally, the most successful poets are a male élite. Though a number of women poets have surfaced, many have had important personal relationships with male poets – Laura Riding with Robert Graves, Elizabeth Barratt with Robert Browning, Sylvia Plath with Ted Hughes, for example. Though these relationships were personal, they were also inevitably professional – and provided the women with a way into a group they might never otherwise have been allowed to enter.

This sort of élitism is natural group behaviour. It results from friendships, contacts, and simple good nature – and the fact that men rarely make close women friends. To encourage newcomers and strengthen the position of accepted members is something every group does; the snag only shows when the group excludes others with a valid claim to be in on the act. In the case of women writers, especially women poets, this can be a real stumbling-block: every writer needs group support.

Achievement in poetry doesn't happen in a vacuum. It requires contact with other writers and an outlet to an audience, whether by reciting, publication, or correspondence. When giftedness leads to achievement, the individual and circumstances have combined to produce a poet we remember. Some important poets write very little; some write a great deal. Some matter in relation to other poets; some because they are unusual; some for their popularity. The way we read their poetry, and sometimes the poetry itself, has been shaped by other writers, publishers, critics, as well as by our own response.

Gifted writers cannot create the environment in which they write. Historically, you get the most remarkable literature where the general achievement has been highest. Shakespeare was one of the Elizabethan dramatists and Sophocles one of the Greek playwrights. They would not have been able to express so much had they been involved in poorer traditions. Some Scottish poets, such as Hugh MacDiarmid, have been hindered by the lack of a surrounding literary culture. I think we can see that neither MacDiarmid, nor Sorley Maclean in Gaelic, hesitated to say 'I am a writer' because of cultural circumstances; but both had to reach beyond their own cultures for support.

Women also need support as writers, and it is only in very recent years, in this country, that they have begun to find it. In the past, women who wanted to fraternize with male poets have found their way impossibly barred. The growth of feminism has led to women-only writing groups – and a number of lesbian poets have appeared, supported by the feminist community. But for those of us working in mixed groups, many of the original problems remain, and feminism has not yet focused much attention on our efforts to be recognized.

Elitist male culture sees writing as a job. 'Becoming a writer' requires more confidence than many women can muster. How can you say you are a writer if you haven't published anything, have little if any contact with other writers, have never been 'admitted' by a sign of favour from an established writer or publisher? You can't even find out where the literary gatherings are. They have in the past predominantly been in pubs, and it is only twenty years or so since a woman could go into a pub unaccompanied.

Publishers and government bodies also work to this definition of 'being a writer'. It is much easier for publishers to market books by cult figures than to evaluate each new book on its own merits. Grants are awarded to 'approved' writers whose success is measured in terms of earnings and 'output', as if a poet or novelist worked in the same way as a doctor or a journalist. What chance has a woman with children of being reclassified by such observers from 'housewife'? Conversely, a young man who has climbed – or been hauled – on to this career bandwagon, may hang on for dear life, not realizing that writing is about life, not life about writing, and he would be better employed as a civil servant. Luckily this situation is changing – and I think time is now on women writers' side.

The old-fashioned version of a literary élite depended on 'literary lions' – young men who were recognized early and spent their careers in the public eye. This pattern is changing. Poets, both men and women, are being published in book form only after years of publishing locally and in journals. Poets like U.A. Fanthorpe and Connie Bensley are cases in point. Naomi

Mitchison's poems were published in 1978 after she had published *seventy books* of other kinds. By the time poets have made their reputations in this way, they are too old to go chasing round the pubs creating gossip which can later be elevated into myth. Dylan Thomas, Eliot, Pound, Yeats and Auden, the men we usually refer to by their surnames as though to place them in our minds with the great names of the past, and MacDiarmid and now Sorley Maclean in Scotland, are probably the last literary lions in the old sense.

As writing lives change, so do ideas of the uses and purposes of writing. A diarist or an aunt who writes wonderful letters is not a 'failed' writer. Nor is a person who goes through a few years of writing and then stops – often in youth. I have also known writers of prose who turn to poetry in a crisis in later life. In some cases to stop writing may be the success. Writing has got someone through a crisis, played a part in their lives, enabled them to read, or watch television plays, more appreciatively afterwards.

Elitism is also losing its credibility as we find new ways of reaching an audience. There are now simple methods of small scale publication – I mean photocopying work and giving it out locally to six people. There are groups in larger cities which may be more or less easily located, where any writer is welcome. There is less reverence for print, to the extent that everyone knows you can be a good writer without having been published nationally.

The embarrassment of saying you were a writer in the past was due to the lack of social involvement as writers for those who had not been picked up, promoted, and published in a big way. Now we can have all the social involvement as women writers we want, and there can be the reverse problem of getting enough time alone to write. I have tremendous difficulty keeping my evenings out with other writers in Edinburgh down to two or three a week. Edinburgh is a very good centre, but I grew up in a small town which had nothing for a young woman writer except a traditional library which shored up the traditional views. That town now has arts centres, writers' groups, evening classes and no doubt a women writers' group or two. Everywhere there are avenues of activity for women who are writers to meet others to improve and hone and shape their work. It is a strange but important truth that you need to be constantly in touch with other writers if you are to develop properly as a writer.

It is only by gaining one's confidence and finding one's level and place in a community of writers that a woman is able to say 'I am a writer' or 'I am a poet' rather than 'I am a housewife' or 'I am a typist', both of which I have said in the past. I expect the person who asks me my occupation to take me seriously when I say 'I am a writer.' I back up my statement if it has caused bafflement. I say 'I go to a group on Thursdays' or 'I've just finished a ballad.'

There would be no point in saying I was a writer if it was not true. Sitting at a desk writing may be intermittent; as a poet, especially, there are patches when I cannot write, because as a human being I need cause for writing, the fuel that comes from a full life with other people, experiences, practical problems, financial problems, problems of the human condition. But I have to be constantly reading, thinking, listening and watching as a writer. And I must get back regularly to that table and chair and pencil (or typewriter).

I no longer think in terms of competition with other writers and am interested only in producing good work. If people write more skilfully than I do I want to read their work, so I cannot resent its being published before mine. I want to see new and better poems so I both take and give within the community I have tapped.

I've also seen behind one last bastion of the oppressed élitists: the idea that there's nothing left to write about. Fast communications are with us these days – except by the post – and there is much more to communicate. The ecology movement, the anti-nuclear movement, the extension of science, medicine, and space travel: along with new publishing methods and new ways of seeing other writers, we have a great deal of new material.

Among the newest is the world of feminism. The predominance of masculine ideas led some women, myself included, to model our writing on male poets' excellence. We forgot there could be feminine excellence as well. With what delight I finally found Eileen O'Leary, Kathleen Raine, Naomi Mitchison. If they could do it in their different ways, so could I . . . and Stevie Smith was one of the first women poets I discovered. Stevie had an irony and detachment I could understand: I was not close to the soft femininity of Elizabeth Barratt Browning or the blood-and-womb imagery of Sylvia Plath. But in Kathleen Raine from England, Naomi Mitchison from Scotland, and Eileen O'Leary from Ireland (though so long ago) I recognized the ferocity and passion, the intensity and drama, and the close links with an old natural world that I wanted to get into words on paper myself – and my community of poets, of which I could at last become a member, was complete.

Women like us

Elsa Beckett

In 1976 Frances, a disabled lesbian, put an ad in *Sappho* magazine asking for friends who would recognize the fact of her disability and accept it. I thought she would have plenty of replies, but was surprised to discover that mine was the only letter she received. Because we were both wheel-chair users (Frances had Friedreichs Ataxia and I am paraplegic), we learned we shared problems of access and of recognition of our existence within lesbian groups – though as I had an able-bodied lover, and we had transport I was not as isolated as Frances was, and at least I could join some mixed gay groups which were accessible.

We decided to try to find other women like ourselves, and so Gemma was formed as a means of lessening isolation, a contact and information point for disabled lesbians (gemma in Latin means a little bud or shoot, something growing). Also we wanted to increase awareness of our needs, and at first believed we could change things quickly in other lesbian groups, but letters and nudges about access had little or no effect and to this day, there are blithely held inaccessible meetings, or groups who hide their access details from us as though they were of value to the Kremlin.

We felt it important not to be a ghetto group (as *they* seemed to be!) and so we welcomed able-bodied members from the start. Some of us would have able-bodied lovers and friends who would want to be in the group and whom we would want to be there; we didn't want to repeat discrimination, and we knew that able-bodied women didn't lead a charmed life and could become disabled also. Isn't it better to belong to a group where you will still be an easily accepted member, disability or not?

Sappho listed us regularly and the Campaign for Homosexual Equality let us use their address until we could afford our own BM box number. As more women came into the group (through ads in the lesbian, gay, and disability press) we were asked to provide social meetings in London, quarterly to begin with and then monthly. The first one-page newsletter informed of the time and place of meetings, and gradually expanded to include news and information as well as the friendship ads, the latter particularly from women who could not attend the London socials (there are now also sporadic socials elsewhere).

I wonder if progress in integration might have been quicker if we had not formed Gemma – if instead we had battered at the doors of the established lesbian groups. Our integrated meetings remain small-scale, and though they are open to non-members, few other lesbians care to come and meet us. Our own members don't attend in great numbers because of illness, disability-related fatigue, agoraphobia, distance etc., and so letters, tapes, and phone calls are our chief means of getting to know and to support each other.

All contact is via the newsletter – members use pen-names for confidentiality in their friendship ads, and replies come direct to me and I then forward them. All initial inquiries and correspondence also come first to me. Very isolated women do have difficulty in learning of our existence. We have little money to advertise in local papers, our info doesn't get put up on noticeboards in, for example, residences for disabled people, but we had one television spot and are occasionally mentioned in disability programmes on radio and in 'agony aunts' columns, and we are increasingly listed in women's resources publications and in disability reference books and newsletters. Sometimes women are referred to us by health workers.

Most members take up correspondence with each other via the newsletter and I get to know no more about them than what was in their intial letter and ad, such as their age, likes and dislikes, whether married, single, bisexual, or in a lesbian couple. Others have kept in touch or have become good letter-friends, especially perhaps those for whom I was the first lesbian, or the first other disabled lesbian, they wrote to. Many women have come and gone in the group since 1976, but some of the early members still work with the group and in 1985 we number 250 nationally, with a few members outside Britain.

Some of us have met friends who became lovers or remained close friends, and some of us have never met the members with whom we have corresponded for years. As I have been 'secretary' from the beginning I have had the privilege of being in touch with Gemma over a long time. What do we write about? The minutiae of our lives, how we manage with money, wrangles with Social Security and hospitals, relatives, hopes and disappointments, joyful news of lovers, children, a new baby, homophobia, politics, books, television, radio programmes, our companion animals. Women abroad write about their lives, lesbian groups (or lack of them), and feminism there.

Many of the most significant letters will not survive. Their writers do not want them to. They are personal, painful, identifiable – I mean particularly those letters where women with disabilities have described their feelings about their bodies and sexual expression, attitudes to lovers, rejection, abuse, despair. Most members do not envisage 'coming out', not even after their deaths. I am regretful that the letters won't be preserved but obviously their wishes must be respected. Perhaps each letter has served its purpose, one woman telling another, and no one else should expect to know the contents of that letter any more than a confidential conversation should be disclosed. While there is a privacy in the support we give each other the effect is one of a network of solidarity.

Letter friendship is a special type of networking. We pass on information, news of campaigns, discuss and argue and sometimes have to settle that we will never agree on a particular point. Some members are not, or say they are not, feminists. As a feminist myself I feel it an advantage belonging to such a mixed group where no one can be taken for granted and one can't assume a consensus of opinion – this individuality is brought home, that perhaps no one woman subscribes to the whole package of our 'alternative culture'. We disagree and we continue writing; feminism is nothing if it is not the community of *all* women.

In many cases this is a group where the more you put in the more you will benefit, for example if you are non-ageist and non-classist you can correspond with women from a wide range of background and experience. At 46 I find it especially interesting writing to women of 17 and 80 to find out how much we share, not only the negative things like being discriminated against because we are lesbian but the positive in the sense of the sisterhood we are creating. Even when you know your letters may be destroyed as soon as read that feeling of spanning, of joined lives, can't be taken away.

Letters are special. You appreciate this when a woman with learning difficulties troubles to write; when a woman because of the nature of her disability has had to dictate her letter to someone else; when a woman caring for a sick parent snatches time to write. Such letters have a special potency. Some I keep a long while before destroying, like the last letter I received from a friend who wrote 'I am so afraid of the next operation. Urine is pouring from this stoma. I think I am going to die.' I felt I had to keep her letter, her last message, because it was important that she had written down her fear and faced it, and had helped me face it also.

And I keep the letters from our co-founder Frances who died in 1978. She hadn't strength to write much, they are short notes written on her electric typewriter on a variety of coloured stationery, brief comments, arrangements to meet – 'You'd better be there!' and they bring back our talks in her garden, her jokes, her seriousness, the pauses in her weak breathing, the strength of her will and spirit – 'Let's see if there are more women like us' – without her there would have been no Gemma. To hold a letter is to be in touch with the writer again.

There's no doubt in our group that we feel we should put in a note, however short, when sending each other magazines, newsletters, cuttings. Sometimes now when sending out the Gemma newsletter I haven't made time to put in a note to each of the members I am regularly in touch with, and I regret this and try to catch up later. For isolated lesbians living in small villages or apparently totally heterosexual dormitory suburbs, women who are at home because of physical disability or unemployment, for women who have little money to go out or to travel, for agoraphobic women, and for many others, letters are especially important. Of course we hope their situations are not permanent, that one day we can meet in our twos and threes if not in larger groups. But some see no change ahead, like the young disabled rural member whose family seem incredibly oppressive, denying her visitors or the use of the phone, so that her only social outlet is letters. Gentle encouragement to rebel has had no result so far, and she seems to accept her life as it is with letters and books being her lifeline to other women.

But for some women letters are not enough, and can't provide even a temporary haven from feelings of rejection, isolation, anger, and bitterness. In their distress and unhappiness they want a circle of friends nearby, or one special person, here and now. When you are content yourself it is difficult, impossible perhaps, to suggest that such women be patient and keep writing. Not all women can feel they are sharing and participating by doing so. Others happily do make friends over long distances and some eventually live together.

Of course, some women cannot write – because of the nature of their disability or because they are dyslexic or haven't learned to write easily. So far I have not been very successful in encouraging them to follow the lead of our blind sisters and tape their letters. This still seems a very new idea to some women, though there have been general tape-corresponding clubs in existence for many years.

Gemma is fortunate in having at present several blind members all of whom are keen correspondents. In the beginning, I have to admit, I did not recognize the full value of these articulate taped letters that I so much enjoyed receiving; then it dawned on me that parts of them were short articles in their own right. I transcribed them and returned them to their authors for editing (if they wished) and of course for permission to print, and the Gemma newsletters have been greatly enriched by their inclusion.

These taped letters are perhaps the ones I enjoy most – they are from members I don't meet regularly yet whom I've come to know best. Other members I meet at socials when there's lots of talk and we don't have time or space to exchange personal confidences so much. Perhaps part of the explanation is that with taping you are half-talking to yourself, therefore there is less inhibition in talking to another woman as you would to yourself. Taping is not like telephoning, it seems to me – it is a correspondence form which produces letters of depth and honesty. Because we don't disguise our voices when we are happy, concerned, annoyed, it shows in the style and content. Perhaps we tend to share more in taped letters, there's an immediacy and spontaneity, everything can come through, and there is the time to develop a theme that we wouldn't have on the telephone. You might think that we 'edit out' as easily as we might tear up a page of writing we've had second thoughts about, but from my experience we tend not to – it feels more like 'cheating' if we do, more like concealment of one's true self – though I must say I *have* deleted an expletive when my cat sent a pile of papers crashing while I was taping.

Some blind women would like to correspond in braille with sighted women and this is something we should be more conscious of. Letters on paper may be more appropriate at some times than a taped letter, some things are better written than spoken, and of course brailled information, addresses, and telephone numbers are easier to refer to; trying to find a 'lost' item somewhere in a long tape is infuriating. Blind women may not always have quiet and privacy in which to tape or listen to tapes. Also a lesbian in a mixed household may be afforded more freedom and sense of security with brailled letters if she doesn't want to 'come out' inadvertently to her family or other residents.

Some sighted women are very self-conscious about attempting to tape and if they won't begin to try it means the number of women with whom blind women can correspond will increase only very slowly. So, as well as encouraging more women to tape we should be suggesting that more sighted women learn braille – grade one is not difficult – either by correspondence courses, teach yourself books or perhaps in small groups at women's centres. All women's centres could look for funding to buy braille-writers in the same way they've obtained typewriters, so that this form of correspondence would become accessible to women who may become tired using a hand-frame or who want to write much longer letters.

It took me a while to overcome my doubts about my ability to learn braille as I regarded it as something so specialized, and I might never have begun if one of my blind friends had not sent me a primer and a 'starter set'. At first I used it just for labelling cassettes but now find it so useful to be able to do letters, though I haven't yet graduated to grade two.

Gemma is only one of several networks, though not all stress integration of women with and without disabilities as we do. Other collectives and groups could raise consciousness of this issue simply by asking all members to state whether they correspond by writing, tape or braille. We need more awareness of different methods of communication and of the potential within many of us to extend our range of correspondence, so that we don't exclude other women from our friendship, so that we are no longer compartmentalized and divided.

Letters are a great force in feminist solidarity. One of our blind members brailles to a woman in prison, and there must be many other isolated lesbians, deaf-blind women for example, who would welcome the support letters can bring. Sometimes we write to women who cannot answer for a time because of disability or depression, but who have let us know they would like to receive letters.

That there is a unifying power in letters is undoubted. We need to increase and improve our links and enable more women to share this. Sighted lesbians, nationally and internationally, taping among themselves, could enjoy a greater sense of sisterhood. Today I have a letter from a Swedish pen-friend pointing out that there is next to nothing written on the subject of lesbians with disabilities. My hope is that out of the circles of writing will come more courage and openness, that letters won't stop there, that women will agree to the collection and publication of their work, and that more writing will grow out of this, to be shared not only with women like us, but with all women.

Broadening visions

Evelyn Conlon

What is feminist writing? Is there such a thing? These questions are being hotly debated at the moment. I took part in a discussion with women writers where the other two speakers *and* the chair thought there could not be such a thing. I felt as I always feel in the company of male writers who somehow believe that art is male and that female success in expression is exactly that – male success. I felt let down by these women because there is no doubt that their writing is affected by the changes happening around them; but they wanted to say that literature knows no sex, no gender. Indeed it doesn't as long as it is mainly male.

I can understand the difficulties associated with saying that one's writing is Ist, but Femin Ist is different from any other Ist, simply because it is not just a doctrine or a philosophy. It is a view of the world, an honest sense of the wrong, a voice for human experience, an insight. The political analysis comes later and is never ever more important than the human insight. Any artist tries to tell the truth, but the story is always only part of the truth: the part seen from the particular artist's viewpoint.

As a feminist my view will be feminist in every way, but particularly in subject matter. I don't write about the life of the man – I look for the unseen woman in the kitchen who is keeping him ticking over, servicing him, and losing her life for him. This is truth as I see it. Talking about it, writing about it doesn't make us popular in the male-identified art world. It might even hurt many people, including our own mothers, and we have been conditioned not to hurt, never to kill, to nurture, to care, but we cannot pretend that we have not seen that truth.

I find that I have little in common with male writers even though I occasionally want to communicate with their writing. It's not just their unacceptable images – the supine, passive woman, the bitch, the whore, the wife, the half person, the cunt, young, beautiful, old, ugly – it's also their subject matter. I didn't need to write a poem about killing a pig – I have enough communion with blood. I don't even need to write about nuclear war or the destruction of the world. You can have those stories, boys. I don't even need to read them.

I have written a play about women in a maternity ward and about the fact that they are none too enamoured with the doctors or with their brand new bouncing babies. Men do not like this play. This used to mean it was no good – but things are changing. For all the flaws I may see in the play in the future, I am glad that it is written. I believe that this is feminist writing, as opposed to a woman writing, because it challenges the belief that women could only be over the moon about a new baby. I am a feminist and I cannot write under cover. I am not afraid to say that, nor to argue the belief that there is such a thing as feminist-inspired writing, even though it would suit me a lot better in this climate not to do so. I believe that the instincts which generate and inform feminist writing – epsecially the writing of women of colour – must be given to the world as well as the writing itself. Otherwise, we are all in trouble.

Like many others I now turn to women writers from all over the world for answers and for pleasure. The influences of these women have been profound. Not just that – essential. I have an empathy and a communication with women writers who are not afraid to write of their real experience and their real insight. More than that, I have a stronger empathy with the work of women of colour because of the slight similarities in our world political positions.

Tillie Olsen has pointed out the low percentage of women who make it to the male top and the even lower percentage of them who have children. I wonder what percentage are Black, poor, or single mothers? My main question on a day to day level is 'Writing versus Motherhood' – and I use 'versus' deliberately. My main influence . . . non-influence . . . consumer of time . . . frustration . . . is that I am a mother. I remember first reading Tillie Olsen's book, *Silences*, and feeling dreadfully depressed because I had had a story almost ready for a long time but I could not get the time to finish it. I do not believe any writer who is not a mother can understand the truth of that. It is not just the time which is not there in the first place (after washing, feeding, drying, putting to sleep, waking, nurturing, scolding – and also something else they call work) – the quality of time is never there. When I hear about writers staring out the window for hours before words come to them, I want to scream – or stop writing.

But I keep on as others have done and are doing. I was born in 1952. I had my first child when I was 23, my second at 25. I thought I knew what I was doing – and maybe would do the same again. I pick up books that are written by men who were born in 1956 – or third books by men born in 1952 – and wonder where the place is for mother writers/artists. Which is of course why the place is in such a state, is it not?

Male organization of the world forces us to be brought up in isolation by women whose intellect men do not respect and whose contribution they stifle. This guarantees a continual stream of subjectable girls and power-conscious boys because children learn young and well. I believe that the first few years of motherhood (I'm speaking of isolated motherhood, because I have not lived through any other sort, nor seen any truly working alternatives) are mentally genocidal tools. Any woman who can still *really* hope and believe in her mind after a few years of enforced solitude with dependent demanding sad youngsters should be given one of those medals for bravery. Put on top of that the frustration of not having time, time, time to do what she must do and you have a recipe for endless depression. Doctors and Valium must have helped kill half the women writers in the world. I make no apologies for my observations – and I do continue to hold men responsible for the huge gaps in women's writing. That is the thing I think of most, in relation to my own work – how little I have done out of what I might have done if I had not had children. I am assured by other writers that this might not be so – but how many of the 'great' writers of the past were mothers?

I look forward to the day in my dreams when women with vision will be nurtured as much as men have been in the past – by women, by men, and by society.

Voice

Sigrid Nielsen

I agreed to write this paper as a dare.

'What is "voice" anyway?' asked a close friend, running her finger down a list of conference workshop topics. (The Edinburgh Feminist Writers' Conference, which we had organized with another woman, was a week away.)

I said that I thought I knew what 'voice' was; or at least, what it might be.

'Could you lead a workshop on it?'

'*Well* . . . I don't have a lot of time,' I said quickly, 'but I could try something. Something short.'

'Voice' sounded like a mildly interesting idea. I did not know much about it, but I thought it was about writing as if you were speaking. I had read a few novels with a strong spoken rhythm, and been powerfully drawn to them. (Later I read Alice Walker's *The Color Purple*, which is written entirely in the voices of its Black American characters.) A few novels hardly seemed like anything that would make a good workshop. I regretted my rashness and doubted that other women would have much to say about an idea that sounded academic.

It didn't turn out quite like that.

The idea of 'voice' may be academic; but I soon realized, as I sat down to think about it, that my reasons for choosing it were personal.

Like much of my life as a woman, my writing life has always been – rather than secret – simply not mentioned. Serious writers, everyone seemed to agree, didn't discuss their writing. I was happy to leave it at that, since I didn't know anyone who wrote in the same way I did.

I wrote, and still write, by listening to the voice inside my head. It dictates: I write. Even when I read, I imagine a voice behind the words, speaking to me as if the author and I were in the same room. This illusion of intimacy probably explains why I wanted to become a writer. But no one ever suggested to me, in all the time I was growing up – or later – that writing was created by any means other than marking words on paper. I even knew a woman who said she could not think without a pen in her hand.

From the point of view of a group of women I did not know, this approach might be even worse than the academic one: even feminism has its limits. I felt I would be exposing myself unnecessarily; but there was just the off-chance that a few other women might think my experience mattered to theirs. It did, but not in any way I foresaw at the time I started to explain my mental voice to myself, something I had never done before.

The voice inside my head is and isn't 'my' voice. It belongs to me, but not to the everyday self my friends would recognize. It takes on many different rhythms and accents, but at its most natural it is like my mother's voice when she read to me as a child: slow, patient, full of authority and a certain excitement. I think my mental voice is probably an echo of some of my earliest memories.

As a child, I told stories to my mother. I told them to myself as well, though I kept that part of my life private. Growing up in a small, God-fearing American town, it was second nature not to mention certain things unless you fancied a visit to the minister or the psychiatrist. I imagined I was a very unstable character, and I wondered if I would ever be a 'real' writer. The writers my mother mentioned, and the ones I learnt about in school, seemed to have written out of some clear inner vision, and not a voice that dictated snatches of this and snatches of that, whether I was trying to write or not. I tried to appear to be the real sort of writer, hoping it might take if I worked at it long enough. It never did, but in the process I learnt how other people believed a proper writer should write, and it was by that roundabout route that I discovered 'voice'.

Real writers may not hear voices, but they use 'voice'. As a literary term, 'voice' implies that speech and the written word are completely different forms – but that occasionally a writer chooses to mimic speech.

Writers of non-fiction, the theory goes, don't use 'voice'. (My voice had a thumping sonorous intonation for non-fiction, such as school essays, but it had to be restrained because I wouldn't have liked anyone to think I was making fun of the form.) And writers of fiction don't often use 'voice' to portray the heroine or hero, who usually speaks 'standard English'. Characters with 'voice' are likely to be set apart by their birthplace, their class, their age, or some other 'eccentricity'. 'Ordinary' characters don't have 'voice'; they speak written English.

Once, when I was 15, I encountered a White middle-class character who had 'voice'. Her name was Libby and she was a character in a novel called *The Group*, by Mary McCarthy. She spoke schoolgirl slang so pervasively that all the other characters avoided her. Even the author described her as pushy and made fun of her ambition as a writer, which was never fulfilled, of course. She was quite obviously not the real thing.

As I tried to think the question over seriously, even so much later, I did not know where to look for other writers who might have something to show me about 'voice' – the literary voice, that is, because I took it for granted they wouldn't mention any other sort. Virginia Woolf crossed my mind, and I leafed idly through her diary. I thought she might discuss talk in fiction, but I wasn't prepared for what I found – a mention of her own interior voice – and in a very down-to-earth context. Her husband was typewriting, she said, and she had decided to make an entry in her diary in order to shut out the sound of the keys. 'I cannot read it down,' she wrote, 'but I can write it down.'

I was surprised. I had never *tried* to drown other sounds with my mental voice, but I knew it was loud enough to compete with teachers, people who shouted at me in the street, and rock and roll. Perhaps Virginia Woolf was talking about something similar; but I thought it was probably just a curiosity, and that she wouldn't say more.

As it turned out, she didn't need to say more; that one sentence was enough to make me think about Virginia Woolf differently afterwards. I've wondered about her sense of isolation – and how much of it stemmed from her fascination with sound and speech in a time when half the art of living, especially for women, was in silence. In Virginia Woolf's novels, everything talks. Even the pigeons in *The Years* don't just coo, they say a nonsense phrase – which happens to be a complete sentence.

The Waves, often considered her best novel, is narrated in six people's interior voices. In her hallucinations the birds spoke Greek; and she drowned herself, finally, when she began to 'hear voices', afraid she would go mad and interfere with her husband's work.

Later I discovered another reference to interior voices in a different kind of writer: Karen Blixen. Unlike the often housebound Virginia Woolf, Blixen led hunting expeditions in Kenya, where she ran her own coffee farm (supported, it should be added, by a large number of Africans). At the age of 48, using the name of Isak Dinesen, she published her first book, a collection of short stories. She had composed them, she said, by telling them to herself over and over, sometimes for thirty years. She added that she had bought the power to tell stories by selling her soul to the devil.

Was it entirely a joke? Both Virginia Woolf and Karen Blixen associated their writing with bad luck and hard times. Virginia Woolf wondered if her novels were an outgrowth of her madness, intelligible only to herself; Karen Blixen saw her stories as a last-minute compensation for her disastrous marriage. Both doubted they were 'real' writers. They disowned both their ambition and their ability, while craving good reviews and honours: Karen, particularly, insisted she was not literary, but secretly coveted the Nobel Prize, which she never won.

The knowledge that Virginia Woolf and Karen Blixen had both understood the idea of interior voices took me some time to absorb. If they had known, why hadn't anyone ever told *me?* Was it really meant to be a secret? Was it something peculiar to women, which men tried to suppress? I didn't know enough to be very clear, but as I looked back over my education, I realized how thoroughly it was weighted against the spoken word, even down to the sign in the school library: SILENCE.

'Don't say something because it *sounds* right,' one of my teachers repeated. 'Don't be like a spider,' said another, 'taking all your material from inside yourself.' Schoolwork, serious work, was meant to be drawn from external sources – and judged by external standards. And those standards were taught by visual means. We diagrammed sentences (*subject/verb/object* – the fact that these were categories invented by grammarians, and not scientific laws, was never mentioned), and we outlined essays – with the important points justified against the left margin and the subheadings indented to the right. We rarely read our work aloud and we certainly did not discuss it with anyone. Any comments were written by the teacher, in red ink, under the letter grade at the top. The height of the visual approach was journalistic writing, which was meant to place all the important facts at the beginning, so that the article could be padded out or hacked off to whatever length looked best on the page.

Much of what we learned was useful. The destructive part wasn't what was said, but what was implied: that writing was a neat and solitary process, a visual art which used words instead of lines and spaces. A real writer, I thought, wouldn't have to resort to mental voices; he or she could make an essay out of nothing but a sheaf of reading notes, or write a story (as one article advised) by making lists of possible first sentences. Everyone, teachers, published (male) writers, and critics, all implied that Life could be turned into Literature without ever speaking to anybody, even oneself. A real writer would have a clean, tidy, *quiet* mind.

I've been told since that the visual emphasis I was taught is peculiarly American, and that English and Scottish educations have a wholly different bias. The bias was different, but as it turned out, the effect was similar. When the conference and the voice workshop arrived, I found out that other women had had parallel experiences to mine, even though their understanding of voice had begun very differently.

Nearly everyone who turned up for the workshop was Scottish or from northern England, and many defined themselves as working-class. They had come to the workshop, not because they thought their interior voices were strange, but because those voices were at odds with written English – as I had believed mine to be, but not in quite the same way. I hadn't been aware of this dimension of voice in writing – that women could see it as related to one's actual speech, or accent; or that the inner voice and the outer voice could be linked. They described voice as a link to class and background, to early memory and strong feeling. Much of their education had been meant to force them to change their voices to something 'standard' – more southern.

Most of them had succeeded in changing outwardly. But they still thought in the accent they had learnt in childhood. Some had felt they should suppress the internal voice as well – even though that meant suppressing the feelings and associations that went with it. Success at school and university and in the job market depended on distancing the part of their minds most deeply connected with their identity – and their writing.

One woman, who did not consider herself a writer, realized in the course of the workshop that the Scottish voice in her mind had to be translated before she could write in English. Phrases which every Scot hears from the earliest age ('Where do you stay?' 'Where're you away to?') have no existence in written English, which cannot express them as the Scots hear them. The words themselves can be written, of course, but they become 'colourful'; they acquire 'voice'. The situation, however, is never explained in those terms, and people whose internal voices don't speak standard English simply decide they can't write.

Those who escaped that judgement did so in curious and roundabout ways. One woman began writing poetry because she had a broken typewriter. Some days it worked, some days it didn't. She made up nonsense sentences in order to test it. Because the sentences were silly and childish, her original voice emerged in them. Eventually she began to listen and let the voice take over; it used expressions she had been avoiding for years; the writing she began this way came more easily than any she had ever done. For others, listening to interior voices meant deep personal change and rediscovery. One woman, whose paper appears elsewhere in this book, called her own mental voice 'a tape recorder just inside my ear'. Listening to this voice was the beginning of accepting herself as northern, lesbian, and working-class, qualities she had spent life's energy suppressing.

I left the workshop with a great deal to think about. In that hour I had learnt new ways to see a reality I had viewed unchangingly and secretly, and tried to suppress, for most of my life. It would take some getting used to.

Virginia Woolf and Karen Blixen identified their internal voices with loss and survival; the feminists in the workshop also remembered loss, but afterwards there was growth.

In the two years since the workshop, I have written more, and more easily, than before. I've concentrated on adapting my rambling, spoken style to the written word – adapting, rather than disguising. I have written a play, but I continue working at short stories and essays. The feeling of intimacy with a single narrator, a single reader, remains a powerful draw.

It was some time before I thought through the things the other women had said about their internal voices as links to their deepest feelings and identity, and remembered my mother, the first person who encouraged me to write. Things were different between us before she realized that I would not have a life she could imagine a woman living. Voice involves memory, and memory can involve pain. But both memory and voice survive, and it's perhaps in accepting them that we become survivors.

The script: a scene for four female characters

Michelle Russell

(*The scene is an empty space. Enter M1 and M2. M1 holds a script.*)

M1: OK, OK, so what is this?
M2: It's for us to read.
M1: Have you read it?
M2: Yeah.
M1: You want me to read it?
M2: I think you'd enjoy it.
M1: Why?
M2: Well, it's about things we've talked about. And anyway –
M1: Yes?
M2: Sigrid is expecting us to have read it by Monday.
M1: Oh. Right. Well, where shall we start?
M2: How about here? (*points to a space in the script*)
M1: OK, we'll start here. What's it about?
M2: Well – it's hard to explain. It's about writing for theatre.
M1: *About* writing for theatre.
M2: Yeah. And about women in theatre.
M1: Right. Women in theatre.
M2: Right. OK.
M1: OK. So I'll start here, shall I? 'I've been in several. . . .' Where do you want me to stand? Is here OK?
M2: Yeah, that's good. Or maybe try it a bit further back.
M1: Back here? (*moves upstage*)
M2: Yeah, that's fine. Try that. Just move as you feel comfortable. If you want to walk, do.
M1: OK. Here we go. 'I've been in several . . . .' Can you hear me from there?
M2: Yeah, that's fine, I can hear you.
M1: Right. I just thought I'd check. (*coughs*) Um-hm. Right. (*deep breath*)

'I've been in several women-only writing groups (and I'm still in one) and also took part in a mixed theatre writing group. Also I have worked in theatre with feminist groups.' How's that?

M2: Yeah, that's great. Don't be nervous!

M1: I'm not nervous! Well, not really.

M2: Just try reading it.

M1: OK.

'In a mixed group, I think it is better if women are in the majority, or at least fifty-fifty; unfortunately this could not be ensured every week as everyone had their own commitments but it was better when there were more women. Although the sharing out of the evening's reading time was done democratically and as fairly as possible, it was difficult to stop some of the men from holding the floor for lengthy periods. This needed quite energetic chairing and was at times quite trying. We were all learning, and were prepared to give each other space to develop our ideas and writing skills and to offer constructive comments. Some men had difficulty in expressing their emotions and took up a large proportion of the group's time in doing so; and, which is worse, discussion could degenerate into argument for its own sake, or theorizing. It seemed like we all had to keep the greedy ones under control, otherwise we all got angry at the amount of time spent on their work and not on others, and I especially got angry at the way women's work got squeezed out and how women didn't say anything when men were going on and on.'

This seems to be all about men. You said before that it was about women. When does it get to the bit about women?

M2: It comes after this bit.

M1: When?

M2: Not long! Just carry on!

M1: Anyway, I don't know if I agree with this. How is that stuff about theorizing specific to a mixed group? Surely some individuals can dominate in any group.

M2: Well, that's what it says. It does go on to explain a bit.

M1: Does it? OK. (*reads*)

'On the whole, group interaction was good and some very good work was produced there. I would say that in a mixed group the attitude of the men in the group is important. The more aware of feminism, the better. The more ready to examine themselves, their egos, their sexuality, the better. Time and attention has to be shared fairly: otherwise

it just becomes a reproduction of existing male/female relationships to do with language, in which men hold the stage and women have to fight to get a word in or else shut up and eventually stop coming. In the mixed group I felt a challenge, a sense of "I have a right to speak and I'm not going to let these men stop me" – this made me assert myself more and take risks as well as articulating my feelings.'
This still seems to be all about men.

M2: Look –

M1: Oh, hang on. I see. It starts here.
'Whereas when working with women in theatre I felt, "I must be careful not to oppress other women", together with a feeling that I needed the women-only group to work so much that I dared not rock the boat. I so often didn't want to cramp another woman's style that I ended up cramping my own quite badly and it's taken quite a long time to sort out the threads and get uncramped. Sometimes I felt overwhelmed with confusion at the anger and misunderstanding I felt, and was unable to express my feelings. In the mixed group I felt more that I had a point to make and I wanted to use the time to best effect. I feel I needed the mixed group as a safety valve as well as enjoying it for its own sake. The challenge of claiming my own space from men gave me confidence. And I came to like the openness and free-for-all discussion that the group engendered.'
Um.

(*pause*)

M2: That's good. (*pause*) Go on. (*pause*) What's wrong?

M1: Nothing, nothing. Is this OK?

M2: Yes, yes, fine, carry on.

M1: (*starts reading again*)
'When working with women, there was a different feeling: more common assumptions about the way we see 'reality', a more relaxed feeling, our abilities coming out more and more as we got to know each other; the feeling of working together to create something, of being self-sufficient, of not having men around, the feeling of achievement, of not being silenced – '

(*enter M3*)

M3: Oh God, I'm *so* sorry, the bus took absolutely ages and I had to take Joanne to the nursery, really sorry. . . .

M2: We had to make a start. . . .
M3: Yes, yes, can I just sit in for now?
M2: We've done a bit already, but –
M3: Maybe I can catch up later? I can read the first bit later. Just carry on from where you are and –
M1: How much more of this do you want to do?
M2: Well, I thought we'd finish it. Why? Have you got any objections?
M1: Well, we have got to get on with the rest of the show. . . .
M2: But I thought it was agreed that we'd keep one morning every week free for going through new stuff and presenting things to each other. I think we should give it a go, and not keep worrying about whether we should be doing it or not.
M1: It's just that this seems to go on a bit. . . .
M2: You haven't even read to the end yet!
M3: I haven't heard any of it yet.
M2: Just carry on, for Godssake.
M1: OK, OK. Now where was I? Oh yes.
' – of not being silenced, of having found a voice together with other women. A hitherto repressed creativity blossoming out. Less basic conflict over content of material, which means more time to spend on detailed advice for improvement. The feeling that your experience is *valid*. But as I've said, there can be a lot of problems sometimes obscured by a superficial common interest, because we live in a patriarchal capitalist world and its ways are out to divide us if we let it.'
M2: Right.
M1: 'Women in theatre have to cope with the more or less overt sexism of a male-dominated profession. The competitiveness filters through. The artistic excellence attained by each woman becomes confused with the competitiveness of the star system. The pressure of competition can be stimulating if one is up to it at any given moment, but its stresses must not be underestimated. If we can counter the offence which patriarchal institutions do to us, for instance by depriving our theatre groups of funding, we can help each other. Fortunately now there is more and more of a network of women in theatre: this has been helped by such organizations as Women in Entertainment.'
M3: That reminds me, I must renew my subscription.
M1: There's a bit here about inter-dependence of skills in theatre.
M2: OK, let's hear it.
M1: 'Theatre writing is not something you do in private, you have to be

fairly public about it. It also involves an inter-dependence of skills. And so understanding and communication is very important. It's true that throughout history the actors, directors, scene shifters, and many others who brought plays to life have been forgotten and the writers have been remembered, because the texts have survived whereas the performances haven't. Thus the notion of the solitary "creative genius" has come about, through the insistence on the written word, and because it suits capitalism and patriarchy to have people think in hierarchies. It has always been a tenet of feminism that *all* support roles are equally important. The temptation of the "star" system is enshrined within capitalism as the greatest achievement we can aim for, claim our hour of glory for us, sod the rest. How can we be unaffected by this ideology? My hope is that we don't have to be conditioned in this way, we can reclaim excellence for our own without stamping on others in the process or allowing ourselves to be stamped on. Patriarchy sets up systems of top dog, underdog, and we don't help each other by obligingly fitting into one of these.'

M3: Could I – maybe read some?

M1: Sure.

(*M1 steps down and M3 goes up. M1 comes and sits down by M2.*)

M3: Right . . . where am I? OK. . . .

'Writing drama is a perilous business anyway. Always there is the other dimension needed to bring it to life. To me this is one of the great advantages of theatre, but it can also be one of its greatest problems – in theatre you have to work with people and you have to have some sort of relationship with people in order to get the work on, and when it's good it's very good, and when it's bad it's a trial and an exasperation all round. But I think it's worth it in the end because it does come back to life, writing, I mean, and I find theatre an exciting form to work in because it has all the characteristics of "life" but is really pretend. I enjoy theatre because it is created action, designed to elucidate certain things for the audience, as well as to entertain them and let them feel part of the society they live in. The process of creating that experience for the audience is one in which many people collaborate.

I enjoy the notion of people getting up and enacting a situation and thus influencing an audience and this process is what I want to be in on.

The collaborative ways of working that I enjoy are and have been where people are committed towards an equality for all members and where there is an openness of discussion about procedure and roles. We have to recognize that this is alien to most institutions in this society and that we have to deal with this in some way, particularly round funding (yet again!). We need guidelines for participation and most importantly we need to believe that it can happen.

Action leads to writing, writing leads to action. The world we live in intervenes in our group relationships, our personal lives, and our interactions around work, competition and recognition. We need people to encourage us in our writing. And we need to want it to happen, in contribution to our own growth and to the growth of a culture that is truly representative of women's achievements and abilities.'

(*stops reading*)

M1: Is that the end?
M3: Seems to be.
M1: (*To M2*) Is that it?
M2: That's it.
M1: It's not very *dramatic*, is it? Still I suppose it's a start.
M3: It does go on a bit, doesn't it? Though I quite like the bit about support roles.
M2: Um. I thought the part about capitalism and patriarchy went on too long. Too agitprop. Needs to be said differently. More subtly.
M3: Where did it come from?
M1: Don't know. We just found it.
M3: Who wrote it?
M2: (*looks at script*) Doesn't say.
M3: Anyway, how about some lunch?
M1: Oh yes, I'm starving.
M2: I'll go and get some milk, shall I?
M1: Right.
M3: Are we going to do any more on this, then?
M1: I think it's a bit stodgy, don't you?
M2: Yeah. Some of it's all right, but it needs more dramatizing.

(*makes to exit*)

M1: Yeah. Look, I want to get some cigarettes so I'll come with you.
M3: Haven't you given up, yet? Thought it was definitely down to one a day this week!

(They all go out, leaving script lying on stage. As they go out, they pass M4 who enters with a broom, coming to sweep up the stage. M4 sweeps up everywhere, is about to sweep up script, then picks it up, has a look at it. Is thoughtful. After a while of reading, takes out a pen and starts to write some notes on the script. Lights fade.)

Resources section

Compiled by Gail Chester

Book publishers and distributors

Authors find publishers by a combination of trial and error, luck, inside information and hard work. We have tried to simplify this process by compiling a list of all British and Irish publishers and distributors who handle significant numbers of feminist books. We sent out a simple questionnaire and most of them replied. We asked them to reply to the following questions:

1 Name of company;
2 Address;
3 Telephone number;
4 Contact person/job title;
5 Feminist series, if any;
6 Number of feminist titles published/distributed per year;
7 Up to twenty words description of what sort of books you are interested in (please bear in mind that this list will be used by women deciding where to send their work for consideration).

One of the publishers sent us the following additional paragraph, with which almost all publishers would broadly agree:

Please tell women writing to us that they should follow the usual procedure when submitting a manuscript, i.e. enclose return postage and keep a copy of their work. We take about six to eight weeks to respond, though if an s.a.e. is enclosed for that purpose, we will acknowledge the manuscript's arrival. We prefer women (and men for that matter) who submit work to us to know what sort of press we are and to have done their homework by looking in the libraries or bookshops at the sort of books we publish. This saves us all time, money, and energy.

While the market for feminist books remains buoyant, almost all publishing houses will include some feminist titles (or at least some 'women's studies' books) in their lists, without having a specific policy to attract them, so many publishers who are not listed here may also be interested in your work. Apart from employing the methods mentioned above, the best ways of finding a suitable publisher are to consult *The Writers' and Artists' Yearbook* (A & C Black, annual) and to visit a bookshop to discover which publishers are bringing out comparable titles. Every year since 1984, the Feminist Book Fortnight group (see Organizations) has produced a list of all relevant titles published in Britain and Ireland that year and Sisterwrite produce a monthly listing of titles newly in stock – prices available on request with s.a.e. These will provide further guidance on who is publishing what.

You will find the distributors in this list particularly helpful if you decide to self-publish your work, as organizing efficient distribution is often one of the most difficult aspects of successful self-publishing. If you decide to try self-publishing, alone or as a group, Ultra Violet Enterprises (see Organizations) is the only agency in Britain specializing in publishing advice for feminists and other radical individuals and groups.

Words to the Wise (Clardy) lists the equivalent publishing houses in North America.

Publishers

1 **Allison & Busby Limited**
2 6a Noel Street, London W1V 3RB
3 01–734 1498
4 Margaret Busby/Director
6 Variable
7 A general international list of non-fiction and fiction (including thrillers) in hardback and paperback by both new and established authors, including Rosa Guy, Buchi Emecheta, Alexandra Kollontai.

1 **Arlen House**
2 69 Jones Road, Dublin 3, Ireland
3 Dublin 786913
4 Catherine Rose/Director
6 10
7 Contemporary fiction, poetry, reprint classic fiction, history, biography, literature, feminist criticism and theory.

1 **Attic Press**
2 44 East Essex Street, Dublin 2, Ireland
3 Dublin 716367
6 14
7 An Irish-based feminist publishing house which produces books by and about women written from a feminist perspective in the area of women's studies, humour, social comment, history and general non-fiction. Launching fiction list in spring 1987.

1 **Berg Publishers Ltd**
2 24 Binswood Avenue, Leamington Spa, Warks. CV32 5SQ
3 0926 29470
4 Dr Marion Berghahn/Managing Director
5 Berg Women's Series

6 4 (of the Women's Series. The women's series is the only feminist series we publish).
7 Works on life and critical assessment of achievements of notable women from any walk of life, profession or period. The Berg Women's Series looks not only at the lives of such women, but also their background, period, influences and achievements.

1 **Basil Blackwell**
2 108 Cowley Road, Oxford
3 0865 722146
4 Sue Corbett/Editor, Feminist books
6 About 10
7 Primarily interested in books on history, literature, sociology and general books.

1 **Bloodaxe Books Ltd**
2 PO Box 1SN, Newcastle-upon-Tyne, NE99 1SN
3 0632 325988
6 2–3
7 Mostly poetry, some fiction.

1 **Brilliance Books/Plain Edition**
2 14 Clerkenwell Green, London EC1R 0PH
3 01–250 0730
4 Jan Cal/Women's Editor
6 6–8
7 Work welcomed from lesbian writers writing fiction on any theme. No poetry and no short stories please. At the moment we are looking for novels between 80 and 100 thousand words long. We are not sure if the classification 'Feminist' is right for the books we publish. We publish work by lesbian writers on most themes, we do not publish feminist polemic disguised as fiction.

1 **Camden Press**
2 43 Camden Passage, London N1
3 01–226 2061
4 Sian Williams/Francis Borzello
5 Women on Art; feminist fiction.
6 12 (about 75 per cent of output)
7 Serious fiction, books on topical issues, health, non-mainstream art, history and criticism, with emphasis on women's approaches.

1 **Federation of Worker Writers and Community Publishers**
2 c/o Centerprise Publishing Project, 136 Kingsland High Street, London E8
4 Rebecca O'Rourke/Publishing worker

7 Some Community Publishing Projects prioritise books by women and other disadvantaged groups. These include Centerprise, Peckham Publishing Project, Commonword and THAP, who all concentrate on local writers. However, groups such as Yer Own Stuff Press and Bristol Broadsides will consider manuscripts from working-class people outside their area. Women writing to Federation groups should note that it is better if they are local to the project and that resources are very limited, so groups publish irregularly and often as pamphlets. The projects publish many types of book: poetry, prose, autobiography, books by individuals and anthologies.

1 **Honno: Welsh Women's Press**
2 Ailsa Craig, Heol y Cawl, Dinas Powys, De Morgannwg, Wales
3 0222 515014
6 Initially 2 in Welsh, 2 in English, hopefully increasing to 6 soon
7 Material or author must have Welsh connection. Novels, short stories, poetry, autobiography, research, children's books, Welsh women's history – anything relevant to women in Wales today, written by women.

1 **Hutchinson Education**
2 Brookmount House, 62–64 Chandos Place, London WC2
3 01–240 3411
4 Claire L'Enfant
6 2–3
7 Publishes writing and research with a feminist perspective on a wide variety of subjects from sexuality and education to labour and the family.

1 **Lawrence and Wishart**
2 39 Museum Street, London WC1
3 01–405 0103
4 Editorial department
6 2
7 Socialist publishers from cultural politics to women and the miner's strike, concentrating on non-fiction.

1 **Macmillan Education**
2 Houndmills, Basingstoke RG21 2XS
3 0256 29242
4 Vanessa Couchman/Humanities publisher
5 Women in Society, edited by Jo Campling
6 About 15
7 Educational and academic paperbacks in the humanities and social sciences. 'Women in Society' emphasizes an interdisciplinary approach, while the new 'Women Writers' series will focus on short studies of women novelists.

1 **Macmillan Press**
2 4 Little Essex Street, London WC2R 3LF
3 01–836 6633
4 Frances Arnold/Literature editor
6 About 10
7 High level academic books, primarily in literature and social science. Also reference books.

1 **Methuen & Co. Ltd**
2 11 New Fetter Lane, London EC4P 4EE
3 01–583 9855
4 Merrilyn Julian/Editor
6 Approx 25
7 Primarily academic studies, particularly feminist theory, literary criticism and cultural studies. We have a very wide ranging academic list and, at present, we have 100 per cent female editorial staff, so a feminist perspective is reflected throughout most of our titles, whether or not they are directly aimed at the feminist readership.

1 **Methuen London Ltd**
2 11 New Fetter Lane, London EC4P 4EE
3 01–583 9855
4 Elsbeth Lindner/Senior Editor
5 Women's Writing List
6 About 15
7 Particularly interested in fiction. Also non-fiction, drama, humour and poetry. Synopsis and sample chapters with accompanying letter preferred as initial approach.

1 **Onlywomen Press Ltd**
2 38 Mount Pleasant, London WC1X 0AP
3 01–837 0596
4 The Collective
5 All our titles
6 4
7 We are a lesbian and radical feminist press publishing poetry, theory, fiction and a lesbian ethics journal.

1 **Pandora Press**
2 11 New Fetter Lane, London EC4P 4EE
3 01–583 9855
4 Candida Lacey/Philippa Brewster
6 40

7 General non-fiction, handbooks, health, fiction, travel, humour, current affairs.

1 **Pluto Press**
2 c/o Allison and Busby, 6a Noel Street, London W1V 3RB
3 01–734 1498
4 Margaret Busby
6 Approx 50 titles in print
7 Radical imprint, with books on feminism, socialism, anti-racism, Ireland, current events and popular culture.

1 **Polity Press**
2 (Editorial) Dales Brewery, Gwydir Street, Cambridge CB1 2LJ
3 0223 324315
4 Michelle Stanworth/Editor
5 Feminist perspectives
6 About 6
7 Interested in all aspects of feminist studies which relate to the social sciences, history, sociology, politics, literature and general books.

1 **Prism Press**
2 2 South Street, Bridport, Dorset
3 0308 27022
4 Gail Chester
5 Feminist series
6 3–4
7 Intelligent non-fiction, with an emphasis on political analysis and debate.

1 **Routledge and Kegan Paul**
2 11 New Fetter Lane, London EC4P 4EE
3 01–583 9855
4 Philippa Brewster
7 Feminist studies for academic and specialized general readership, mainly cross-disciplinary in the areas of history, politics and popular culture.

1 **Sheba Feminist Publishers**
2 10a Bradbury Street, London N16 8JN
3 01–254 1590
4 Raeann Robertson
6 6–8
7 Fiction, poetry, new women writers, black women's writing, non-fiction, lesbian writing, children's books.

1 **Stramullion**
2 c/o First of May Bookshop, 43 Candlemaker Row, Edinburgh
3 031–225 2612
4 Liz Burns
6 3
7 Books specifically of Scottish interest or with a Scottish connection.

1 **Tavistock Publications Ltd**
2 11 New Fetter Lane, London EC4P 4EE
3 01–583 9855
4 Caroline Lane/Gill Davies
7 Social policy, social welfare, third world, health.

1 **Virago Press**
2 41 William IV Street, London WC2
3 01–379 6977
6 Approx 85
7 Feminist company publishing books which illuminate and celebrate all aspects of women's lives, including fiction, poetry, autobiography, health, women's studies, literary criticism, both new books and reprints.

1 **Women's Community Press**
2 44 East Essex Street, Dublin 2, Ireland
3 Dublin 712149
4 Marianne Hendron
6 6
7 Irish community publications, collections from writing groups, information booklets, feminist, lesbian and gay writing. No fiction, poetry or manuscripts from individual women. We also undertake distribution for other feminist/community presses.

1 **The Women's Press**
2 34 Great Sutton Street, London EC1V 0DX
3 01–251 3007
6 About 50
7 Feminist publisher publishing books by women. Interested in fiction (including science fiction), politics, history and art history, psychology, health, humour and other issues concerning women.

1 **Womenwrite Press**
2 PO Box 77, Cardiff CF2 4XX
3 0222 496062
6 About 3

7 Committed to publishing non-sexist and non-racist academic and literary books of social relevance by collectives and individuals, in English and Welsh. Intend to publish a set of feminist postcards.

1 **Zed Books**
2 57 Caledonian Road, London N1 9BU
3 01–837 4014
5 Zed Books on Third World Women
6 5–10
7 Zed is the leading independent socialist publisher in the English language of books concerning the Third World. Our strong women's series reflects our international orientation. The majority of our authors live and work in the Third World countries which they write about.

Distributors

1 **Airlift Book Company**
2 14 Baltic Street, London EC1Y 0TB
3 01–251 8608
4 Susan Daley/Promotions/Feminist titles
6 About 50 new titles per year
7 Some emphasis on importing American small press titles. Feminist titles, fiction, and non-fiction, for distribution only.

1 **Central Books**
2 14 Leathermarket, London SE1
3 01–407 5447
4 Kate Dean
6 12 to 15, plus 5 periodicals
7 Concentrates on Marxist titles. Most of our books are non-fiction, e.g. current affairs, gay issues, photographic books.

1 **Element Books Ltd**
2 Longmead, Shaftesbury, Dorset SP7 8PL
3 0747 51339
4 Annie Walton/Director
6 25
7 Feminist psychology, transpersonal psychology, mysticism, health and healing, philosophy, yoga.

1 **Housman's Distribution**
2 5 Caledonian Road, London N1
3 01–837 4473
4 Mia Moseley

6 About 10
7 Specialize in pamphlets and books on peace, anarchism and socialism.

1 **Password Books Ltd**
2 25 Horsell Road, London N5 1XL
3 01–607 1154
4 Sarah Peel
6 About 20
7 Our publishers concentrate on poetry, fiction, drama and literary criticism. I must stress that we do not publish, nor are we in a position to act as literary agents for women seeking a publisher.

1 **Third World Publications**
2 151 Stratford Road, Birmingham B11 1RD
3 021 773 6572
6 50
7 Promotes and sells books from and about the Third World, and aims to make Third World women's (and men's) writing as widely available as possible.

1 **Turnaround Distribution**
2 27 Horsell Road, London N5 1X1
3 01–609 7836
4 Ruthie Borthwick/Teresa Stephenson
5 Women's Press of Canada/Trouble and Strife/Women's Review, etc.
6 Many
7 We specialize in distribution of radical and independently published material – books and journals – furthering understanding of feminist, anti-racist, and gay politics.

Periodicals

This list contains the major feminist periodicals currently appearing in Britain. In addition to the more general publications which welcome contributions, there are many magazines and newsletters connected with specific campaigns and organizations. They tend to publish more specialized material, and a small selection of them is included here. There are also a number of regional women's newsletters which concentrate on news and opinion of local interest.

Periodicals are born and die with great frequency, and sometimes one seems defunct when another issue unexpectedly appears. If your thriving publication is missing from this list, many apologies, and please let us know. The Feminist Library (see Organizations) has a comprehensive – but by no means complete – collection of periodicals from many parts of the world, including copies of many which have stopped publishing. It is well worth visiting.

Words to the Wise (Clardy) contains a wide-ranging guide to North American periodicals.

Arachne
c/o A Woman's Place, Hungerford House, Victoria Embankment, London WC2.
Newsletter of the Matriarchy Research and Reclaim Network.
Association of Radical Midwives Newsletter
62 Greetby Hill, Ormskirk, Lancs L39 2DT.
Aurora – creative writing by women
PO Box 4, Liverpool L17 7EE.
Two-woman partnership, publishing bi-monthly, interested in all forms of creative writing.
Battleaxe
8 Aubyn Square, London SW15 5NT.
A new labour movement paper for women, committed to women's liberation and socialism.
Bi-monthly
BM BI, London WC1N 3XX.
Magazine for bisexual women and men.
Birmingham Black Sisters Newsletter
c/o Trade Union Resource Centre, 7 Frederick Street, Birmingham 1.
Quarterly local Black women's paper.
Cassoe Newsletter
44 Well Close Rise, Leeds 7.
Campaigning and information about sexism in education.
Children's Book Bulletin
4 Aldebert Terrace, London SW8.
Information on anti-racist, anti-sexist, children's books.
Everywoman
34a Islington Green, London N1 8EA.
Monthly news magazine.
FAN: Feminist Arts News
195 Station Road, Kingsway, Birmingham 14.
Discussion and coverage of the visual arts.
Feminist Review
11 Carleton Gardens, Brecknock Road, London N19.
Socialist feminist theory journal.
Gemma
BM Box 5700, London WC1N 3XX.
For lesbians with/without disabilities of all ages. Available on tape. See Elsa Beckett's article in this book.
Gen
ILEA Drama and Tape Centre, Princeton Street, London WC1.

Anti-sexist education magazine. Available on tape.

Gossip

Onlywoman Press, 38 Mount Pleasant, London WC1.

A journal of lesbian feminist ethics.

History Workshop Journal

c/o Routledge and Kegan Paul, 11 New Fetter Lane, London EC4.

Social and feminist history.

International Working Group on Women and the Family Newsletter

245a Coldharbour Lane, London SW9.

Concentrates on issues of concern to immigrant women and women of colour.

Iranian Community Centre Women's Section Newsletter

465a Green Lanes, London N4.

Published in Persian.

Kardinalrin Sesi

129 Newington Green Road, London N1.

Newsletter of the Union of Turkish Women in Britain.

Lesbian and Gay Socialist

c/o 119 Riversdale Road, London N5 2SU.

Mama Africa

c/o Africa Centre, 38 King Street, London WC2.

Magazine of the African Women's Confederation.

Mothertongue

BM Box 6790, London WC1N 3XX.

'Women making statements'. Available on tape.

Mukti

213 Eversholt Street, London NW1.

Asian women's magazine.

National Childcare Campaign Newsletter

Wesley House, 70 Great Queen Street, London WC2.

Older Feminists' Newsletter

c/o A Woman's Place, Hungerford House, Victoria Embankment, London WC2.

Older Lesbians' Newsletter

c/o A Woman's Place, Hungerford House, Victoria Embankment, London WC2.

Outwrite Women's Newspaper

Oxford House, Derbyshire Street, London E2.

Monthly, internationalist feminist. See Shaila Shah's article in this book.

The Radical Bookseller

265 Seven Sisters Road, London N4.

Monthly trade journal, includes lists of new radical publications.

Revolutionary/Radical Feminist Newsletter

17 Kensington Terrace, Leeds 6.

Women-only forum for political discussion. Available on tape.

Sisters Against Disablement Newsletter
c/o Mayrav Dover, 241 Albion Road, London N16.
For women with and without disabilities. Available on tape.
Spare Rib
27 Clerkenwell Close, London EC1.
Monthly women's liberation magazine: news, features, some fiction. Available on tape.
Speak Out
Mary Seacole House, 41a Stockwell Green, London SW9.
Newsletter from Brixton Black Women's Centre.
Third World Women's News
Kwame Nkrumah House, 173 Old Street, London EC1 6NJ.
A forum for discussion of, by, and for women in the Third World.
Trouble and Strife
c/o The Women's Centre, 50 Bethel Street, Norwich.
Radical feminist magazine of politics and debate – Britain's finest. Available on tape.
Voices
61 Bloom Street, Manchester M1 3LY.
Deceased journal of FWWCP. Back copies available.
We Are Here
c/o A Woman's Place, Hungerford House, Victoria Embankment, London WC2.
Black feminist newsletter, by and for Black women only.
Women Live
5 Middlehill Road, Colehill, Wimborne, Dorset BH21 2SA.
New magazine of autobiography. Each issue will concentrate on a different area of experience. All types of writing welcome.
Women's Health Information Centre Newsletter
52–54 Featherstone Street, London EC1.
Regular information and resources on women's health. Available on tape.
Women's Review
1–4 Christina Street, London EC2A 4PA.
Monthly cultural magazine, covering all the arts.
Women's Studies International Forum
41 Rosetti House, Flood Street, London SW3.
Quarterly academic journal.
Women's Studies Newsletter
9 Upper Berkeley Street, London W1H 8BY.
Published by the WEA, but of much wider interest.
Working With Girls Newsletter
National Association of Youth Clubs, 30 Peacock Lane, Leicester.
Writing Women
10 Mistletoe Road, Newcastle upon Tyne NE2 2DX.
Journal of mostly poetry and some fiction.

Your Health
c/o Forward, Africa Centre, 38 King Street, London WC2.
Magazine of the African mother and child health campaign.

Courses

Over the past few years, women's interest in writing, both their own and other women's, has rocketed. This is reflected in the number of courses that are available to women at every level. These tend to come in two main categories – those which concentrate on helping women develop their own writing and those which study other women's writing.

Your local adult education institute and the WEA (see Organizations) can be approached about providing day and evening courses, if they don't already do so, as can the extra-mural department of your nearest university. In some places, steps are being taken to make women's writing courses more accessible and responsive to the needs of different sorts of women. For example, some classes have started which concentrate on Black women's writing, others are aimed at women who have never tried 'creative' writing before. At the Albany, a community theatre in Deptford, South London, Caeia March runs a course which she describes as 'community education and support in everyday language', while there are an increasing number of adult literacy and English as a second language courses aimed primarily at women.

The Open University has recently established a course called *Women, Writing and Culture*, which costs £12.50, where you study Femininity and Women's Magazines (via *Woman's Own*) and Reading, Women and Writing (through Doris Lessing, Agnes Smedley and Snow White) independently at home. The Arvon Foundation (see Organizations) concentrates entirely on running residential courses in creative writing, and many of these are led by women writers and feminists.

Each issue of the Feminist Library newsletter (see Organizations) contains details of the latest courses in Women's Studies; otherwise *What About Women?* (Cowley) may help you find a course.

Writing groups

Many women have joined writing groups to get regular support, both directly, through having their writing read and commented on, and indirectly, by having somewhere to discuss problems which may be preventing them writing. Finding a writing group can be difficult, but ways of contacting other compatible women include: putting up a notice in your nearest alternative bookshop (the Federation of Radical Booksellers – see Organizations – has an up to date list); contacting the FWWCP or the NFVLS (see Organizations) to find out if there is a group near you or people who would like to start one; putting an ad. in *Spare Rib* or *Women's Review* (see Periodicals); joining an adult education class and continuing as an informal group once the course ends. West Midlands Arts was sponsoring someone to collect information on women's writing activity in that area, so it might be worth contacting your Regional Arts' Association to see if they can help.

Organizations

Amazon Press Ltd
75 Back Piccadilly, Manchester M1 2AZ, 061 228 2357.
Women's printing, typesetting, design and finishing co-op.
The Arvon Foundation
Totleigh Barton, Sheepwash, Devon EX21 5NS and Lumb Bank, Heptonstall, Hebden Bridge, West Yorkshire HX7 6DF.
Short residential courses for people seriously interested in writing. Wheelchair access now available at Lumb Bank.
Association of Little Presses
89a Petherton Road, London N5 2QT, 01–226 2657.
Black Women in Media
c/o Outwrite, Oxford House, Derbyshire Street, London E2.
Campaign for Press and Broadcasting Freedom
9 Poland Street, London W1, 01–437 2795.
Has active women's, Black, disabled, lesbian and gay groups. Supplies mail-order media books.
Cinema of Women
27 Clerkenwell Close, London EC1, 01–251 4978.
Distribute many films and videos by and about women.
EOC Information Centre
Overseas House, Quay Street, Manchester 3, 061–833 9244.
The Fawcett Library
City of London Polytechnic, Old Castle Street, London E1, 01–283 1030 x 570.
Particularly good historical collection.
Federation of Radical Booksellers
c/o Housmans Bookshop, 5 Caledonian Road, London N1.
Keeps up to date list of radical shops (about 150), most of which have a substantial feminist section.
Federation of Worker Writers and Community Publishers
c/o Janet Burley, 35 Nursery Road, London SW9, 01–737 6929.
The Feminist Archive
c/o The University of Bath, Claverton Down, Bath.
Feminist Audio Books
52–54 Featherstone Street, London EC1, 01–251 0713.
Collective of women with and without sight, making British feminist books available on tape.
Feminist Book Fortnight Group
7 Loddon House, Church Street, London NW8.

Group consisting mainly of publishers, who co-ordinate this annual publicity venture. Contact them to invite authors to your locality.

Feminist Library

Hungerford House, Victoria Embankment, London WC2, 01–930 0715.

Contemporary collection of books, pamphlets and periodicals. Some borrowing allowed.

Gay's the Word Bookshop

66 Marchmont Street, London WC1, 01–278 7654.

The Hall-Carpenter Archives

London Lesbian and Gay Centre, 67–69 Cowcross Street, London EC1, 01–608 1737.

Lesbian and gay archive containing books, periodicals, press clippings, and papers of groups. Bias towards gay men at present.

Lavender Menace Bookshop

11a Forth Street, Edinburgh, 031 556 0079.

Scotland's lesbian and gay community bookshop. Mail order anywhere – regular lesbian list. Free book search.

Letterbox Library

5 Bradbury Street, London N16, 01–254 1640.

Book club specializing in anti-sexist, anti-racist children's books. Produce full-colour catalogue with reviews, and newsletter.

Material Word

Unit 53, 16–20 George Street, Moseley, Birmingham B12 9RG, 021 440 1977.

Translators' co-op which concentrates on serving the local community and working with publishers.

National Federation of Voluntary Literacy Schemes

Cambridge House, 131 Camberwell Road, London SE5 0HF, 01–703 8083.

Brings together voluntary and community groups with an interest in informal learning and basic education.

National Union of Journalists, Equality Council

Acorn House, 314 Grays Inn Road, London WC1, 01–278 7916.

Handles complaints against its members, as well as campaigning for improved journalistic standards.

The Open University

Milton Keynes, MK7 6DH.

Order 'Women, Writing and Culture' (no. PU712 from the Learning Materials Service Office). The OU also runs other women's studies courses.

Sheffield Women's Printing Co-op Ltd

111A Matilda Street, Sheffield S1 4QF, 0742 735180.

Silver Moon

68 Charing Cross Road, London WC2, 01–836 7906.

Women's bookshop, also organizes some events.

Sisterwrite
190 Upper Street, London N1, 01–226 9782.
Women's bookshop, including mail-order service and monthly list of new books. New gallery space upstairs.
Theatre Writers' Union
c/o The Actors' Centre, 4 Chenies Street, London WC1 7EP.
Transaction Co-operative
Redlands, Tapton House Road, Sheffield S10 5BY, 0742 661103.
Women's co-op offering translation, interpreting and tuition in 32 languages.
Translators' Association
84 Drayton Gardens, London SW10, 01–373 6642.
Offers help to members with disputes and advice on fees. Keeps list of recommended translators.
Triangle Translations
25 Horsell Road, London N5, 01–609 9740.
Co-op of femnists and gay men providing translation into and from most European and Asian languages.
Ultra Violet Enterprises
25 Horsell Road, London N5, 01–607 4463.
Offers publishing advice and assistance, especially to feminists, community groups, trade unions and others interested in self-publishing.
Wiser Links Library
173 Archway Road, London N6, 01–341 4403.
Women's international information exchange and solidarity project.
WEA (Workers' Education Association)
9 Upper Berkeley Street, London W1.
Women in Entertainment
7 Thorpe Close, London W10 5XL, 01–969 2292.
Women in Libraries
c/o Elaine Falter, 52D Westbere Road, London NW2 3RU.
Women in Printing Trades
Box 13, 2a St Paul's Road, London N1, 01–250 3320.
Women in Publishing
c/o Liz Hartley, 43 Leamington Road Villas, London W11, 01–727 1885.
Organizes monthly open meetings, training courses, etc.
Women's Media Action Group
c/o A Woman's Place, Hungerford House, Victoria Embankment, London WC2.
Concentrates especially on campaigning around sexist advertising.
Women's Press Bookclub
34 Great Sutton Street, London EC1, 01–253 0009.
Quarterly catalogue offers 80 new titles annually (plus extensive stocklist) from British and foreign publishers.

Writers' Guild
430 Edgware Road, London W2 1EH, 01–723 8074.
Has an active women's committee. TUC-affiliated trade union.

Books

The titles in this list are generally about writing, rather than being the writing itself. There is a substantial body of academic feminist literary criticism (often from the USA) which is not represented here. *The New Feminist Criticism* (Showalter, ed.) contains a comprehensive bibliography of such titles. Unfortunately, some books on this list may be out of print, in which case you are unlikely to obtain them from a bookshop. Where available, this list gives publication details for the British edition of books.

Abel, Elizabeth (ed.), *Writing and Sexual Difference*, Brighton, Harvester, 1982.

Baker, Bob and Harvey, Neil (eds.), *Publishing For People and Fighting Censorship*, London, London Labour Library, 1985.

Batsleer, Janet, Davies, Tony, O'Rourke, Rebecca and Weedon, Chris, *Rewriting English: Cultural Politics of Gender and Class*, London, Methuen, 1985.

Beauman, Nicola, *A Very Great Profession: the Women's Novel 1914–39*, London, Virago, 1983.

Boyce Davies, Carole and Adams Graves, Anne (eds.), *Ngambika: Studies of Women in African Literature*, Trenton NJ, Africa World Press, 1986.

Browne, Susan E., Connors, Debra and Stern, Nanci (eds.), *With the Power of Each Breath: a Disabled Women's Anthology*, Pittsburgh/San Francisco, Cleis Press, 1985. (Available on tape from Womyn's Braille Press, USA.)

Bryant, Dorothy, *Myths To Lie By*, Berkeley, Ata Books, 1984. (Especially final section, 'Being a Writer'.)

Cadman, Eileen, Chester, Gail and Pivot, Agnes, *Rolling Our Own: Women as Printers, Publishers and Distributors*, London, Comedia, 1981.

Carey, G. V., *Mind the Stop*, Harmondsworth, Pelican, 1971. (Old-fashioned but accessible aid to punctuation.)

Clardy, Andrea Fleck, *Words to the Wise: a Writer's Guide to Feminist and Lesbian Periodicals and Publishers*, Ithaca NY, Firebrand Books, 1986.

Clausen, Jan, *A Movement of Poets: Thoughts on Poetry and Feminism*, Brooklyn NY, Long Haul Press, 1982.

Coghill, Mary and Scott, Diana, *If Women Want to Speak, what Language do they use?* London, Beyond Patriarchy Publications, 1977. (Probably out of print.)

Cowley, Ruth, *What About Women? Information Sources for Women's Studies*, Manchester, Fanfare Press, 1986.

Delany, Sheila, *Writing Woman: Women Writers and Women in Literature, Medieval to Modern*, New York, Schocken Books, 1983.

Dickey, Julienne and CPBF London Women's Group, *Women in Focus: Guidelines for Eliminating Media Sexism*, London CPBF, 1986.

Evans, Mari, *Black Women Writers 1950–1980: Arguments and Interviews*, London, Pluto Press, 1985.

Faust, Langdon Lynn (ed.), *American Women Writers – a critical reference guide from colonial times to the present* (abridged in two volumes), New York, Frederick Ungar Publishing Company, 1983.

Finn, Frankie, *Out on the Plain*, London, The Women's Press, 1984. (See the introduction.)

Goldsmith, Jane and Wright, Mary (eds), *Knowing Women: Women and Educational Alternatives Worldwide*, Oxford/London, Third World First/WUS, 1986.

Grahn, Judy, *Another Mother Tongue: Gay Words, Gay Worlds*, Boston, Beacon Press, 1984.

Grahn, Judy, *The Highest Apple: Sappho and the Lesbian Poetic Tradition*, San Francisco, Spinsters Ink, 1985.

Grier, Barbara, *The Lesbian in Literature*, Tallahassee Fla, Naiad Press, 1981 (3rd edition). (A comprehensive bibliography.)

Griffiths, Stuart, *How Plays are Made*, London, Heinemann Education, 1982.

Hackney Women Writers' Group, *Some Grit, Some Fire*, London, Centerprise Publishing Project, 1984.

Jacobus, Mary, *Women Writing and Writing about Women*, London, Croom Helm, 1979. (Out of print.)

Malpede, Karen (ed.), *Women in Theatre: Compassion and Hope*, New York, Limelight Editions, 1985.

Miller, Casey and Swift, Kate, *Handbook of Non-Sexist Writing for Writers, Editors and Speakers* (revised British edition), London, The Women's Press, 1981.

Miller, Jane, *Women Writing about Men*, London, Virago, 1986.

Millett, Kate, *Flying*, St Albans, Paladin, 1976.

Monteith, Moira (ed.), *Women's Writing – a Challenge to Theory*, Brighton, Harvester, 1986.

Ngcobo, Lauretta (ed.), *Let it Be Known: Black British Women Writers*, London, Pluto, 1987.

O'Connor, Flannery, *Mystery and Manners: Occasional Prose*, London, Faber and Faber, 1972.

Olsen, Tillie, *Silences*, London, Virago, 1980.

Petersen, Karen Holst and Rutherford, Anna (eds.), *A Double Colonization: Colonial and Post-Colonial Women's Writing*, Oxford and Sydney, Dangaroo, 1986.

Rainer, Tristine, *The New Diary – How to use a Journal for Self-Guidance and Expanded Creativity*, New South Wales and London, Angus and Robertson, 1980.

Rule, Jane, *Lesbian Images*, Trumansburg NY, The Crossing Press, 1982.

Russ, Joanna, *How to Suppress Women's Writing*, London, The Women's Press, 1984.

Sarton, May, *Writings on Writing*, Trumansburg NY, The Crossing Press, 1980.

Showalter, Elaine, *A Literature of their Own: British Women Novelists from Brontë to Lessing*, London, Virago, 1978.
Showalter, Elaine (ed.), *The New Feminist Criticism*, London, Virago, 1986.
Spender, Dale, *Man-Made Language*, London, Routledge and Kegan Paul, 1980.
Spender, Dale, *Mothers of the Novel*, London, Pandora Press, 1986.
Spender, Lynne, *Intruders on the Rights of Men: Women's Unpublished Heritage*, London, Pandora Press, 1983.
Steinem, Gloria, *Outrageous Acts and Everyday Rebellions*, London, Fontana, 1984. (The introduction is particularly about her development and career as a writer.)
Sternburg, Janet, *The Writer on her Work*, New York, Norton, 1980.
Stratford, Teresa, Dickey, Julienne and Davies, Kath (eds.), *In Whose Image? Writings on Media Sexism*, London, The Women's Press, forthcoming 1987.
Swindells, Julia, *Victorian Writing and Working Women: the Other Side of Silence*, Cambridge, Polity, 1985.
Taiwo, Oladele, *Female Novelists of Modern Africa*, New York, St Martin's Press, 1985.
Tate, Claudia (ed.), *Black Women Writers at Work*, Harpenden, Oldcastle, 1985.
Todd, Janet (ed.), *Gender and Literary Voice*, New York, Holmes and Meier, 1980.
Walker, Alice, *In Search of our Mothers' Gardens: Womanist Prose*, London, The Women's Press, 1984. (Especially part 1.)
Wandor, Michelene, *Carry On, Understudies: Theatre and Sexual Politics*, London, Routledge and Kegan Paul, 1986.
Wandor, Michelene, (ed.), *On Gender and Writing*, London, Pandora Press, 1983.
Washington, Mary Helen (ed.), *Any Woman's Blues: Stories by Contemporary Black Women Writers*, London, Virago, 1980. (See especially the introduction, 'In pursuit of our own history'.)
West, Celeste, *Words in our Pockets: the Feminist Writers' Guild Handbook on How to Get Published and Get Paid*, Paradise CA, Dustbooks, 1986.
West, Celeste and Wheat, Valerie, *The Passionate Perils of Publishing*, San Francisco, Booklegger Press, 1978.
Wilson, Katharina M. (ed.), *Medieval Women Writers*, Manchester, Manchester University Press, 1984.
Women's Community Press, *Making Your Mark: Producing Your Own Publication*, Dublin, Women's Community Press, 1986.
Woolf, Virginia, *A Room of One's Own*, St Albans, Triad, 1977. (Originally published in 1929.)
Woolf, Virginia, *Women and Writing*, London, The Women's Press, 1977.
Wordsworth, Dorothy, *The Journals of Dorothy Wordsworth* (edited by William Knight), London, Macmillan and Co., 1930.
Worpole, Ken (ed.), *Reading By Numbers: Contemporary Publishing and Popular Fiction*, London, Comedia, 1984.
Worpole, Ken and Morley, Dave, *Republic of Letters: Writing, Culture, Publishing and Politics*, London, Comedia, 1982.

Articles

Arnold, June, 'Feminist presses and feminist politics', *Quest: a feminist quarterly*, vol. 3, no. 1, 1976.

Klepfisz, Irena, 'The distance between us: feminists, consciousness and the girls in the office', *Sinister Wisdom*, winter 1985.

Spender, Dale, 'The gatekeepers; a feminist critique of academic publishing', Helen Roberts (ed.), *Doing Feminist Research*, London, Routledge and Kegan Paul, 1981.

Videos

No Set Type

Produced by women printworkers, principally aimed at encouraging school-leavers into the trade. Very informative. Accompanied by a 24–page booklet (also available separately price £2.00), hire from Cinema of Women (see Organizations).

Eden Grove

Part of the video called 'Print It Yourself', this episode is about a women's adult literacy class who produced their own book. Available to hire from Concord Films, 201 Felixstowe Road, Ipswich, Suffolk, tel 0473 73900/715754.

Notes on contributors

Rosemarie Ademulegun The Libra woman. And so she went on taking first one side and then another and making quite a conversation of it altogether. . . . She generally gave herself good advice, though she seldom followed it. . . . And in a nut shell, that's me. . . . (The above is an extract from Linda Goodman's sun signs.)

Dena Attar has been active in the Women's Liberation Movement for the last fourteen years. She has taken part in the collective writing of leaflets and conference papers in London, Oxford, and York, and has also written a few articles which have appeared in *York Feminist News, Trouble and Strife* and *Shifra* (a Jewish feminist magazine).

Elsa Beckett was born in 1939 in Northern Rhodesia (now Zambia). Lived in Britain since 1969 with my mate Kathryn. Besides Gemma I work with the British Council of Organizations of Disabled People, Newham Employment and Disability Group, and am a campaigning member of the Campaign for Homosexual Equality.

Rosalind Brackenbury I am a poet and novelist, 43 years old, the mother of two teenaged children, and live in Edinburgh. At present I teach creative writing at the extra-mural department of Edinburgh University. A new novel, *Crossing the Water*, is being published by Harvester Press in 1986, also a collection of poems, *Telling Each Other It Is Possible*, by Taxus Press.

Hilary Bourdillon has been working in comprehensive schools as a teacher and adviser of teachers for the past fourteen years. It is this experience which has caused her to write materials for the classroom and on women's history. She is currently Director of Studies in a South London comprehensive school.

Eileen Cadman is a rather parochial person, having lived only in London. Worker in libraries and publishers. Written some good poems and a bad play. Co-author of *Rolling Our Own*, about women in the book trade. Hope to publish massive volume of erotica when I'm 70 – that gives me 35 years to work on it.

Marsaili Cameron was born in Inverness in 1951; school in Ross and Cromarty and Edinburgh; degree at Aberdeen University. Worked for a medical publishing firm in Edinburgh; then at the Open University in Milton Keynes. Contributed to the old *Gay News* from 1973 till its demise. Since 1977, freelance writer and editor, living in London.

Chris Cherry Self-employed, I'm active in women's education and training; practise as a Gestalt therapist and write educational material and poetry. I'm currently working on a myth, expanding images received in a waking dream, through my own process of psychic transformation.

Gail Chester was born in 1951, raised orthodox Jewish, is now a born-again atheist who has been active in the Women's Liberation Movement since 1970. She is an organizer, writer and publishing advisor who believes in the political importance of feminist and radical publishing. Non-fiction is her strength, though she is becoming a closet story-teller.

Penny Cloutte is a much-unemployed arts graduate, political activist, teacher, mother. Now struggling to get my feet on the ground and find my voice. Current obsessions: food supply (global, and tonight's supper); Africa; and the unconscious. In spite of threats by government to all life-support systems, approaching fortieth birthday with optimism.

The Common Thread project came into being as a result of the widely felt need for a collection of working-class women's writings. The group has existed since 1984 and works collectively. At the time of writing this chapter there are nine women in the collective, from a variety of working-class backgrounds. We are committed to challenging the dangerous and insulting stereotypes of working-class women that the media in all forms continue to perpetuate, and to the idea of giving working-class women a voice, both through the book, and through evenings of readings by new working-class women writers.

Evelyn Conlon was born County Monaghan, Ireland. Travelled in Australia and Asia. Have written poetry, two plays, and a collection of short stories, *My Head is Opening* (Attic Press, 1987). Have also published essays and sex education books for children. Live in Dublin with two sons.

Sally Evans is English but lives in Edinburgh. She has had various jobs in London, Italy, northern England and Scotland, but now writes poetry for as much time as possible, while looking after her two children and taking part in poetry events and publishing groups. She has published books and pamphlets of her own.

Kath Fraser was born 1947 in London. White, lesbian. Live on my own in Colne. Have been involved in and supported by women's networks since the early 1970s. I have had two poems published in *One Foot on the Mountain* and a short story in *The Reach* (both from Onlywomen Press).

Berta Freistadt lives in London, where she was born, and writes poetry, plays, and short stories. She has always been a writer but didn't notice until recently. Now that she has, she does supply teaching to support the habit.

Ellen Galford My first novel, *Moll Cutpurse: Her True History*, was published by Stramullion in 1984; my second is soon to be published by the Women's Press. Poems have appeared in the Stramullion collection *Hens in the Hay*, and a short story in The Women's Press anthology of lesbian feminist fiction, *Girls Next Door*.

Caroline Halliday is a writer of women's poetry and fiction and only a beginner in writing for children.

Kirsten Hearn is a 30 year old blind feminist who has been active in the disability and women's movements for the last five years. When not working in local government, she enjoys making tactile sculpture, writing, reading, cuddling teddy bears, eating, and drinking barley wine.

Joy Hendry was born in Perth in 1953. She graduated from Edinburgh University with Honours in Mental Philosophy and taught English at Knox Academy. Since 1972 she has edited the Scottish literary magazine, *Chapman*, and is now working as a freelance writer and editor, writing criticism, general articles, poetry, and reviewing for radio and newspapers. Her first full length book, coedited with Raymond J. Ross, *Critical Essays on Sorley MacLean*, will be published early next year by Scottish Academic Press.

Maggie Iles Born in Kingswood, near Bristol, in 1931. She left school at 16 to work at a variety of jobs: for British Rail, insurance, the advertising section of a local newspaper. It wasn't until 1982 that she started writing full time.

Susie Innes Born in the south of England in 1948 but have lived most of my life in Scotland. Since student journalism I have worked as a journalist, broadcaster and sometimes as a gardener; I now divide my time between journalism, graphics, and caring for my two small daughters.

Catherine Itzin was born in Iowa in 1944, and works as a writer, counsellor, and mother. See my notes (pp. 70–1) for further details.

Anna Livia was born Dublin 1955; childhood in Africa; adolescence in London; mother in Australia. Lesbian radical feminist currently working at Onlywomen Press. Published work: *Relatively Norma*, a novel (Onlywomen Press, 1982), *Accommodation Offered*, a novel (Women's Press, 1985), *Incidents Involving Warmth*, lesbian love stories (Onlywomen Press, 1986).

Pearlie McNeill When is a writer not a writer? Anytime when the demands of being a woman overlap or interfere with the passion and need to be a writer. In the gaps I live, work, love, enjoy, pick my nose but still refuse to carry a clean handkerchief.

Sara Maitland's most recent book, *Vesta Tilley*, was published as a Virago Pioneer in 1986. She was part of the *Tales I Tell My Mother* Collective and has also published two novels, short stories, non-fiction and journalism.

Rosemary Manning I have worked both in business and teaching and only began to write when I was forty. I have written about ten children's books, several of which are still in print, four adult novels and an autobiography, *A Time And A Time*, republished 1986 by Marion Boyars. Women's Press will publish a new autobiography in June 1987.

Caeia March was born Isle of Man, 1946. Both parents white, working-class. Raised in industrial south Yorkshire. Came to London, to study, in 1964. Married for 12 years until 1980. Now lives alone. Works full time in clerical work; tutors a creative writing class, and a woman's discussion and support group in adult education. Needs more time for writing fiction.

Suniti Namjoshi was born in Bombay, India, in 1941. Her books include *The Jackass and the Lady, Feminist Fables, The Authentic Lie, From the Bedside Book of Nightmares*, and *The Conversations of Cow*. She teaches English Literature at Scarborough College, University of Toronto.

Sigrid Nielsen grew up in rural California and lived in Santa Fe, New Mexico, before coming to Scotland in 1979. Her short story, 'The Marina Trench', was published in *Girls Next Door* (Women's Press). She is the author of a play, *Vita*, and of *Speke's Visions: An Explorer's Biography* (as yet unpublished).

Pratibha Parmar was born in Nairobi, Kenya, in 1955, is an Asian feminist and socialist. A product of the Indian diaspora, now struggling and living in London. She currently works in a racially mixed feminist publishers and is committed to coalition politics.

Joy Pitman has worked as a teacher of English and creative writing, an archivist, a mother, a publisher, and an administrator. My poetry can be read in collections by Stramullion and Macdonald. I have completed a first novel and I am working on the second.

Moya Roddy was born in Dublin 1949. Lives and works in London. Has been writing seriously for four years. Presently looking for a publisher. Anyone interested?

Michelle Russell lives in a housing co-op in New Cross, south-east London, having arrived there via Worcester and Cambridge, where she studied French and Greek. She writes plays and is also at present following an acting course at Morley College.

Ros Schwartz 'dropped out' of university here and fled to Paris, where she lived for eight years, doing a variety of odd jobs, and ended up teaching English. She obtained a degree from the then radical University of Vincennes and now works as a freelance translator and agent, specializing in women and ethnic minority writers.

Shaila Shah is Indian, feminist, a founder member of *Outwrite Women's Newspaper*, and proud to be all three.

Diana Shelley, born in 1943, lives in London. She has worked as a secretary, actor, and journalist, and is now writing a history thesis. Besides articles, leaflets, and legal briefings, she has co-written two editions of the *Squatters' Handbook; Piecing It Together: Feminism and Nonviolence;* and *A Legal Advice Pack for Nuclear Disarmers*. Politically active for twenty-seven years, she now works mainly in the peace movement.

Jo Stanley is a 37 year-old writer and journalist. A Marxist and feminist, she lives in London, though originally from the North. Her current work includes two collections of short stories – one about Carmen; a play about Pre-Raphaelite model Lizzie Siddall; a non-fiction anthology on women and their socialism.

Billie Hunter is 31, a midwife, and mother. She is about to start writing her first book, an oral history of midwifery.

Margaret Quigley is 27. She is a community worker in Hackney.

Jennifer Wallace is a mature student, working on a project on women and mental health in Hackney. She is 24 and originally from Luton.